keepers OF THE flame

keepers OF THE flame

UNDERSTANDING AMNESTY INTERNATIONAL

stephen hopgood

CORNELL UNIVERSITY PRESS   ithaca and london

First published 2006 by Cornell University Press
First printing, Cornell Paperbacks, 2006

Printed in the United States of America

Design by Victoria Kuskowski

Library of Congress Cataloging-in-Publication Data
Hopgood, Stephen.
   Keepers of the flame : understanding Amnesty International / Stephen Hopgood.
      p. cm.
   Includes bibliographical references.
   ISBN-13: 978-0-8014-4402-9 (cloth : alk. paper)
   ISBN-10: 0-8014-4402-0 (cloth : alk. paper)
   ISBN-13: 978-0-8014-7251-0 (pbk. : alk. paper)
   ISBN-10: 0-8014-7251-2 (pbk. : alk. paper)
   1. Amnesty International.   2. Human rights workers.   I. Title.
   JC571.H66 2006
   323.06'01—dc22

                                        2005027434

Cornell University Press strives to use environmentally responsible suppliers and materials to the fullest extent possible in the publishing of its books. Such materials include vegetable-based, low-VOC inks and acid-free papers that are recycled, totally chlorine-free, or partly composed of nonwood fibers. For further information, visit our website at www.cornellpress.cornell.edu.

Cloth printing   10 9 8 7 6 5 4 3 2 1
Paperback printing   10 9 8 7 6 5 4 3 2 1

contents

preface and acknowledgments

of the many shocking things I heard during my fieldwork, the one I find most disturbing is the story of a man who was kept in a box by his torturers. His name is Luis Muñoz. This was Chile in the 1970s, under Pinochet, and Luis was among thousands who suffered from the brutality of the general's Cold War regime. One day they opened the box just to tell him they had killed his wife, and then they shut it again. This haunting image remains in my mind as the very essence of human misery: alone, physically and emotionally broken, but alive. Most of all I found it unbearable to imagine what he must have felt in the darkness after the lid closed.[i] It must have been as if pure evil ruled the world. As if hope had been permanently extinguished. As O'Brien tells Winston Smith in George Orwell's *1984*, "If you want a picture of the future, imagine a boot stamping on a human face—forever."[ii]

If one organization is synonymous with keeping hope alive, even as a faint glimmer in the darkness of a prison, it is Amnesty International. Amnesty has been the light, and that light was truth—bearing witness to suffering hidden from the eyes of the world. Picture the Amnesty campaigner sitting in front of a television in 1997 watching videotaped testimony in Spanish of a Guatemalan peasant woman whose husband was taken in 1992 from their house by the police in a truck. He was beaten so badly during the journey that she could follow the trail of blood to the police station. They refused to release her husband's tortured body, demanding payment. Through a local human rights lawyer she found her way to Amnesty International and a researcher, sent out from London, who came to take her testimony. The volunteer watching this woman, five years later, found himself reaching out to the screen. "I actually remember speaking to this woman and saying we'll try, we'll try to do something," he says. "I felt I had to do something. I felt it was my problem."

In 1984, O'Brien tormented Winston by trying to destroy this hope: "Remember that it is forever. The face will always be there to be stamped upon. The heretic, the enemy of society, will always be there, so that he can be defeated and humiliated over again. Everything that you have undergone since you have been in our hands—all that will continue, and worse. The espionage, the betrayals, the arrests, the tortures, the executions, the disappearances will never cease."[iii] It was precisely this heretic, this enemy of society, on whom Amnesty fixed: the prisoner of conscience. It is a potent and seductive ideal still. One early Mexican evening in August 2003, walking up the stone steps into a large meeting hall, I along with the gathered leaders of Amnesty was confronted by an ex-brigadier-general, Jose Gallardo, and his family, surrounded by 35,000 letters. These were the messages he had received in prison from Amnesty members. They spilled out across the floor, different sizes and colors, in loose piles and crammed into boxes, postmarked from all over the world. There were even Christmas cards. And in the middle of them all someone had placed a lighted white candle wrapped in barbed wire, flickering gently in the gathering gloom. Letter after letter expressed the same sentiment: you are not alone; don't give up hope. Here was an almost tangible kind of moral force. No wonder released prisoners talk with such wonder about receiving these letters. This scene seemed to contain an answer to the first question that had provoked me: Why should I join Amnesty? What follows will ask of you the same. In order to answer it, we have to understand what Amnesty is. It is not as straightforward as you might think.

Caught between sympathy and doubt, I wanted to know what human rights organizations were *really* like. I soon discovered a void existed where work on the culture of human rights ought to be found. A comparative study based on primary research was impossible. The foundational work does not exist. How could so many international relations scholars, institutional sociologists, political philosophers, and others talk so confidently about the meaning of human rights norms when so little was known about the social origins of those norms, how they assume the form they do, and what motivates those who make them their life's work?

Acquiring the sociological depth necessary to see how morality takes concrete form meant a period of intense empirical study. It seemed best to do an analysis of one organization over time. In this respect, only one candidate would do and that was Amnesty International. From September 2002 to September 2003, I spent twelve months inside the International

Secretariat (IS) of Amnesty in London. Although it is important to stress that, as we will see, the IS is not wholly representative of the 1.7 million members of the Amnesty movement, it is inside the IS that the second question motivating this study—what is practical morality in action?—has been puzzled through for forty-five years.

My research included more than 150 loosely structured interviews with present and former staff, observations at numerous meetings at all levels of the IS, and attendance at gatherings of the Amnesty membership's core governing body, its International Executive Committee (IEC), and its supreme policy-making forum, the biennial International Council Meeting (ICM). This observational and oral research was augmented by work in the IS archives, tracing features of the IS's and Amnesty's organizational culture as they have evolved over many years.

This way of proceeding had various limitations. Most crucially, interviews were undertaken on the basis of anonymity, at all levels of the IS and Amnesty. I have tried wherever possible to use original material from these interviews. Using the words IS staff and Amnesty members use, including the hesitations, pauses, and changes of direction, gives a certain richness to the text, but these personal accounts are exemplary and not part of an exhaustive and fully representative sample, which would have been impossible to collect if it were to reflect contemporary diversity and historical change.

The interviewees were initially self-selected, responding to a posting on the staff's electronic bulletin board, IntSec Forum. After these, I sought interviewees out more directly by taking up suggestions about who had institutional knowledge, an interesting perspective, or an important historical or contemporary role. This group included staff from the research, campaigns, and resources parts of the IS, as well as members of long-standing, ex-senior staff and others no longer at the IS. The idea was to get at something of the *quality* of practice through the use of practitioners' words. Some readers may find the lack of context about the speakers off-putting. I can only sympathize and say this was unavoidable; in most cases, the words are those of still-serving senior and junior IS staff, and taking care to protect their anonymity was my first consideration.

The vast amount of paper generated by Amnesty was a further limitation. Despite the efforts of archivists, most of this material is organized according to date and simply stored chronologically in paper form or on microfilm. Many documents, memos, and notes from the past do not have proper identification and are scattered through various files. There is no way to do a thematic search. If you want to know about Amnesty's budgets over time, for example, you have to look at the financial part of quarterly IEC meetings year by year—1964, 1965, 1966, and so on—hoping to pick up the thread. Or you have to find later documents that summarize earlier material. In the end, I concentrated on the Secretary General's Office and IEC files. You need to know in advance what you are looking for, in other words, heightening the role played by staff and members with institutional memory. This gives us a first inkling of how important evolutionary processes have been to Amnesty's identity. Much material has been lost, misplaced, or buried in the filing cabinets of various individuals in the IS and the movement. Only the prisoner files, with their compromising contents, are securely locked away to avoid the unwanted attentions of states. Furthermore, the IS—the seat of Amnesty's research work and organization—holds only movementwide material. The major sections, such as AIUK, AI Netherlands, and AIUSA, all have their own archives, papers that may tell the story differently given national experience and perspective. This diversity within the movement is matched by the great variety of subcultures within the IS. There were simply no regular meetings you might have gone to, or papers you might have read, or staff you might have spoken to that would have been representative of Amnesty and the IS as a whole. It is, as we will see, a remarkable mix of uniformity and autonomy, and contested internal authority has been its hallmark.

All of which is to say that the following account is an interpretation, not a definitive history. It is a pieced-together account, told in as compelling a manner as possible both to engage the reader in the inner life of Amnesty and to make the moral and practical dilemmas clear. These are our dilemmas too. Amnesty is not an elsewhere—it is *us*, however we might define and understand that awkward idea. Its agonies, obligations, fears, opportunities, and challenges are our own.

Thus, the third question: What does Amnesty's experience tell us about our own future in a world of globalized capital and transnational organization? Does it help us understand how we might get from the system of sovereign nation-states to new forms of social and political association that might be more like a genuine global society? Or does it tell us that such hopes are illusory? Amnesty has been a pioneer on this voyage. While others—politicians, activists, intellectuals, and revolution-aries—have given their attention to the destination, Amnesty has under-stood that it is the journey that matters. We can see that *there*, on the far horizon, appears to be more equal, just, fair, and desirable, but we do not know with any certainty if we can steer that course. And, crucially, we have to begin from *here*, from where we are and as we are now. For Amnesty, at least, everyone gets a seat. Imagine it as a lookout on the prow of the ship, lamp in hand, trying to see a way through the dark, forbidding water.

Over four decades of careful navigation, Amnesty's practical achieve-ments have been significant, as evidenced by the high level of public esteem it enjoys. It is an impressive record to which I do not need to add. A worthy testament to this enviable reputation as a moral authority is the extraordinary scale of U.S. government and press reaction (let alone right-wing commentary) to Amnesty calling Guantanamo Bay "the gulag of our times" in its 2005 Annual Report. An angry *Washington Post* leader claimed:

> It's always sad when a solid, trustworthy institution loses its bear-ings and joins in the partisan fracas that nowadays passes for political discourse. It's particularly sad when the institution is Amnesty International, which for more than 40 years has been a tough, single-minded defender of political prisoners around the world and a scourge of left- and right-wing dictators alike.[iv]

Amnesty's moral authority ensured that its condemnation hit home and could not be ignored.

Since 1961, Amnesty has kept hope alive, advanced the cause of human rights especially in areas such as torture and the death penalty, and created an unrivaled global reputation for moral integrity. In other ways, however, it has fared less well. Little of its distinctiveness has been per-manently embedded in any kind of social space separate from territorial sovereign states, its transnational appearance disguising various national economic and social structures that significantly constrain its global aspi-rations. It has also struggled to deal with the integration of difference, of gender, race, or nationality, making it a surprisingly masculine (cultur-ally), white, Western, and middle-class organization.

Most of all, it is struggling with globalization. Intensified capitalism has whipped the sea into a frenzy. Amnesty is a moral authority in an era when all authorities—from priests to politicians, from parents to pro-fessors—are under scrutiny and when the opportunities for and attrac-tions of consumption and self-expression are rampant. Capital increasingly knows no bounds. What it wants is to buy Amnesty's moral authority, now consolidated in the AI brand.

Can Amnesty survive such a buffeting? When it was launched in 1961, there was nowhere else for the faithful to go. Now there are innumerable choices, many of which focus directly on the narrower interests and iden-tities of the new young. Can a morality that imposes significant obliga-tions on us to distant others gain any purchase in this world? Young Westerners no longer join organizations such as Amnesty on the terms they once did. They do not make long-term commitments of this sort, preferring involvement in networks and issues that are more fluid, easier to join, and easier to leave. Life-long association, like life-long local factory employment, is a declining feature of the modern West. Yet I often heard people say of Amnesty, it's a good thing that they're there. They saw it as a fixed point on the moral landscape, as a sentinel. For many staff and members, this is Amnesty's very reason for being. For others, the age of institutions, of permanent authority, is thankfully over. Such unques-tioned authority was always ideology, and Amnesty needs to fight the politics that lie beneath that ideology. AI needs to leave the deck and enter the cabin to pore over the charts and play its full and proper role in making decisions about the ship's final destination. Which of these two Amnesties should prevail? You can judge for yourself. What did I decide? Did I join Amnesty when the book was finished? If you will forgive a small conceit, I leave the answer to that question until the end.

The debts I have incurred doing this research are impossible to repay. First of all I am endebted to my family, Helen, Ellie, and Lucas, for their love, support, understanding, and patience. Thank you for helping me to see both the light and the shadow. Second, I am grateful to my colleagues in the Department of Politics and International Studies at the School of Oriental and African Studies (SOAS), University of London, especially

Steve Heder, Tom Young, Mark Laffey, and Louiza Odysseos. I also thank SOAS as a whole for its flexibility about my sabbatical leave. Third, I am endebted to the Social Science Research Council (SSRC), and its Program on Global Security and Cooperation based in Washington. Its generous funding and deep-seated commitment to such an ambitious piece of research made it the ideal sponsor. I record my particular thanks to John Tirman, Petra Ticha, Itty Abraham, Daniel García Peña, and Tom Biersteker. I also thank the John D. and Catherine T. MacArthur Foundation which funded the SSRC initiative. Fourth, various friends and colleagues read and commented on the draft or discussed various of its issues with me. I thank in particular Daniel Attas, Michael Barnett, Tom Buchanan, Diego Gambetta, David Gellner, Helen Jenkins, Daniel Large, Robin A. Redhead, John Sidel, David Stoll, and Rob Waygood. Christopher Lake provided detailed comments on parts of the draft twice, for which I am very grateful, and Karen Melham was the perfect research assistant, providing invaluable help with the transcription of material and adding significantly in intellectual terms through her command of ethics and theology. Finally, I thank Roger Haydon at Cornell University Press for his encouragement and support.

Which brings us to Amnesty. The decision to allow me into the International Secretariat was a brave one; made by Irene Khan, the secretary general; Kate Gilmore, her deputy; and by the staff as a whole. With agreement on only minimal safeguards to protect the confidentiality and anonymity of staff and to allow Amnesty to meet its wider legal obligations, they took a leap of faith within an organization that is instinctively wary of external critics. The staff members themselves cooperated with and became engaged in the research in ways that, I hope, some have found positive and at the least thought provoking. I know, of course, that many will feel they have been poorly served by their generosity. The account that follows makes hard reading in places, even though my interpretation is anchored fundamentally in the experiences of staff, then and now. All I can hope is that the internal debate the book will spark sheds some light in those darker places that hamper Amnesty International as a whole in the era of globalization. The membership, especially on the IEC and in sections such as AIUSA, AI Netherlands, and AIUK, have been equally generous with their time and allowed me to witness some very private moments. For this I can only say thank you.

To all these people, those who built Amnesty, some of whom have been in the IS and the movement almost from the beginning, and to those who are trying to take it forward toward and past its half-century, I am inexpressibly grateful. I have thought long and hard about whom to name and have decided, with the greatest regret, that it is better to name no one than to risk identification, omission, offense, and selectivity. Many of those whose insights proved most illuminating may not even have been aware they were providing them. Others were, and to them (and they know who they are) I can only say thank you once more. It is to all these IS staff members, past and present, that this book is dedicated.

STEPHEN HOPGOOD

London

keepers OF THE flame

1

BETWEEN TWO WORLDS

an open letter lies on the large, rectangular wooden table in the library of the International Secretariat (IS) of Amnesty International (AI) in London. It is late July 2003. The letter, which has dozens of signatures on it, is addressed to the secretary general, Irene Khan, and her deputy, Kate Gilmore. It comes after a packed meeting at which many members of staff expressed fears about the way in which the work of the IS is being transformed. The letter claims there has been a "lost opportunity to use IS expertise and experience" and a failure to appreciate "the possible consequences of expected decisions on the quality of Amnesty International's work." This last point concerns the dropping of traditional areas of work, "including 'forgotten prisoners', the very raison d'être of Amnesty International—in certain countries." The letter is driven not by conservatism, it says, or resistance to change but rather by a commitment to Amnesty. It concludes, "We owe it to the victims of human rights violations and to the members who believe in Amnesty International's research and action."[1] This is the kind of letter Amnesty usually sends to governments. Now it is the stuff of staff disenchantment with their own management.

The library has a place at the heart of Amnesty mythology. Work compiling and registering prisoner cases began there in 1961, in the dank basement of a British lawyer's chambers a few miles from where the IS now lives. From these unpromising beginnings, Amnesty became an iconic global symbol of moral authority built on the foundations of the very ethos that the letter claims is under threat. On the library wall, watching over the staff members as they sign, is a framed black-and-white photograph that encapsulates this ethos well. It shows a large, serious-looking man in a dark tie and jumper, wearing thick glasses. He is using an enormous pair of scissors to cut stories from the newspapers spread before him. His name is Colin Leyland-Naylor. The picture is headlined "The Volunteer Spirit." Underneath is the candle in barbed wire and the following caption:

> Amnesty International began as a volunteer movement in the 1960s, and to this day it remains overwhelmingly an organization of dedicated individuals freely giving their time and energy to the cause of human rights worldwide. The International Secretariat too began as a volunteer operation, and has always relied on unpaid volunteers in many areas of its work, as well as the dedication of its staff. Two of the very earliest volunteers at the International Secretariat were **Rhyl Andrews** and **Colin Leyland-Naylor.** Both came in regularly to read, cut and paste newspaper articles. From the earliest days of Amnesty International right up until it was no longer possible for either of them to come to work because of failing health, their contribution was essential to the life-saving work of the movement. In their own distinctive ways, both expressed extraordinary courage, determination and humour in the face of personal adversity—and enduring commitment to the principles for which Amnesty International stands. Quietly and persistently they exemplified the qualities of character and service that built Amnesty International and preserved in it the ability to value and defend the human spirit.[2]

Almost all the key elements of the ethos are here: voluntarism ("freely giving their time and energy"), individualism ("dedicated individuals"), practicality ("read, cut and paste newspaper articles"), self-discipline ("courage, determination and humour in the face of personal adversity"), self-effacement ("quietly and persistently"), and moral import ("life-saving work of the movement"). These "qualities of character" mirrored those of the individuals for whom the volunteers worked: prisoners of conscience (POCs).

This ethos is learned and absorbed. Thus, paid staff can possess a voluntary ethic (leading to amateur professionalism) and quiet persistence can coexist alongside a global media profile. "Life-saving work" is a reference to victims, Amnesty (according to the ethos) serving as a means to an end rather than an end in itself. It is the messenger, not the message. In the words of a female researcher, an IS veteran of more than a decade:

> I have no ties to Amnesty as an organization. As I said, I didn't join Amnesty because I wanted to be part of Amnesty, but because it gave me the opportunities to continue working on human rights in the region. So theoretically, if there were another organization that allowed me to continue that work on the region or develop it in different areas, then I might consider moving. I have not come across another organization that gives you the sort of scope Amnesty does. And the sort of involvement, level of involvement that Amnesty does. In the region. Human Rights Watch . . . does some great work and I'm a great admirer of Human Rights Watch, but I think they are a bit theoretical, because what they do is they do research and then they go and write their report and launch their reports. They don't have the, the same degree of ongoing involvement in cases. Because they don't do individual casework. Every single day, we're working on individual cases that come. And so they don't have the same relationship with the people, with the victims.

Working tirelessly from these foundations, Amnesty International became the prime example of a principled nongovernmental organization (NGO), a key component of transnational advocacy networks and an exemplary transnational actor.[3] Although great attention has been paid to its role as a shaper of ethical outcomes in the world, we know next to nothing about what Amnesty is like on the inside. As the chapters that follow show, Amnesty has not only never been an NGO, it has not really been a human rights organization either (in the sense that human rights provide its ethical momentum). Reformers would quite like it to be more of both these things, but historically the social institution it most resembles is a chapel or a meeting house. The key to understanding it lies less in how it presents itself, therefore, and more in its internal organizing principles and their relationship to moral authority.

Accumulating and protecting that authority has been Amnesty's main achievement. It has led, as we will see, to intense disputes—the letter being the latest in a long line of clashes going back decades. The cost of challenging the legitimacy of states, and generating an enviable reputation for truth-telling in the process, has been a deeply fractured internal authority structure.

The Nature of Moral Authority

Authority is more than force and different from the capacity to prevail through rational persuasion. The word of an authority is enough to create a reason for us to do what the authority says simply because the authority says we should do it.[4] At its extreme, genuine authority may even require us to do things that we think are wrong but still do because we accept the legitimacy of the authority. Crucial to being recognized as legitimate in this way is not what is said but the identity of who says it—"who the speaker is."[5]

It is conventional to distinguish formal authorities (those in authority such as police officers) from theoretical authorities (those who are an authority such as doctors). Roughly speaking, the former have authority because they have power and the latter have power because they have authority. Moral authority is a special kind of theoretical authority. It combines two elements. First, privileged access to knowledge that is inaccessible to the ordinary person. This much is true of all theoretical authorities—they tell us what we have reason to believe.[6] It is the usual province of the "expert." But moral authority has a second component. The word of these privileged intermediaries also claims to be a reason to act on that belief regardless of our own interests and inclinations (unlike a doctor's diagnosis, for example). Moral authority tells us what we should do.

Few ever confront moral authority in this pure form, of course. Moral authority is better used more loosely as a synonym for strong (out-of-the-ordinary) reasons to act in a certain way, usually against what are taken to be our wants and desires. Essential to elevating this special class of authority to its moral status is that it convinces us it is more than merely a veiled attempt to promote the subjective preferences or advantages of some. It must claim a certain objectivity in speaking for the truth. As Stephen Toulmin puts it:

No one takes wholly seriously the moral opinions voiced—whether in outrage, sorrow, or excuse—in the General Assembly or Security Council of the United Nations, as they are always presented by official spokesmen for the Member States, whose status marks them as "interested parties." The only institutions whose opinions command general respect and are generally heard as stating "the decent opinion of Humankind" are Amnesty International, the World Psychiatric Association, and similar organizations, which are devoid of physical power or "armed force."[7]

A tension exists, therefore, between speaking the truth and deploying that truth in an argument for social change. This balancing act, undertaken skillfully by Amnesty since 1961, has become harder and harder to carry off. Just at the moment when Amnesty began building its store of moral authority, numerous critics began to ask whether such a privileged space, a space of objectivity and unquestionable truth, could even exist. For them, the very idea of a detached vantage point of this sort, let alone its practice, was no more than self-serving ideology, a way for authorities of all kinds—paternal, colonial, patriarchal, and so on—to suppress dissenting voices and interests that had just as much right to be heard.

In this vein, Richard Wilson, an anthropologist, describes how Amnesty constructs, as do other human rights groups, an appearance of objectivity out of subjectivity (eyewitness accounts), creating "human rights violations" out of criminal murder: "Human rights reports are written with an unflinching realism which bluntly recounts one fact after another in an unmitigated and relentless barrage of short case summaries. Only a literalist chronicle passes the twin test of authenticity and authority, leading to a suppression of the authorial voice and the deployment of a language purged of all tropes, metaphors and figurative elements."[8] For Wilson, this "unflinching realism" disguises interpretation as fact. In what follows, in my own interpretation of these interpretations, we trace aspects of this process of construction in detail. We leave the question of whether we can conceive of something "objective," a kind of residual moral truth lurking behind human rights reporting, until the conclusion where I argue that such a truth does exist and that the Amnesty-

style "literalist chronicle" shows an intuitive and sophisticated understanding that this truth is the foundation of moral authority. When Wilson
says of human rights reports, "my intention has not been to undermine
their effectiveness, but to raise questions about the manner in which they
are produced," he may want more than he can have, in other words.[9]

Once you have authority, you protect it. This has created a further
dilemma for Amnesty: How can it take an interest—in the two senses of
looking after itself and moving from abstract to specific concerns—when
its authority and identity are predicated precisely on not having an interest to take? How can it move from an objective view to an active choice?
As Bernard Williams puts it, theoretical reasoning enables us to "stand
back," but action is always "first personal."[10]

To begin with, Amnesty simply extrapolated the foundational symbol
—the POC—to other areas, keeping its prisoner orientation and concentrating on casework as its basic method. Even in the newer domains of
the death penalty, torture, and disappearances, the same basic features
held, especially the fundamental fact that these prisoners could not speak
for themselves, whether because of incarceration or execution. This
enhanced their symbolic power: they embodied in a pure form the idea
of innocent suffering. This solitary moral hero—Christ being the most
obvious example—is among the most powerful cultural archetypes of the
West.[11] As time went on and Amnesty became more of an actor in the
world—running campaigns and pressing for international legislation—
problems of prioritization increased. The difficulty of choosing came not
from organizational arrangements or from bureaucratic inadequacies but
from the foundational moral structure and the effect this had on working
culture. A presumption in favor of moral detachment and objectivity was
built in. Once this became doctrine, Amnesty was loathe to question such
a basic cornerstone of its identity. We begin to see, therefore, the importance of looking at concrete practice.

The Practical Origins of Moral Authority

During my fieldwork, the preeminent liberal political philosopher of the
post-1945 era, John Rawls, died. If Amnesty has done more than any other
organization to spread the message of universal rights, Rawls did more
than any other modern philosopher to argue for their vital role in moral-

ity. Was I naïve to think someone would notice his death? An IS director said that only five people in the building would really know who he was. We might ask what all those students of political philosophy are doing if their work has no impact on the world? They certainly are not providing a grounding for human rights activists. Policy work looks like theory to activists, and it looks like practice to academics.

One ex-researcher, who had studied the philosophical foundations of rights theory, and was certainly a "keeper of the flame," described Amnesty as "tactical, action oriented": "I think it is the conviction. I think it's actually a very practical thing. I don't think Amnesty's a place for intellectuals. If you're going to work . . . within it . . . you have to make an effort to remind yourself of the intellectual side of things." Amnesty devised a highly practical method—letter-writing—to publicize innocent suffering. Yet the explanation for this was not functional. It was integral to Amnesty's structure and cultural background.

Amnesty has no building blocks, no entry requirements in terms of values, beliefs, identity, or experiences. It is not organized around a shared interest (like a labor union) or a shared identity (like a women's rights group) or a common god (as in a formal religion) or a shared ideology (like a political party). Unlike the Red Cross or Oxfam or Médecins sans Frontières, it is not organized to meet a need or provide a service. There was and is no single characteristic to which we can point and say, "This shared thing draws these people together." It is not embedded in an identifiable social class or group whose objective life-situation and subjective qualities unite them prior to Amnesty membership. Initial joiners simply recognized something in the archetype and the letter-writing campaign and were drawn to it.

The founder, Peter Benenson, used the notion of wavelength to describe what attracted these supporters. He saw Amnesty as a form of collective action that might succeed where religion and socialism were failing. The purpose of Amnesty, he said, was to "Re-kindle a fire in the minds of men. It is to give him who feels cut off from God a sense of belonging to something greater than himself, of being a small part of the entire human race."[12] Launched in May 1961, the initial Appeal for Amnesty aimed "To find a common bond upon which the idealists of the world can co-operate. It is designed in particular to absorb the latent enthusiasm of a great number of such idealists who have, since the eclipse of Socialism, become increasingly frustrated. . . . those whom the Amnesty Appeal primarily aims to free are the men and women imprisoned by cynicism, and doubt."[13]

The idea of natural rights comes closest to a theory of the wavelength. As Peter Jones describes these keep-out notices, "They proclaimed that each individual should be left free to worship God in his own way, to express his thoughts, to tend his property, without interference from others, particularly without interference from the state."[14] Natural rights had reinforcing attractions. Central to Christian theology, *and* precursors of human rights, they are also part of the tradition of radical English popular dissent stretching back to Quaker-born Thomas Paine and his hugely influential *The Rights of Man*.[15] This dissenting tradition emphasized democratic accountability, moral equality, and social reform. It was a crucial part of the British Left's political heritage, as well as allying Free Churches with political liberalism in causes such as women's rights and antislavery.[16] The sense of natural rights suffuses, for example, an angry 1963 editorial Benenson wrote when Spanish communist Julian Grimau was executed: "If the AMNESTY movement had more influence, no Government would dare flout the basic principles of humanity, because there would be an enraged international public opinion strong enough to protect lonely beings from senseless vengeance."[17] This set Amnesty's cultural and social background within the tradition of ecumenical European Christianity, what I later call religionless Christianity, giving it from the start symbols (such as the candle), organizational principles (nonviolence), and operational mechanisms (witnessing) that at once resonated with early supporters. Of all the dissenting groups and nonconformist denominations within Christianity, it is perhaps the Society of Friends, the Quakers, whose foundational ethos most resembles Amnesty's: witnessing, testifying, the inner light of conscience, speaking truth to power, and nonviolence. Letter writing was a practical form of moral action that presented no doctrinal problems for Catholics, Jews, Muslims, the many varieties of Protestantism, Atheists, and others. Amnesty was, in effect, a secular Free Church, combining skepticism about higher authorities, worship without restrictive doctrine, conscience, and more, all allied to a belief in moral equality and a concern with the alleviation of suffering. The use of the term *human rights* is misleading in this respect. Although Amnesty cited the 1948 Universal Declaration of

Human Rights (UDHR), it did not do so as foundation but as corroboration. It was saying "and history is with us," not "the UDHR is why Amnesty exists."

The privatization of religious belief in modern Europe had by 1961 robbed the churches of their preeminent role in defining morality for society at large. Amnesty was an early response to this aspect of globalization. Its task was to reconstitute authority in some form, with aspirants to such privileged status required now to demonstrate their functional worth as providers of social goods such as justice and empowerment.[18] All of which leads us to a startling paradox. The routine account of universal human rights has them and their advocates as gravediggers for traditional forms of authority. Amnesty was subtly different. It sought to question the traditional while trying to rescue the authority. In an era of tumultuous social change, it had no special affection for the historical authority of states or the established church, about whose power it was skeptical. It sought resurrection of the idea of a more profound authority than that embraced by these temporal and spiritual institutions. In this endeavor, it encompassed both ecumenical Christianity and those, especially on the Left, who would form the new social movements of the 1960s and beyond. Both of these were responses to the erosion of traditional authority, one seeking a renewal in moral (that is secular) terms, the other thriving on the new freedom that the opening up of postwar Western societies seemed to promise.

Contested Authority

For senior IS management, the letter of July 2003 was a sign of staff anxiety at their "existential encounter with the future." At an IS staff meeting to address the letter, the feeling of guardianship was made clear when one researcher, not long-serving, warned that dropping traditional areas of work and moving away from country-based research might result in Amnesty's reputation suffering irreparable damage. She wanted, she said, to hear the secretary general "recognize these are dangers" and "let us know you care about that as well." In her impassioned response, the secretary general told the staff that her commitment to Amnesty's cause went as deep as anyone's and that no one in the room had better be in any doubt about that.

The guardians of Amnesty's heritage, those skeptical about the direction of change, are just one side of the story. A senior campaigner described the emotive term *forgotten prisoners* as "shorthand for a creation myth . . . what Amnesty was forty years ago and isn't anymore and can never be." Another said it confirmed his view that the movement would eventually lose patience and "asphyxiate" the secretariat because die-hard researchers did not want to change. A third responded to the title *keepers of the flame* by exclaiming, "I don't know when or what moment they handed the flame to a small number of paid staff!" We knew we were talking about the researchers, one of whom described the dismantling in the 1990s of the Head of Research Office (HORO), the citadel of the ethos, as a coup. Even in Mexico, just two weeks after the letter, at Amnesty's biennial International Council Meeting (ICM), a candidate for the International Executive Committee (IEC) made a plea for election by walking a fine line between the past and the future. "I am in touch with Amnesty's past," he said, but "we are not a museum or a case study."

That well-established organizations struggle with intergenerational change is a common observation. But in how many could those fearful of its risks argue that something of worldwide symbolic importance was at stake? This view is not just that of veteran staff; many newer researchers feel the same way, as do many Amnesty members. Symbolic power must be handled with care. In altering what the symbol symbolizes, an organization risks fracturing the umbilical link to the source of moral authority (here, the principled suffering of POCs). In Amnesty's case, the danger posed by precipitate change is seen by many as too great. Symbols that inspire intense feelings tend to conservatism over time, in other words, sacrificing breadth to depth (i.e., not more members but members with more commitment). When Amnesty reached the high phase of its symbolic moral authority in the later 1970s and 1980s, there was even talk of making parts of the internal lore[19] permanent, erecting a higher entry barrier to new members lest the value of this scarce authority be diluted.

That the movement now talks of the Amnesty brand, the commodification of its hard-won status, seems an almost sacrilegious association of something so pure with the ultimate profanity—money. There is, for example, an Amnesty International Platinum Visa Card, available to IS staff and Amnesty International United Kingdom (AIUK) members (described as "attractive, silver and bearing the AI candle logo"). I mentioned the word *brand* to a former and very senior IS manager, who visibly blanched and said, "So people use that language now? Really?" In comments appended to the critical letter to the secretary general, one person wrote, "The 'AI' brand image so proudly referred to in the last 'Day Out' was the fruit of years of painstaking and thorough research focused on areas clearly identifiable and understood by public and media." Contrast this with the view of a current senior IS manager about the letter: "I always knew at some point steel would hit steel. You know. The steel of our resolve to reclaim some authority over the place. And to ask people to be servant of the movement's will was going to hit the steel of their conviction that they were right."

For much of its history, the preservation of moral authority has dictated institutional priorities. But, as new members and staff have joined, established AI culture has become more porous to the society around it. Amnesty's detached identity has been destabilized, its walls breached by those as concerned about the human rights of women, minorities, the poor, and nonheterosexuals *in their own societies* as about POCs. These reformers seek to use stored authority for more openly "potitical" ends, in other words, wanting Amnesty to be a sentinel no longer but a player.

The story of this long contest over Amnesty's symbolic moral authority must be simplified to be comprehensible.[20] We will meet people who regret the receding past and people who dream of a transformed future. Some I characterize as *keepers of the flame*. They are the guardians of the Amnesty ethos, found in its purest form in researchers at the IS but also found in many parts of the membership of Amnesty sections worldwide, especially volunteers who coordinate work in sections on individual countries and who possess a deep attachment to those countries and a long-standing relationship with IS researchers. There are only about sixty or so designated researchers in five Regional Programs (Asia, Africa, Middle East and North Africa, Americas, and Europe, and Central Asia) at the IS, although a similar number of regional campaigners work closely with them doing research, albeit with less institutional status. It is in the Regional Programs that the ethos is strongest. There are also campaigners in the Campaigns Program, and the rivalry between the research staff, on the one hand, and campaigners, on the other, can be intense. At times

I effectively use the term *researcher* as shorthand for keeper of the flame, although there are people in policy, legal, publications, information, and press work who share a strong attachment to the ethos. There are also researchers who want change.[21]

In contrast with these keepers, I characterize a group of Amnesty staff and senior members as *reformers*. This group taps into options submerged at the moment of creation: demonstrative protest, political solidarity, and social change. This Amnesty is more engaged, more of a movement. Reformers exist within the IS at senior levels and within Amnesty's membership and leadership. They, too, are a less-than-homogenous block.

I adopt two further distinctions for indicative purposes. On the one hand, there are reformers who see the need for Amnesty to take on thematic human rights issues, such as economic and social rights, and women's rights, and to campaign in new ways (more direct political action) and in new areas (focusing more on societies in the West). They are also in favor of greater democracy within the Amnesty movement and of a reining in of the researcher-dominated IS. These people I categorize as *campaigners*. On the other hand, there are those who see AI as needing professionalizing to survive in the more market-oriented world of globalization. They seek a distinction between employed staff (with management, research, campaigning, financial, and infrastructure skills) and voluntary members who work for Amnesty unpaid. For this group of *modernizers*, key reforms include better fund-raising and handling of money; consolidation of the Amnesty brand in competition with other NGOs, especially Human Rights Watch; and more effective accountability and evaluation procedures. According to them, the IS should be like a civil service under the direction of the Amnesty movement. Many reformers share some element of both of these approaches—campaigning and modernizing—and so are defined together. When they differ, it is principally on the question of Amnesty's relations with the corporate world.

Both strains of thought, the ethos-inspired keepers of the flame and the more political/professional activists, vied for supremacy even within the motivation of Peter Benenson himself. They are not merely tactical differences. They imply distinctions in attitudes toward the justification for, and practice of, moral action. Most obviously, if the world is not listening, do you try to shout louder or do you change what is being said? Moral philosophers characterize this as roughly a difference between deontology (what's right is right) and consequentialism (if it's not working, try something else). Keepers of the flame tend to be deontologists; reformers tend to be consequentialists. For how long would you fund a disappearance case? Ten years? Twenty? As long as it takes? If it is the right thing to do, isn't it right regardless of the cost? Isn't that what morality means? For deontologists, yes. But even if the cost for one POC is $1 million? And even when there are so many others whose rights could be improved with that money? Then again, isn't this the logic of utility, the language of needs but also of consumption and the market, just the kind of thing Amnesty is sworn to resist by looking in the places where the spotlight does not shine? This is not just an esoteric issue. As a senior member of the IS staff said, "I do actually still think I am doing it out of, sort of, principles. I'm not concerned about . . . results, at least not necessarily in the short-term. I usually have very low expectations of having an impact, which I guess helps. And all of which is to say that if for every year I know of only one person to whom we've made some sort of difference, that's good enough for me." While a veteran researcher told the following story:

> A young boy disappeared with his parents in Uruguay in the mid seventies during the height of the repression. And was discovered earlier this year. Identified. Living with adoptive parents in the military. And the moment that that family that had been searching for that baby for the last twenty, thirty years discovered that, you know, yes it sounds trite, but yes, suddenly it was all worth it when you see one family that you helped to keep going and you helped somehow to manage to support through adopting their case.

Disappearances are not to have the same kind of organizational priority in the future as they have had in the past. Priorities, now defined as part of a "mission," are to be set with a more conscious focus on opportunity and impact rather than existing preference and practice. Amnesty needs to change to survive, say reformers, one senior manager arguing that it is now "in the business of selling hope."

In the chapters that follow, I contrast Amnesty's ethos-inspired protection of *moral authority* with the reformers' search for more *political author-*

ity. Although the former has been dominant since inception, the latter is increasingly resurgent with its emphasis on a more political approach to the doctrine of human rights. Here I mean the political (with a small *p*) in a broad sense that refers to both the right to speak as a legitimate representative of an interest or identity (whether organized as a community or not) and the competitive process of establishing that right.

If moral authority is enhanced, classically, when the speaker does not possess marks of belonging (he or she is seen as an honest broker who has no interest and therefore acts morally), political authority is only possible when someone possesses those very marks.[22] Can a man speak just as effectively for women's rights as a woman? Can a white Briton speak as persuasively on racial issues as a black Briton? Can a straight woman enjoy legitimacy leading the cause for gay and lesbian rights? Can a Christian speak with authority for Islam? Ask yourself, would he or she be taken seriously, trusted, treated as an authority? And—a highly subversive question for Western human rights activists (and Western academics as well)—can a nonnational ever really be taken as a political authority (not just listened to, but observed) on the life of another nation?

Of the trajectories possible for the newly-formed Amnesty in 1961, it was the moral rather than the political that prevailed, the practical result of which was the ethos and an operational culture that embraced the idea of bearing witness. Bearing witness became research, the documentation of individual cases and the recording of human rights abuses on a country-by-country basis. At the core of everything Amnesty has done lies this method of human rights activism. It came to be seen as integral to maintaining moral authority. In the words of a very senior ex-IS member who spent twenty years at Amnesty: "For me, what was special about it was what it purported to try and deliver. Which was objective information about individuals in particular parlous situations vis-à-vis their governments. That it was accurate, it was careful, it was not grinding political axes. It was providing the information that others could grind political axes with if they wanted to. That's fine. But that it was just simply a voice of cool, calm documentation to prevent history being written by the victors." This sacred core, monitored from London, was kept safe from pollutants such as money, interests, and politics by its border guards, the intermediaries between the source itself (suffering POCs) and those who sought knowledge and understanding of it.[23] These are the keepers of the flame. Thus, the permanent staff at the IS are our main empirical focus. They are the ones who have been responsible for investigating, writing up cases, interpreting Amnesty policy, and generally creating the identity of this seemingly identityless organization. Without building blocks and with only a family association with the language of human rights, Amnesty's internal lore—the principles and practices through which moral authority was protected and augmented—came to be identified with Amnesty as a whole. These guarantors, committed to an ideal that by its nature was indifferent to their own particular lives, have given much for the privilege of tending this legacy.

Morality and Self-Sacrifice

Moral and political authority impose specific kinds of burdens on their proponents. When people work in an ethical environment, feelings run high anyway. Where the very ethos and functioning of the organization are constantly at issue, even as the work is done and the organization grows, they run higher still. Here is the vivid recollection of one former IS staffer: "The last ICM that I went to was in Ireland [Dublin, 1989] and that was the one that really broke me, because it was so vicious. It was so vicious. I mean, the IS . . . you would have thought the IS, we were torturing people. We were the ones killing people. We were the torturers. . . . Everything was doubted. Everything was suspect. Every motive was questioned." He said, "I realized I had to leave . . . I would have ended up on the [roof], you know, like a sniper up there shooting members." But there was still an Amnesty International poster on the wall behind him.

The work of documentation has been undertaken in the main by members of the IS research staff. It is they who have imbibed and disseminated the ethos, supplemented by a handful of policy, legal, and publications staffers. The intensity of their commitment is evident in the words researchers use about their work: "I love my job. I love, you know, I love the fact that I feel I make a difference. . . . [But] I work as though it's a crisis all the time. . . . you can never take holidays. . . . I've got so much leave built up already . . . because if you go away, you just know that no-one else is going to look after it. You know. Who, who on earth is going to take care of it?" This was from a new researcher. Another, very senior ex-IS manager said he felt grateful for his time there, whereas an experienced researcher recalled that at first she "adored working for Amnesty . . . if I went on holiday, I couldn't wait to get back." These emotive words, expressing sentiments shared by many at the IS, show the spirit of the ethos. But we must add to this both the indifference that ideals, utopian and boundless in their scope, show towards their champions, and the particular issues that attend working on someone else's behalf.

Moral altruism is demanding, in other words. Advocating for others but not as their designated representative leaves the altruist in the position of making crucial moral decisions, such as when is enough effort enough, about others who are suffering but have no say. The price of moral authority is anxiety and guilt. Representation—acting under some form of instruction—leaves the responsibility for tough choices with those whose interests are the ones at stake. This is more like political authority. In the past, human rights workers have had to draw moral limits for themselves, the obligation they feel to help adding to a sense of self-blame for failure. Consider the rest of Benenson's 1963 editorial on Grimau:

> It is easy on the occasion of a birthday to look back with satisfaction, or forward with anticipation. In the case of this movement, when we look back it is with a sense of deep shame that we have at times thought more about ourselves than others. And when we look forward, it is in the knowledge that our resources—and we ourselves—are inadequate to meet a challenge which is not of our making. But if we fail, let it never be said that we have not thrown the last ounce of energy into the struggle, or scraped the skin off our knuckles rapping at the prison doors.[24]

Motivation is deeply bound up with why individuals want to do the work *themselves* (as opposed to supporting it financially).[25] At the beginning, there was no meaningful distinction between staff and members; all were unpaid. As the staffers were transformed into employees, they kept (and passed on) a commitment to the ethos that was not professional but vocational ("not a job, but a life choice"). It was like a calling. Thus, the keepers of the flame form a kind of amateur (vocationally oriented) profession inside a bureaucracy. This has made problematic the integration of those with commercial skills who could not, almost by definition, be "part of the heartbeat" (to use one fund-raiser's words). It raises the vexed question of paying high wages to attract senior staff whose expertise may not even be in human rights.

Contested authority, graphic and disturbing images and stories, lack of resources, guilt, vocational versus nonvocational commitment—all these things have their effects inside the IS and in the personal lives of the staff. Amnesty is a very human organization, in other words. Yet an ethical organization should be different, shouldn't it? Did I think life inside the secretariat would be like "Walt Disney?" I was asked in one of my first staff interviews. I suppose I did think that. This was, after all, the international staff of Amnesty International—*the* organization committed to the dignity of the individual. I felt the weight of moral inferiority just watching staff members go in and out of the security doors that protect the IS inner sanctum. Were these not the good people with the good hearts? My interviewee said she too had expected Disneyland, but she had been wrong, she said emphatically. (Someone later said that this is what Disneyland is really like.) Ideals are a heavy burden to carry.

And yet this purity is precisely part of the attraction. It is what creates "fire in the belly," as one young volunteer put it. It is a siren call. A senior manager said she had been attracted by this, "the magic of Amnesty," even though, she said, "the word was out, you know. . . . And I'd asked around. I was still shocked. I mean, I was absolutely appalled by how bad it was." She spent the first three weeks wanting to resign.

The culture of the IS is, unsurprisingly, messy. Often pained and suffocating, it is full of commitment and determination alongside unhappiness and resentment. The nature of the work—filing cabinets full of pictures of torture, walls covered in posters about suffering, endless stories of executions and the roll call of the disappeared, mission visits to prisons, and dealing with phone calls from desperate relatives—manifests in the staff an anger that must be repressed in order to do the work. Long and late hours, untaken holidays, and unrelenting stress are for many the norm. It is not an easy life and clockworklike efficiency is not one of its virtues. As further evidence that morality is at work, that the reasons for action have nothing to do with their advocates' own interests, the negative effects of human rights work are hard to beat. But still the flame burns and still the power of the ideal is strong, and the volunteers to work for Amnesty line up around the block.

A Secular Religion?

Amnesty staff and members often use religious language and ideas when talking about the organization even if they are not religious themselves. Any naïve assumption that you are entering a wholly secular space is soon dispelled when a senior member of the Amnesty movement tells you, "I don't see why we can't take sides. Jesus took sides all the time." Or a program director recalls being told his radicalism would fail because "the cardinals will get you in the end." One young IS staffer on the research and policy side said working at Amnesty was "almost like being a professional Catholic," whereas an elderly unpaid volunteer in the Americas Program, who joined Amnesty in 1961, put the ethos succinctly in the words of Christ: "If you visit a prisoner, you visit me."

Christianity, culturally and spiritually, was an integral part of Amnesty's origins. Yet it was secular in doctrine, drawing only on the UDHR for external support and developing, internally, a set of rules and principles to guide its way. There is no mention of a god in its statutes, and many staff and members are either nonreligious or non-Christian. And yet we can already see that if we use the idea of an NGO or a social movement (organized around interests and/or identities) we fail to capture precisely what Amnesty is. It is one of the key thinkers in sociology and social theory, Émile Durkheim, who comes to our aid.

For Durkheim, churches were not divinely inspired acts of shared worship but no more (nor less) than a community's recognition of itself, of its own collective reality. He defined religion as *"A unified system of beliefs and practices relative to sacred things, that is to say, things set apart and surrounded by prohibitions—beliefs and practices that unite its adherents in a single moral community called a church."*[26] Amnesty became this kind of moral community. Integral to religion for Durkheim was a division between two worlds, the *sacred*, where communal identity and one's place within it was reaffirmed, and the *profane*, the world of day-to-day existence. All religions must keep these worlds apart because, if the profane pollutes the sacred, the renewal of the society will be impossible. This line between sacred and profane is also the boundary between moral and political authority.

From where does this sacredness come? For Durkheim, "when collective life reaches a certain degree of intensity it awakens religious thought," creating a "state of effervescence."[27] Although faith initially underwrites this effervescence, an answer soon has to be found to the question all constructed communities need to ask themselves: "Why are we here together?"[28] Durkheim argues, "Men cannot celebrate ceremonies for which they see no rationale, nor accept a faith they cannot understand. To spread it, or simply to maintain it, one must justify it—in other words, generate a theory of it."[29] It was the role of the IS and the few senior members of the burgeoning movement to generate this theory. As Durkheim says, "For society to become conscious of itself and sustain its feeling of itself with the necessary degree of intensity, it must gather individuals together in sufficient concentration. Now, this concentration determines an exaltation of moral life that is expressed by a set of ideal conceptions in which the new life thus awakened is portrayed."[30] This was the situation in which the IS found itself. As Amnesty evolved, its symbols, doctrine, and internal lore took on the significance of "things set apart," and, although the growing membership met once a year (at this stage) and its executive four times a year, it was in the IS—an institution permanently in session—where the sufficient concentration was found, out of which the ideal conceptions, what Amnesty was and ought to be, were fashioned. Here we also find clues to other aspects of Amnesty's internal life.

In regard to personal sacrifice, for example, Durkheim points out that some kind of distinction is to be expected between the moral life, that which is different, and therefore sacred and therefore authoritative, and the ordinary profane life, which is less pure but more human. Such devotion requires "discomfort and renunciation"[31] (as we see in chaps. 2 and 7). Sacrifice through self-denial is a signal of morality.

Amnesty's practical origins and aversion to theorization, based on a shared wavelength, has made it resistant to critique and often extremely skeptical about outsiders. For Durkheim, faith was a "predisposition for belief which precedes proofs, [and] leads the intelligence to bypass the inadequacy of logical reasons" allowing an individual to make the "leap to believe" that is "precisely what constitutes faith; and it is faith that gives authority to rites in the believer's view." Even those who may question their religion at the intellectual level do not shift automatically into doubt: "The very fact that among them faith has lost its intellectual roots lays bare its deeper rationale. This is why facile critiques, which sometimes submit ritual prescriptions to a simplistic rationalism—generally leave the faithful quite indifferent."[32]

Finally, we know that efforts to decenter the permanent staffers, who have carried the ethos since the 1960s, have met considerable resistance. As Durkheim concludes:

> A society is not simply constituted by the mass of individuals who compose it, by the land they occupy, by the things they use, by the movements they make, but above all by the idea that it fashions of itself. And of course it may hesitate over its conception of itself: it feels pulled in divergent directions. But these conflicts, when they erupt, take place not between the ideal and the reality but between different ideals, between the ideal of yesterday and the ideal of today, between one that has the authority of tradition and one that is still evolving.[33]

Amnesty should be understood as a kind of church, and in what follows I provide a great deal of evidence in favor of this way of thinking. In the book's conclusion, I elaborate further on the implications and limitations of such an approach.

Conclusion

Moral energy once flowed through the words Amnesty used. It is the reformers' case that those words, a thicket of internal lore, are now dissipating and diverting that energy. For them, in the end, words are no more than an instrument, a conduit, for moral energy. They channel it; they neither create it nor legitimize it. To allow the words such sacred status is to give permanence to contingency and re-create the kind of authority structures that limit the capacity for social change. To these campaigners must be added the modernizers, for whom intensified competition about Amnesty's future in a globalized world means making the most of its most lucrative commodity, its reputation, as a brand. Both strands of sentiment—keepers of the flame and reformers—exist throughout the movement as well, among the 1.7 million current members, international office holders, and national section staffs. In rejecting much of the logic of change, the guardians of the ethos fear Amnesty's moral authority is eroding. Under pressure to commodify itself they believe the sacredness that attends its historical work is under serious threat.

Yet all of this may seem somewhat abstract and unreal. To remedy this, we look in chapter 2 at life inside the IS, concentrating on how the ethos has impacted on physical and emotional space. Chapter 3 gives a fuller account of Amnesty's foundation and the religionless Christianity that proved such fertile soil. In chapter 4, we move on to the evolution of secular religiosity in Amnesty's practice of bearing witness and the research culture in which it was embedded. It was here, in the IS of the 1970s and 1980s, that symbolic moral authority was nurtured. Chapter 5 introduces the struggle for political authority and recounts the first concerted efforts at reform of the ethos. At the forefront of this drive was a newly empowered Amnesty section in the United States. Chapter 6 gives us a sense of what is at stake for Amnesty in a world where being good is as important for one's authority as doing good. Chapter 7 then brings the story up to date, dealing with contemporary reform efforts within the IS and the Amnesty movement. In the conclusion, chapter 8, we return to various issues touched on in the introduction: subjectivity and objectivity in morals and social action, identities and choices, and personal morality.

2 SHADOWS AND DOORS

what should we expect working life inside the International Secretariat of Amnesty International to be like? Going through the front doors is a daunting enough experience on its own. The IS is based on Easton Street, a side road just off Rosebery Avenue in northeast central London. Amnesty owns and occupies most of both sides of Easton Street, the separate buildings joined high in the air by an enclosed bridge, in the center of which is a large circular window.[1] The older part of the building, a decaying former paint factory, is No. 1 Easton Street, which has been the home of the IS since 1983. The building cost about £1.25 million to buy before renovations and was the first IS premises that Amnesty owned.[2] It was later renamed Peter Benenson House in honor of Amnesty's founder. No. 1 Easton Street is heavy and somber. Grayish walls rise straight up several stories from the pavement.

If one word sums up the impression this austere structure made on me, that word was *institution*. In this, the IS building reflects its historical ethos. From the first instant it feels heavy, physically and emotionally. Ought we to expect a senior director in the world's foremost transnational human rights organization to say, for example, "Sometimes you do feel you're running a sheltered workshop, for the socially challenged"? Or expect another senior manager, with a private-sector background, to reflect that "it is the least caring organization I have ever worked in"?[3] One staffer, with many years experience in not-for-profit work, remarked, "I just thought, isn't it just sad, really that . . . the experience of that collection of people in the organizational form can produce so much hurt, actually. And quite a lot of callous behavior. And yet if you sat those individuals down they'd all be motivated from pretty good ethical values. . . . There's a sort of shadow side, or whatever, in the organization." We return to the shadow in a moment. Forty years of painstaking, disturbing, unglamorous, unfeted work has taken its toll. It is an ethos-inspired institutional understanding that Amnesty does not claim its successes, that the anonymity of the researchers is a strongly held principle, and that explicit praise is rare.

This organizational culture may seem to be a side effect of longevity, but the point cannot be made too strongly that it is not. The experience of the first person to run what would later become the Research Department, a German émigré named Christel Marsh, echoes that of today's salaried researchers; she started work in 1961, just four days after the Appeal for Amnesty was launched. Almost immediately she had to deal with fledgling members pressing her for copious and detailed information, cope with the lack of resources (she had to buy her own card index, for example, to record case material), and deal with the poor physical environment in Benenson's office basement.

In an *Amnesty Bulletin* published at the time, she wonders aloud if it is worth it, saying she relies on her conscience to keep her going (although, she says, doubts creep back when she emerges through her door into the sunlight).[4] As for workload, her husband and fellow Amnesty stalwart, Norman Marsh, recalled:

> People don't realize but Christel spent not only an enormous length of time at the thing, but worked all through the night. I helped her with it. She would come home with piles of letters, drafting letters to people and causes and groups and who knows what else all over the world. She did most of the work at home because the conditions in the office, to begin with, were such that they were so crowded. It was funny, you could go downstairs, you could see down the steps of Mitre Court, down in the basement you'd see people writing letters on the floor, in one corner, all in little corners. It was an extraordinary situation.[5]

From the first, the work was hard and underresourced, yet the ethos made of this no more than an occupational hazard, Durkheim's "discomfort and renunciation." The emotional impact of this working culture is the subject of a later section. The next section begins with a fuller account of the interaction between moral idealism and tangible space.

Doors

For a movement legitimized by universal principles, Amnesty is strongly defined by the system of sovereign nation-states. Members are organized into national sections—AI Peru, AI Senegal, and so on—and the movement's political economy is almost entirely national. The IS gets its £25 million a year (as of 2003) from money raised not by the members of Amnesty International but of AIUK or AI France. Each section jealously guards its national media and fund-raising space, national boards paying an assessment based on declared income to keep the IS afloat.

This form of international organization—the Red Cross model—must have seemed natural in 1961. What was less obvious, perhaps, was that the work itself would be organized along national lines. States, even postcolonial ones, controlled security and information, and those whom Amnesty sought to free were locked away in the least accessible places of all, prisons. This is where researchers had to begin, committing themselves to negotiated rather than clandestine entry.[6] In the first *Amnesty* newsletter of June 1961, Benenson wrote: "We have not the slightest intention of dabbling in the domestic affairs of other nations. We are concerned only with the basic human right of any man or woman to give visual or vocal expression to sincerely held beliefs. But when this right is infringed then we shall strive to mobilize world opinion to the point where it can no longer be flouted by the abusers of political and religious liberty."

For scholars of international relations, especially the so-called realists, this states-system is familiar. Anarchy has been its defining feature, meaning not disorder but a system in which independent units are subject to no superior authority, making interstate relations entirely questions of force and interest rather than trust and morality.[7] One legendary IS staffer, now retired, called the researchers "kings and queens," and she was right. Just as monarchs and modern nation-states have sovereign equality, so the Research Department came to recognize no superior authority. Researchers became the authorities on their national domains, reinforcing the territorial state as the prime unit of analysis. Practical knowledge production made the state appear more, not less, natural, despite Benenson's hope for a revived sense of global community and the commitment researchers held and hold to the idea of moral solidarity. It is this international space, beyond the state, that reformers want to flesh out.

Scarce resources made regions the initial focus. In 1966, Maureen Teitelbaum, then in effect the head of research, wrote:

> It seems to me the Investigation Bureau can only work really efficiently if we have 5 people in the office dealing with the five main regions. They would allocate and supervise the work of volunteers who would then specialize in a particular country. The 5 people (who could be part time) in the office would be specialists in the affairs of a whole region and would watch the developments as to political or religious prisoners in the various countries of that continent. They would then decide what was to be investigated really closely and prepare briefs for the volunteer investigators.[8]

In the original draft of the memo, the first two mentions of *region* are inked in over the word *continent, continent* surviving once at the end. As the size of the research staff grew, expertise would be more narrowly defined as country specific. Early on, however, some researchers worked even on countries from different geographical regions.

I asked one researcher from the 1960s about country expertise, and she replied, "How else could it have been organized?" I said, "Thematically?" She went on:

> If your task, your mission, your job is to get these people out of prison, then you have to know as much as possible . . . About who they are and the context in which they are imprisoned. . . . And if you say, let's concentrate on journalists, then if you have journalists in prison in forty countries, you have to have a professional research competence in forty countries . . . and that's more difficult than having a professional competence . . . in journalism. So it seems to me that to work thematically presupposes a very strong research infrastructure . . . Because that's essentially the first step . . . and the thematic research is the second.

For a world of separate sovereign units without superior authority read a building with separate sovereign researchers in their individual offices and skeptical about the claims to superior authority of both management and the leadership of the movement.[9] This has a strongly practical dimension. Reading through material, conceiving of and writing reports, and checking information—the key elements of research—necessitate concentration and so require seclusion. However, because research has been the primary organizational output, its production structuring everything downstream, from campaigns to membership action, the culture of research has become the dominant feature of everyone else's working life. Amnesty researchers see research as action, Amnesty as a whole talks of "research and action," but the reality has been research, then action (as we see in chap. 4). This is the crucial division of labor. Despite numerous efforts at integration, this essentially linear relationship has never been overcome. It is not just about the temporal priority of research (i.e., that it must come first); it is about the key role research plays as Amnesty's foundational practice, that of bearing witness. It has special, moral authority. Research practice embodies the ethos. It admittedly puts huge pressure on the researchers—everyone is waiting expectantly for the material, the cases and reports, to flow from them. Even without the sacrificial demands of the ethos, this clamor from below reinforces the researchers' commitment to private space as a protection from being overwhelmed. This was already Christel Marsh's experience in 1961, within months of starting work.

Space was an issue for Secretary General Thomas Hammarberg when the IS moved to Easton Street:

> I took the line that I would respect the opinion of people on their own future working conditions—but that I wanted people to be open-minded and learn about different alternatives before making up their minds. Many staff were shown "landscape" and "open plan" offices in that process. There were a lot of discussions in the IS. The final conclusion was that people wanted to be able to close a door behind them. This conclusion may be seen as disappointing, but I feel it should still be respected. It was not reached lightly and some of the arguments were convincing. There is no "right" or "wrong" on this.[10]

We return to open-plan offices shortly when considering a £10 million refurbishment of the IS, but first let us consider the building as a whole. Amnesty members and the 400-plus-person staff refer to *the IS* in such a way that it is impossible to disentangle the building from its occupants. A phrase used by the current management in its efforts to change secretariat culture has been "Getting the IS out of the IS." The desire has frequently been expressed by some sections that the IS be moved out of Britain entirely (when Benenson parted with Amnesty on bad terms in 1967, he made the same plea).

The small entrance space at the IS is dingy: a worn carpet, shelves of Amnesty publications, a smoking room, and a handful of chairs under the gaze of a glass-fronted reception desk. Rubbish frequently litters the streets outside. On the one poster wall in the lobby—wedged in front of the entry doors—are a variety of letters, news cuttings, and publicity about Amnesty's latest campaign. These are often cut out by hand, stapled onto colored paper, and appended to message boards wrapped in black plastic dustbin liners. Whatever message this self-made culture sends, it is not a corporate one. It is a different world from the offices of Amnesty's only real rival in the global human rights field, Human Rights Watch, which are cramped to be sure but command stunning views of Manhattan from midway up the Empire State Building.

To get further inside, you must enter the "airlock," two electronically activated doors that cannot both be open at the same time. While states busily hide what they do from Amnesty, Amnesty—fearing infiltration—hides what it does from states. Prisoner files are locked away in the archive for decades. One interviewee recalled that years earlier in the Middle East Program a senior manager would walk down the corridor at the end of the day shouting, "Security, lock your windows and your cabinets." There are still internal electronic security doors that lock at 6 PM. These arrangements are not obsolete; in 2001, they prevented members of a Turkish Leftist group who stormed the lobby (on the day Secretary General Pierre Sané left the IS) from entering the building proper (the facilities manager was kept hostage before police freed her).

Once through the airlock, you are certain, without guidance, to lose your way in the sprawling Amnesty occupation of its two premises. Through many physical incarnations, the IS has grown into its buildings, fashioning them through practice not design into a rabbit warren of offices, corridors, and overcrowded space deluged in paper. The walls of the main stairwell, painted in pastel shades of pink and blue, have occasional posters of POCs or Amnesty milestones, the odd congratulatory letter or award. But the many corridors that run off the stairwell are decorated in program-specific ways—from pictures of staff members as children to (in the regional programs) maps of subregions of continents to Amnesty posters to letters of thanks to paintings of executions to ethnic wall hangings.

Almost all of this visual culture relates to Amnesty's work in some way, but none of it is corporate in the sense of institutionally managed to create a favorable impression. A corporate style is only evident in the offices of the Human Resources Program, where large glass windows are embossed with Amnesty candles and orange and red chairs are purposely intended to symbolize the flame. As the IS support staff has grown, the distance between these new employees and the candle is inevitably greater. They are far from the ethos and the core work, have generic skills, and have no authority within a building where some researchers started work for Amnesty in the 1970s. As the proportion of staff members who are not close to the main work increases, more effort has to be made to create a sense of common purpose. A certain skepticism, even a disdain, of the keepers of the flame for the profane work of housekeeping, the running of the IS physically and financially, has been a recurring theme.[11]

It should be clear already that a coterie of core staff members feel alienated neither from their work nor their workplace, recalling fondly small eccentricities such as the mouse that used to inhabit the Research Office, the staff member who would bring her dog to work or practice her violin, and the stray cat in the Africa Program who is fed rather than ejected. There is a kind of reassuring domesticity about all of this, as there is about the small kitchens on each floor, with the attendant politics of mugs and food in fridges. There are no vending machines here. And the Nobel Prize citation from 1977 is nowhere to be seen.[12] As with the entrance hall, whatever is on the walls is there because someone has chosen to put it there. This is not a building where internal culture is managed by a single overarching authority, and because outsiders rarely get access only the initiated see this eclectic kaleidoscope. On the inside, AI's image is left to the IS staffers to fashion—it cannot be sold to them because they already own it. Given this radical autonomy, who cares for the structure as a whole? The answer, until now, has been no one.

The building is dying. They would be lucky if it made it through another winter, the facilities manager told the staff in 2003. When consultations were held in 2001 and 2002 on raising IS morale, the building was a major source of frustration. Its basement offices flood with drain water, the heating breaks down, rain seeps through the roof causing power cuts, fleas inhabit the carpets in some ground-floor offices, and the passenger lifts are in terminal decline. When newly arrived Deputy Secretary General Kate Gilmore tried to boost spirits by making small improvements, this was the response:

> One of the first things I remember about Kate when she first got here was that there were complaints that the place was awful. It was shabby and it was rundown and it was an awful place to work, which it is. One of the things Kate did was she . . . ordered a firm to put flowers in. Plants. A really nice gesture. Inexpensive. Relatively inexpensive . . . and then the very next morning afterwards she was crucified by a couple of people from the . . . other parts of the building who just thought that it was just a waste of money. It was a disgraceful thing to do. I mean, that sums this place up.

Some staff even see virtue in the dilapidated offices, which are luxurious they say when compared with the poverty experienced by many of those they try to help. Here are the views of a researcher who has been at the IS since the late 1970s and recalled the pre-Easton Street building:

> I mean, when the people that I work with, when they see this office, my God, it's . . . we look like the UN, don't we? You know. And I can remember being really embarrassed in a sense. When we moved from our shabby old place in Covent Garden and we came here. And that was the embarrassment. I mean, we are working with the poorest of the poor. And the, the most powerless people in the world. And they come here and of course what do they think? You know. We are, we are a rich Western organization.

The only real collective space is a low-ceilinged, suffocating room with fixed square pillars, an enormous television, and a large cardboard cutout of the Amnesty candle. When fully opened, it is big enough to hold only perhaps half the staff. The canteen has long since been dismantled. There is nothing welcoming, functional, or attractive about any of this space at all, especially in the old building where everything is very square and solid, straight lines, hard edges, and right angles. Even an earlier attempt to create a more transparent meeting space for senior staff—the curved fishbowl outside the secretary general's office—resulted in a stifling oppressive room whose single overhead fan is necessary but too noisy when turned on.

One of the first people I talked to about the building took me to see what she had found on her first day—a teaspoon chained to the wall above one of the kitchen sinks. Another said, "When I joined here, I was very aware that perhaps superficially, the building seems okay. It's a bit dingy, its not really been cared for. It's not bright, airy, open. But I think by far the worst thing is that, for me, it encapsulated everything that I thought Amnesty was supposed to be campaigning against in the world." She drew a parallel with Greenpeace's UK offices where "they use reclaimed timber . . . [and] the building is sort of managed in an energy efficient way . . ." so that the staff's "campaigning work is manifest in the physical space." She said of Amnesty, however, "For me here, it was a prison. Lots and lots of dark, dingy corridors with little cells of offices off them, and I just thought this is, is not going to positively contribute at all to the staff of the secretariat seeing the world that they want to be in their work."

In reality, the hitherto dominant conception of Amnesty's work *is* manifest in the physical space—country-based research, an antipathy to money, and a strong sense of staff ownership. This was the house the ethos made. Now, however, a £10 million refurbishment of the IS was to reverse the usual polarity—function would follow form in a purpose-built space. This change in working organization was principally about creating space for extra staff and increasing the value of the building, which had fallen because of its dilapidation. But part of its rationale was, as one IEC member put it, "dethroning the emperors." Reformers hoped for a different kind of atmosphere, more noise, more of a campaigning feel—not what a human rights activist from Africa found entering the IS as a staff member: "I can remember the first thing that surprised me was going for a walk down the corridor . . . of the Africa Program . . . And seeing a sign saying 'Do Not Disturb.' . . . I had never ever, ever in my life seen that before. That shocked me."

Changing this culture, reformers knew, meant displacing the researchers, thereby changing the linear relationship (and, because research and the ethos are so heavily aligned, displacing the ethos as well). We have seen how Hammarberg fared. A senior manager from the post-Hammarberg era recalled, "It's funny you mention this thing about moving, because one of my goals, or one of my jobs was to reorganize the building. And this was, like, one of the greatest nightmares. Because to ask a researcher to move down the hall to a new office, you would have thought you were saying, you know, give up your first born child and throw it in the Thames." It was, he said, because people felt so besieged that the IS became like a kind of fort (others called it "the bunker"). It was, he said, "where people sort of hid . . . and that's why open plan generally was regarded with horror. Because at least you could close your door. And you'd get away from the pressure. It was just an enormous pressure cooker."

This private space is where filing cabinets bulge with years of research, from newspaper cuttings to testimony, and where shelves groan under the weight of papers, books, and the Annual Reports that many researchers have lined up as markers of the annual cycle in which they deliver a definitive judgment on their countries. A member of the Facilities Management Program (FMP), which manages the building, recalled trying to get a researcher to let them fix a dangerous shelf in her office:

It was wobbling, and it was completely overloaded with papers. I mean, it was very unsafe. And so [we] asked if it could be moved. And . . . were abused. I went up and asked, and I was told, I haven't got time to do this fucking filing. Do it your fucking self. And slammed the door. . . . We tried to move the papers and we got abused again. You can't touch these, this is my stuff. Complete disregard for the fact that this . . . could burn the building down, let alone it could kill people. . . . And it's not acceptable for the regional program specialists to treat the resource programs the way they do. . . . it really does feel sometimes like they treat you like a servant.

Senior managers in FMP talked about the personal abuse their staff had experienced, calling themselves, with irony, the "bottom feeders." As one IS senior director told the heads of all programs, research staffers treated FMP in a way they would never treat the legal staff (a sign of the IS internal class system, they were told). FMP staff bore the brunt of efforts to resist open-plan offices. A major clean-up campaign to remove the "IS paper mountain," so that the building did not lose its fire-safety certificate, also proved a long drawn-out affair, resulting, for example, in a senior director eventually telling reluctant staff forcefully that being closed down by the fire inspector "isn't going to help anyone's human rights."[13]

Maybe reformers see "walls as [the] researchers' last bastion," said a senior researcher as she emphasized the necessity of "private space in which one can, as a researcher, analyze and produce these reports." Offices clearly reflect status—they mirror proximity to the ethos—but functionality, making sensitive long-distance phone calls on poor lines and thinking through reports, was the nub of the researchers' argument for retaining private personal space. One veteran who joined in the 1980s said, "As a researcher, I felt very much that you close the door on what's happening in the IS because it's a distraction. And things are happening in the IS constantly. There's constantly a process of restructuring, there are changes, things good and bad changing all the time, but they are a distraction. And the focus is always external." Another said imperiously that if the walls were removed there would have to be a "culture of no talking," whereas a third said that life inside the building was not "real work," and so "[I] shut it out of my life." "I think probably a lot of people in the research team have that ability. That we can look out much more easily. And it's actually a problem because it means we don't engage enough with the building," said another. As far as one experienced Asia researcher was concerned, the proposal for open-plan offices was "devoid of any insight into the reality of the way we work," so much so that "I certainly felt it couldn't be taken seriously."

For many Amnesty staffers and members, this very certainty needs shaking in order to transform Amnesty back into a *movement* from what it has become, an *organization*. One senior IS staffer from the campaign side described the (literally) Herculean task that she saw as required: "You do an Augean stables. You just divert a river through here. . . . the only thing that scares these people is the movement. . . . So I just figure . . . what you do is wash the sections through here." This necessitated lobbying members: "We got them whipped up into such a state that, you know, they were like tabling resolutions all over the place. And the buzz that went through with those decisions. And change started to happen. . . . This isn't me anymore. This is the sections. . . . And if you do that with the campaigning sections, and the fund-raisers, and the regional coord[inators]. . . . And you just keep throwing change through this place, it will happen. But it will be nasty."

The Amnesty movement wants the IS to do a new kind of work, exemplified by the campaign launched in 2004 called Stop Violence Against Women (SVAW) and in the title ("Globalizing Justice!") of Amnesty's six-year (2004–2010) Integrated Strategic Plan (ISP). The ISP's preamble describes Amnesty's evolution from a prisoner-oriented organization to one embracing economic, social, and cultural rights. To deliver this, the ISP's organizational strategy, entitled "Releasing energy!", contains goals such as "build a dynamic architecture" (the financial strategy is simple: "Grow!"). The movement's leaders want to "recreate the energy people felt in the early days of Amnesty working on prisoners of conscience" (as one IEC member described it). The phrase *dynamic architecture* captures this perfectly. *Architecture* in this sense links the movement's body with its purpose. As senior IS managers told trade union members concerned about open-plan offices, "We also need to move to an architecture that stimulates exchange and facilitates more open and cooperative ways of working."

This shift is about engagement and social change, change that may require the private sphere—whether home, office, work environment, or Amnesty as a demarcated identity with clear boundaries—to be opened up. An SVAW campaign strategy document launched within the movement in December 2002 suggested as a campaign slogan "Bring Human Rights Home."[14] Among other things, the campaign challenges "governments to take down the barrier between 'public' and 'private' acts of violence," and aims "to change the public perception that human rights are an abstract concept and not relevant to daily life, especially at home where basic respect for individual life should begin." In order to make Amnesty itself more gender sensitive, the campaign was launched internally first (at the Mexico ICM in 2003) and externally only in March 2004.

Many staffers did not want to lose their offices during the 2004 refurbishment, but none could make the case that researchers could. The argument rumbled on for months. An email from directors denied that the secretary general had decreed open-plan offices before consultations even began. At a senior management meeting, grids that revealed which programs had agreed to the open plan and which had not were collected from directors lest they leak out and affect negotiations. Eventually, things were decided at a meeting of the heads of Amnesty's fifteen programs—an All Programs Forum—when it became clear that of these fifteen, eleven, including one regional program (the Americas), had accepted the open plan. Of the four regional programs that refused to budge, all the members of the Europe Program had requested offices (thirty-six of them) along with twenty-three members of the Middle East Program (which the meeting was told was an improvement). Eventually a deal was struck whereby the regional programs would each get a small and proportional allocation of glass cubicles, not private offices and not enough for each researcher to have one. Allocation was then left to the programs.

In defending their decision, directors named the inefficient use of space but also concerns about equity and the privilege of a minority of staff. This turning of the spotlight on Amnesty itself, an act of transparency, echoed comments that managers had made about reallocating space as a way to change Amnesty into a "community of shared purpose." The researchers fought back. "Having an office is not a privilege for me, it's a must," said one, while another argued that some IS staff *did* have greater responsibility for its core work than others.

I give the last word on this to an IS staff member who had also worked at Human Rights Watch. He captured the seductive but pained nature of a commitment to the Amnesty ethos. Human Rights Watch, he said, had a buzz about it that the IS did not, linked to its "performance kind of culture." But Amnesty was, he went on, "This incredible institution and organization and . . . people and the extraordinary work that's being done . . . and you walk in the front door foyer area and it just felt [he paused] depressing. It felt sad. . . . it sapped your energy."

Shadows

So why do people work at AI? The diversity of interview responses and the impossibility of getting a representative sample make only generalized inferences about background conditions possible. Many staff have a religious background, especially some form of Christianity, even though they may not be religious themselves.[15] Some said they had wanted to work for Amnesty for years, and in quite a lot of interviews it was clear that staff members came from backgrounds that were somehow socially engaged, with parents who did noncommercial work, for example. Relatively few had parents who had been Amnesty members. Although some recalled a formative event—either their own or their families' suffering or witnessing an act of great barbarity or courage—this was infrequent.

One stronger observation was that few staff members had any interest in commercial work, even if they had transferable skills. They liked being in an organization such as Amnesty, the political sympathies of the IS as a whole firmly on the liberal wing of the Left. This fuels a certain skepticism about corporatism and money. The majority, although not all, had a higher education (post-eighteen), especially the research staff (although to gauge this accurately for the staff as a whole a much more representative sample needs to be drawn). Measuring class would have been time-consuming and of limited use, although staff members do come from a variety of class backgrounds. The mix of morality and intellect was also a particular attraction for some. In the words of a former secretary general, it was a combination of "strong emotional commitment and intellectual discipline." The necessity of intellectual engagement inherent in the working culture and internal lore is partly what attracts motivated, educated people to come to and stay at Amnesty. It engages the mind as much as the heart, especially on the research and policy side.

A further attraction is Amnesty's reputation. Saying you work for Amnesty International usually elicits respect and admiration. It certainly leaves few people indifferent. One researcher told me that whenever he gets the chance to explain what Amnesty does (on this occasion to a taxi driver taking him home after a BBC radio interview) he gets a new member. He himself had applied eight times to work at the IS before being successful. Each time the Human Resources Program (HRP) advertises for volunteers, it is deluged. These are often young, educated, multilingual people, more women than men, who are soon frustrated with the mundane nature of volunteer work (filing and stuffing envelopes). HRP has even contacted local churches looking for older volunteers. It is particularly the regional programs—with their combination of stimulating work, travel, and reputation—that attract volunteers, unpaid young people who may have to begin with administrative work in a resource program (even with master's degrees). From here, they look for a volunteer opening in a region where, if they are successful, they find the same basic work required of them. The prize, for some, is permanency and eventually, for a few, researcher.

Some researchers recognize the dual nature of their positions:

There are parts of the building that don't travel. And in that way . . . aren't exposed and on the front lines . . . and I suppose in the politics of the building, we're the ones who people would want to be, because you're the ones who do the exciting adventurous stuff. And go off and, you know, see the situations and meet the people and all of that. And it's true, it's amazing and it's an amazing experience. And it's something I'll value forever.

This reflection came after a somber one, in which this young researcher said, "I've been on two long trips. I haven't been on that many. But by the end, I'm saturated with suffering, really. . . . And you just think, well I can't take any more of this. I can't, you know. . . . where does it go, or what can we do?"

This pattern was familiar. Whenever researchers talked about difficulties in their working lives, they almost always compensated with a reference to *privilege*, the most frequently used word to describe what working for Amnesty meant to them. One veteran researcher described it thus:

I think it's something much more personal than [solidarity]. I think it's something that comes from a sense of sharing a danger. Sharing real humanity which doesn't exist outside of these situations. And it's a privilege to be part of that. It really is. Even though we share the danger from, from Amnesty, to a much lesser extent . . . there are risks but they are very much reduced in comparison to these people who are on the front lines every day. And I think to, to have the privilege of being part of that is, is something that keeps a lot of people here going.

Within a few minutes another veteran researcher went through the following emotions:

It's very difficult to turn your back on people when that's what you do it for . . .

You can sometimes influence things or make a difference. Or even just listen . . . you know, you're. . . . God knows why, these days, trying to maintain Amnesty's reputation that, you know, that Amnesty does care and it does listen and it is there.

I would put it back to my upbringing. You know, a ghastly sort of Christian acronym . . . Jesus first, others next, yourself last. Well, if you're going to put Amnesty at the beginning of that, then you're going to come up with a, sort of cry of pain is probably, you know, how you end up. But . . . you're in a building where everybody else, that you're working with is, you know, has the same attitude. And you have enormous, you know . . . I had a great time as well.

You know I traveled a great deal. I've done things . . . as an Amnesty researcher you do a whole gamut of things. Which are, you know, sound incredible to other people. You do CNN interviews, you go lobby the UN . . .

I like writing up, I like . . . getting the essence of something and putting it down. . . . it's a job I really love.

A cry of pain coupled with love? How many commercial firms could engage such emotions? Being at the IS is like being in a family, rewarding and painful. Not that either the cry of pain or the love is much in evidence. When you are "saturated with suffering . . . where does it go?" The answer is, into the shadows. In his memoirs, the psychoanalyst Carl Jung recalled one of his most vivid dreams:

It was night in some unknown place, and I was making slow and painful headway against a mighty wind. Dense fog was flying along everywhere. I had my hands cupped around a tiny light which threatened to go out at any moment. Everything depended on my keeping this little light alive. Suddenly I had the feeling that something was coming up behind me. I looked back, and saw a gigantic black figure following me. But at the same moment I was conscious, in spite of my terror, that I must keep my little light going through night and wind, regardless of all dangers.[16]

The light was his consciousness, the specter his own shadow inescapably cast by the flame. As a metaphor for Amnesty, this dream is unsurpassable. The shadow, the first Jungian archetype, is something we *all* possess, whether we think so or not. As the totality of our repressed tendencies, "the sum of all those unpleasant qualities we like to hide,"[17] it comprises the feelings, frustrations, and inclinations, the mastery of which has been seen as the hallmark of Western civilization. Jung sounds sympathetic to the ideology behind disciplinary power over children, women, colonies, and labor when he says, "If the repressed tendencies, the shadow as I call them, were obviously evil, there would be no problem whatever. But the shadow is merely somewhat inferior, primitive, unadapted, and awkward; not wholly bad." But he rescues himself: "It even contains childish or primitive qualities which would in a way vitalize and embellish human existence, but convention forbids!"[18]

When AIUK, a section whose traditional ethos is close to that of the keepers of the flame, undertook a rebranding survey, one observation from focus groups was that members got "passionate and upset" and were "often inarticulate when expressing how they feel." These members said things such as, "I believe in lost causes," "you just have faith," "I'm a member because I can't bear it," and "You make someone else's problem, your problem. Once you've joined, you have to accept that you are going to get upset on a regular basis." The survey found "a certain *child-like* quality to how members talk": "It's like when you're a child and you stamp your foot and you say, 'IT'S NOT FAIR!' " Fairness, it concluded, was central to Amnesty's appeal, its "buried treasure" being "the basic package of goodness that we have as a child (fearlessness, passion, sense of justice) that we spend most of our time as adults trying to reclaim."[19]

Benenson stamped his foot, invigorating those around him with his formidable zeal. This energy cannot be denied, and it cannot (always) be positive because we have darker feelings too. These have to be faced or eventually the shadow will "burst forth suddenly in a moment of unaware-ness," in Jung's words. This can result in very un-Amnesty things, as one staffer put it, implicitly dividing the moral world into two halves in which Amnesty/not-Amnesty mirrors good/bad, ideal/real, and inside/outside. She said, "I think people are basically good. I really do. I think there's a lovely bunch of people that work at Amnesty . . . but I think that they have, or we, we have, the same flaws as you would experience in wider society. So, even if people here are concerned and knowledgeable about, you know, human rights violations going on in the world . . . it doesn't mean that the lens they see through is completely clear." She was talking about racism, a very un-Amnesty thing (see chap. 6). Seeing people as basically good is a glimpse of the shadow. IS staff may have the same flaws as others, but they labor for an ideal that requires they remain on one side of the Amnesty/not-Amnesty line. Feelings of bitterness, frustration, anger, and self-interest do not fit. Indeed, feelings of any sort, even fatigue, may hamper the staffers' ability to go on, mired in the awful-ness of work on imprisonment, torture, violence, and death. Amnesty has been a light in the darkness at the cost of denying the darkness within itself.

It is part of being professional to limit your feelings of direct respon-sibility and control negative emotions. And yet the motivation and justi-fication for doing human rights work depends on these things not being true. This is an inescapable dilemma and the most stressful aspect of moral activism when you do not face a direct threat yourself (which would justify resistance in more obvious terms). Human rights workers must feel moral solidarity with those they help and must believe such an attachment exists to legitimize, to themselves and others, the work they do. It is not service work, despite efforts to evaluate outcomes using market notions such as utility and efficiency. Morality is more than and different from this. If staff members are alienated, they may as well work in a commercial job with better terms and conditions, and ethically speak-ing they probably should.

Medics face similar dilemmas, but their sense of obligation is profes-sional and vocational, not necessarily moral (although it often is, to be sure). Their authority over patients is theoretical of the nonmoral type. They act as skillfully as they can in the best interests of the patient. But to be good doctors does not require they feel solidarity. Their work is service provision, patients in reality paying for their expertise directly or through the taxation system. Some of the problems humanitarian orga- nizations face in terms of professionalization and bureaucratization stem from their failure to fully comprehend the implications of this fact. What human rights activists provide is not a service—it is a self-defined, and self-funded, mission. If IS staffers were "gambling something," as one staff member who had once risked a great deal described it, the question of moral responsibility would not arise because they would be *being* not *doing*. Consider this view from an African human rights activist compar- ing his work for rights in Africa, "in the jaws of the lion," with coming to work at the IS: "We never took ourselves seriously. We laughed. You go to a, a demonstration, get beaten up by the police. Some people are arrested, some people die. But . . . you come out and laugh. Have a drink and laugh about it. [At the IS] I had never seen such a serious place! It bothered me. Why people took themselves so seriously here." Performing the role of an external, self-appointed champion fuels the sense of guilt. There is always more to be done. As one veteran of twenty years explained, "There's a lot of stress. Because . . . you don't want to let anybody down. . . . This is the dilemma we're facing. When they first started asking us to plan . . . it's impossible. I can't tell somebody we are shut. I told them, you can't say you are shut. You can't do it! . . . but it's up to you. So really, you are left to deal with it the way you see fit. So you just have, you have to do your best." Some researchers even feel that they, not the organiza- tion, are personally responsible for prisoners. As one explained, "There's, there's this terrible weight of expectation. You know, you can't leave it. You can't not do this. Just one more action. Just one more urgent action, one more letter to government. But however much you do, you're never going to begin to respond to . . . everything that's happening in the coun- tries you're working on." Saying no on missions was even harder than saying no at the IS, said another: "I've found myself in the situation of, you know, twelve o'clock at night, holding hands with a priest and five other prisoners in a circle on our knees praying. Which isn't a situation you really want. At twelve o'clock at night, you just don't want to be in a prison." Often, sources and contacts in the country, some who expose themselves to great risk, become friends. It is on these mission visits that the energy that comes from meeting people in the field, face to face, is generated.[20] The missions also serve to replenish the authority of researchers inside the building—they have direct contact with the suffering from which Amnesty draws moral strength. Working on the violent threshold between life and death exerts a strangely compelling pull, transcending the mundane and the profane.

Feelings of obligation are pervasive. A very senior staffer from the 1980s talked about "this enormous guilt, that you're not doing enough": "At the end of the day, people are responsible for people's lives. That's how Amnesty's set up and that's what makes it great. That's what makes it work. Unlike Human Rights Watch, which doesn't really have a kind of personal relationship to . . . a prisoner or to a family whose person has been killed in an extra-judicial execution or someone on death row. Amnesty did. It was built on it." This staff member had just described his job at Amnesty as impossible and his time there as "Frankly a nightmare, I mean, [to be] totally honest with you, these were the worst . . . years of my life." Still, he said, he would consider going back to Amnesty (although not to the IS).

For researchers, feelings of personal responsibility partly explain their determination to defend the primacy of research: "As a researcher you feel sometimes if you fell under a bus, the next day it would be really difficult for anybody to make a decision on anything in your country." She went on, "One of the reasons you become perhaps a little paranoid is because you know that the buck will stop with you. And I can remember coming from a session with a campaigner where I sort of said, listen, if you publish what you want to say it's over my dead body. Because you won't have to bear the brunt from that. It'll be me answerable to the press on all of this. And the public." This veteran researcher was scathing about the idea that experienced researchers should, during crises, swap "holding the fort, making sure that everything that went out was coherent and accurate," for "being an activist in the field, dancing around with a microphone."

Reformers see things differently. One intent on making changes to the ethos was acutely aware of how much a sense of guilt suffuses the organization:

I was talking to one of the . . . regional people who was at the ICM [Mexico]. And, you know, I was just saying that I felt . . . that the researchers . . . we allowed them to become terribly brutalized.

And she took real issue with the word brutalized. Because it implied in her mind that they *were* therefore brutalized. Well actually that is the truth. I'm sorry, but it is the truth. . . . And having been a researcher herself, she sort of just started to talk about it. . . . And she was saying, you never forget. You never forget the ones you didn't help. And, you know, I just thought my God, it's so alive. You know. It runs terribly deep.

Others are less tolerant of the kind of heroic individualism that binds the researchers to the POCs and the disappeared. No researcher would say, as one nonresearch senior manager did, "I bet your average prisoner of conscience is a pain in the butt. They're arrogant, they won't listen to anybody. . . . they're individualized. They stand out, they hate community. You know . . . they'll challenge everything, they're afraid of nothing."

Much more familiar for research staff is agonizing over whether a hotel was too luxurious, a meal too expensive, a drink and a swim after visits to prisons an indecency. Even the counseling available to IS employees is offered by a private firm off-site, as if the shadow must not be acknowledged as part of Amnesty because it somehow profanes the suffering of the real victims. The "palpable strain of the place," as it was described, should come as no surprise. Many of those I interviewed said they found the interviews cathartic ("the best free therapy I ever had," said one), and my two feedback sessions to the assembled staff seemed to be well received because of their frankness about problems inside. I was not a consultant, and I had only questions not answers. These sessions simply acknowledged the issue from a vantage point outside, always a place treated with suspicion by IS staff.

Alongside the sense of personal responsibility is the material itself, especially interviewing prisoners, hearing their testimony, and seeing pictures of their injuries. One researcher on Asia gestured to her filing cabinet, stressing how some graphic photographs had to be kept securely locked away for fear someone might see them accidentally. For her, it was part of being a professional that she could view this material without being incapacitated. This is not a concern just for researchers. Campaigners, audiovisual and publications staff, and others often have to deal with this aspect of the work. Many have found it difficult.

I mean, the first time I went around to the photo library, I remember this clearly. I'll never forget this picture. I'd been here . . . three days or something. And that . . . I mean, I've been in the Lebanese civil war . . . you know . . . I've been in real life horrendous situations, so it wasn't like I was completely green. And I went down and picked this picture up. And I couldn't grasp what it was. I couldn't sort of understand that it was an execution. And that I suddenly . . . it was like my brain wouldn't register the horror it was seeing, and then it suddenly did. Which was a decapitated head. Lying on the ground. Next to the guy that had been tied to the pole. And I just started to vomit, you know, retching. And I had to run from the room. I mean . . . I just think that is just straight irresponsible for an organization.

Humor is one way to deal with this awfulness. This interviewee went on: "In this corridor we're terrible about it. You know . . . the torture picture's no good. It's not nearly gruesome enough. . . . you just try to neutralize it through black humor. . . . you're saying, look this . . . is a pathetic case of torture. You know, I need a bit more detail and, and you hear yourself and think . . . that's revolting. But it's true! You need to wake people up with this!"[21]

One staffer measured how much he was affected by using "a very simple device": "I can show somebody a horrible photo and they screw up their face and turn away and say, that's horrible. And I can look at it and I just say, no, it just shows you . . . a person's head." The photos, he said, were bad but "you just get used to images of bodies and so forth." He went on, "What's more touching is, is testimony . . . because that's a real person telling you a story. And, and sometimes they're so painful . . . that I couldn't, for example, tell somebody. I would not feel like I could download it to somebody else. Because it's too horrible."[22]

For some Amnesty staff these experiences have been all too personal. They or their relatives have been tortured or imprisoned. One told me about his father whose eyes were pulled out under torture.[23] Another recounted the story of her sister who was disappeared. There are even a handful of staff members who are at risk enough to have close protection from Special Branch police officers in London. The risk of burnout is ever present, and many interviewees had stories of people who failed to cope or of their own difficulties coping. One senior campaigner described it as a "stress related fear of drowning."

This stress is a fact of life inside Amnesty. The anecdotal stories I heard were numerous—people sleeping under desks or saving emails they wrote at 11 PM to send the next morning to disguise their real hours or forgoing having children in order to keep working for Amnesty. And many accounts of breakdowns and health problems. One symptom of stress has been a very high incidence, since the introduction of computers in the early 1990s, of repetitive strain injury, and many staff members I talked to through the year had suffered or were suffering from it. I asked a member of the IEC whether it was possible to be in Amnesty and have a private life? "That's easy, no," came the instant reply. At the Mexico ICM, as the movement prepared to pass its ambitious strategic plan, an IEC member joked, "I hope the IS has a good mental health plan, that's all!"

Much of the stress staff members feel is caused by their own behavior toward one another. One interviewee recalled listening to two senior researchers discussing how much they hated their initial experience, that it seemed like the worst mistake of their lives and that their confidence was badly shaken as a result. The interviewee went on:

> These are very ambitious people you know . . . and it was difficult for them to handle. Anyway, twenty-five years on they're still here. But they talked about that in such a way, if there's anything we can do to, you know, go against that. Two minutes later we mentioned a report by another researcher. . . . And without even a second thought one of them said, well what do you expect? That idiot's just producing garbage like that. . . . And I just thought, you didn't even see, you've become the very thing you hated when you got here. And that you're saying you're fighting against now. . . . You're pretty intimidating yourself and you're saying that to me. I'm an external person [external to research]. How have you got that much of a blind spot? How can you not see your behavior like that? Very dismissive, you know. Expressions like . . . oh you wouldn't expect anything from them. Action is hardly their middle name is it.

Some complained of bullying, some of being reduced to tears by being shouted at in person or on the phone. The Media and Audio-Visual

Program (MAV) had a name for being savaged by researchers—they called it *munching*. It was a regular occurrence. Even the architects planning the IS refurbishment were shocked at their treatment in meetings with regional staff. One campaigner recalling experiences in a regional program described it as "the least agreeable, least friendly place I have ever been in," full of "deep rooted conflicts" where people would "take it out on each other." There were "fantastic people" at the IS, she said, but as a whole it was "the opposite of what we try to do in the outside world." She said, "Someone should be writing letters to Amnesty saying treat your staff better."

As an example, take the experience of a young woman with a university degree and private-sector experience. She was highly motivated to work for Amnesty, coming as she did from a religious background, and saw compassion as the key to her commitment. Highly articulate and thoughtful, she worked in a regional program first of all, where she said she was "bullied appallingly, a horrible situation." (It was difficult to believe of this confident and articulate young woman.) Things improved when she moved to another program; she talked of her admiration for specific research staff members whom she felt did very impressive work alongside "the dead wood." But her obvious competence meant she was now being given an increasing workload, leading to what she felt as "simmering resentment." She had, she added, sometimes been "just strung out and taken on far too much," staffers being expected to "sink or swim," while management could be "extraordinarily rude." But then she said, "A lot of its wonderful and I do love it [and] look forward to going to work. [It's] a real privilege to work here but it could be so much better."

This ethos-derived culture is not simply the product of long-serving staff members or a complex bureaucracy, the compacted sediment, as it were, of forty years. Already by 1967, the first systematic report into the secretariat, compiled at a time of near-fatal financial and management turmoil, talked of the "vicious circle . . . [of] officers overloaded with work, really important and absorbing work" who sacrificed timetabling, prioritization, delegation, and budgeting (planning, in other words) to cope with the short-term incessant demands of the core casework.[24] The report said, "The workload, consequently, was allowed to increase further without any guarantee that the most important tasks were carried out and that each task was carried out by the right person or in the best way. Attention to practical details was always neglected as there was always something more urgent to do." This could easily have been written now, word for word. Barely six years in, the stressful working environment was seen as an unavoidable side effect of dedication. The ethos was already embedded. The 1967 report went on:

> It is only through efficient administrative procedures that loss of time and effort-consuming confusion or uncertainty can be avoided. All this is really self-evident. However, during the hearings we felt that several of the officers did not like to think along these lines. The argument was put forward repeatedly that hard-working volunteers would resent an efficient organization. Efficiency was evidently associated with bureaucracy and lack of personal freedom. Adherence to administrative efficiency was believed to compete with dedication to the main tasks of Amnesty.

The last sentence says it perfectly. How can so little have changed? Amnesty staff are selected to challenge authority ("managing activists" was an oxymoron, said one director), and an aversion to management is a part of deep culture. Here is the view of a veteran researcher: "There is something magic about being unprofessional for a volunteer organization. Because the spirit is there. And you destroy the spirit with . . . too much legislation."

Management is deeply antithetical to the Amnesty spirit. Senior managers met in the 1980s under the name Group of Eight, and the internal phone directory is still organized alphabetically by first name, not surname, reflecting a time when the IS was more compact and staff turnover was low. More than one interviewee while reminiscing mentioned that secretaries general of old would serve a turn on the front reception desk and eat in the canteen and that most new staff—especially researchers—could expect a personal meeting with the secretary general at some point.[25] The divergence that grew in the 1990s between top and bottom salaries, when Amnesty accepted it had to pay to attract high-quality staff to senior positions, still rankles. In one of the first interviews I did with a senior researcher, for example, she remarked that Irene Khan was paid too much.

Amnesty has no real career structure, and for many reaching the post of researcher and Grade C is to reach a ceiling that cannot be surpassed because there have, historically, been few management jobs to move into and doing management would take these researchers away from the work—the countries and the victims—that is their reason for being involved in the first place. The managers there have been almost all followed the amateur-professional model, being activists-turned-managers, which means that actual management—by professional managers with management, not human rights, skills—has hardly ever taken place.

Whenever I asked in interviews about the workload and stress, almost everybody sighed, deeply. The workload is heavy, but the problem of workload has just as much to do with the lack of management and planning. In September 2003, the Human Resources Program conducted a stress audit throughout the IS. The return rate, out of more than four hundred staff, was on some questions close to 50 percent, where those responding chose one of four answers: often, sometimes, seldom, never. The six questions asked of staff, anonymously, were:

1. I am able to cope with the demands of my job. (Demands)

2. I am able to have a say over the way I do my work. (Control)

3. I believe that I receive adequate support and information from my colleagues and superiors. (Support)

4. I am subjected to unacceptable behaviors (e.g., bullying) at work. (Relationships)

5. I understand my role and responsibilities within the organization. (Role)

6. The organization engages staff frequently when undertaking organizational change. (Change)

The responses are shown in Table 2.1. The numbers for Support were considered low enough to be a priority area and the numbers for Change low enough to need attention. For Relationships, that 66 percent reported seldom or never was judged acceptable, even though 72 out of 210 respondents reported unacceptable behavior either often (fifteen staff members) or sometimes (fifty-seven staff members).

TABLE 2.1
Stress Audit Results for the International Secretariat as a Whole[a] 2003

	Often (a)	Sometimes (b)	Seldom (c)	Never (d)	Total (a + b)
Demands	112 (53%)	71 (34%)	21 (10%)	6 (3%)	87%
Control	110 (52%)	76 (37%)	21 (10%)	3 (1%)	89%
Support	57 (27%)	76 (36%)	62 (30%)	15 (7%)	63%
Relationships	15 (7%)	57 (27%)	57 (27%)	81 (39%)	(66%)[b]
Role	57 (27%)	89 (43%)	51 (24%)	13 (6%)	70%
Change	54 (25%)	78 (38%)	52 (25%)	26 (12%)	63%

[a] n = 210. All percentages are approximate; some have been rounded up or down to make the total equal 100%.
[b] The total here is c + d because the hoped for answer is in this case negative.

TABLE 2.2
Stress Audit Results for Regional Programs[a]

	Often (a)	Sometimes (b)	Seldom (c)	Never (d)	Total (a + b)
Demands	34 (42%)	30 (38%)	12 (15%)	4 (5%)	80%
Control	38 (47%)	31 (39%)	8 (10%)	3 (4%)	86%
Support	16 (20%)	29 (36%)	24 (30%)	11 (14%)	56%
Relationships	8 (10%)	18 (23%)	21 (26%)	33 (41%)	(67%)[b]
Role	17 (21%)	25 (31%)	26 (33%)	12 (15%)	52%
Change	13 (16%)	31 (39%)	22 (28%)	14 (17%)	55%

[a] n = 80. All percentages approximate; some have been rounded up or down to make the total equal 100%.
[b] The total here is c + d because the hoped for answer is negative.

The scores for the five regional programs—where the combination of researchers and nonresearchers make up about one-half the IS total staff—are shown in Table 2.2. Of the fifteen programs, the Asia Program and the Europe Program returned the most negative results, with every Europe Program result and all but one Asia result being ranked as for priority attention.

The areas where the main problems come all have to do with internal interpersonal and management matters: Support, Relationships, and Change. Support is a chronic problem and was scored even lower than average by the regional programs. With the regional programs firmly at the heart of the IS workstream, what many resource staff mean by "lack of support" is the way the regional programs treat them and vice versa. Many regional program staff members are unhappy, for example, about the support they receive on and after missions. Some feel isolated, with a high premium put on self-reliance. One researcher described his experience thus: "The first time I went away on mission . . . I was out there interviewing victims and there's no sort of counseling or any debriefing. . . . You weren't given the tools to deal with it. And I found, psychologically, I was just, you know, I came home and I was . . . very affected by it. That I was quite depressed for a period of about two or three months after this. I really burned myself out working . . . doing actions practically every day as a result of what I had seen." This had, he said, made him "pretty cynical about people who aren't from regional programs." The implication was that support staff do not understand. The danger of not sharing is clear—it feeds the shadow—but internalization is a common response. Another researcher recalled, "When you come back from mission, there's nothing worse than nobody wanting to hear. . . . I always assumed that people outside would be so interested in all that, but they, they don't want to hear. . . . They don't want to know. You go through all this experience, you go through all that and I suppose in the end I've kind of lost that need to share, but in the beginning I was desperate. Desperately wanting to talk to people about it."

At a 2003 meeting of the heads of the fifteen IS programs to discuss occupational health with a consultant, one regional director acknowledged that "the question of denial is very important in the regional programs," describing this "culture of self-sacrifice" as "whatever is happening to me it's worse for the people out there we are dealing with." This was followed by an illuminating exchange in which the consultant was invited to attend program meetings to discuss stress. How many programs are there, she asked? "Five," someone replied, to which others quickly responded, "there are other programs too."

Nothing, however, more starkly illustrates the split within the organization than the fact that, of the cohort of permanent staff members who have done the work that has made Amnesty's reputation, the stress audit found that only 52 percent said they understood what was expected of them (Role). As one researcher in the Europe Program described the current process of change, "But the chaos. I mean, there's no attempt. . . . I have absolutely no . . . sort of input into my work from anybody else apart from colleagues I would have asked for. . . . I don't know whether I'm actively being discouraged from . . . continuing to be interested in it and they're hoping I'll go away. I don't know. But that's the sort of feeling you get. That they wish you'd just disappear."

Stress is a combination of workload, a pervasive atmosphere of unease, and failed management in the past. One senior director from an earlier era, who quickly left, recalled first coming to work at the IS, "I knew the kind of workload. I knew the kind of hours and all that, but I didn't really quite, I think, understand the . . . sort of chaotic style of it all. The stress of it all. . . the constant, I suppose pressure. I mean . . . self-imposed pressure, or . . . just the pressure of the place, or the pressure of human rights cases. Or . . . even the pressure of the work to do. It's just so constant." This is borne out by time-keeping within the IS. It is a place that starts late and finishes late, with an eerie sense of quiet before 10 AM and many staff members still working late into the evening. At weekends, the facilities program has trouble regularly with staff members who are not authorized to use the building but who insist on coming to work, setting off the burglar alarms in the process. The majority of the meetings I went to in the year started late—some by an hour—and others were called or canceled at only a few hours notice. Because I was, certainly at first, often punctual for these meetings, various staff members took to saying things such as, "I knew you'd be here on time because you have to be" and "I hope you're taking a note of who is on time." When I went to see an Asia researcher for a prearranged interview and found her racing out of the door to catch a plane, she apologized and said, "I guess this happens to you all the time." In Human Resources, one staffer brought me emails showing how late some senior directors sent requests for urgent work (2 or 3 AM). The culture of late hours goes right to the top, in other words, constant meetings driving people to do their "real" work at the end of the day. I recall a senior director coming in for a morning management meeting and saying something like, "It's only ten o'clock and already I'm exhausted."

Many staff self-select for this kind of intense work, part of its attraction lying in its all-encompassing vocational nature. Yet some felt that Amnesty as an organization based on an ideal, with a voluntary ethic and a shortage of cash, has exploited this inclination. Here is the view of a Human Resources officer: "We'll throw at it whatever it takes, whether that be people hours, because we know we have the support of people to work around the clock, or whether that be financial cost and we just cut back on something else. It's almost as though we've got this self-belief that it'll just work itself out. It'll just happen. And that's incredibly damaging because at some point down the line it's just not going to happen." A veteran IS senior manager told me, "I've been a workaholic all along." "I don't mind doing it out of my own choice. But I resent it when it . . . becomes an expectation. . . . I want to decide whether I want to do it or not. . . . And I remember, what happens when you fall sick or . . . you know . . . you don't have any buffer for an emergency because you've killed everything." The danger, he said, was in the IS becoming a "club of obsessed . . . workaholics" who deter those who want a "normal life." "I'm not sure it's fair. . . . I worry about that, tearing myself. It's crushing the individual for a greater cause."

What a graphic image for an Amnesty staffer to use: Amnesty can consume your life. When former Secretary General Thomas Hammarberg visited the IS, he was introduced as living proof that "there is life after Amnesty." It was not meant entirely as a joke. Even the most senior staff pointed out how family unfriendly Amnesty is. One campaigner, who said she found the IS "like a prison," said, "I don't want to be just an Amnesty person. I want my own life."

It is little wonder researchers want doors they can close. The culture of self-sacrifice is learned because so much of the ethos is absorbed through a kind of thrown-in-at-the-deep-end apprenticeship. Despite the recent addition of more sophisticated training and induction, researchers learn on the job what it means to be an Amnesty researcher rather than a researcher per se. Without the protection of private space, should one person take on this much responsibility? The movement wants to take a lot of it away, turn the researchers into research managers, and decide for itself what they do and do not work on. It wants to decenter them, as we have seen, physically and culturally. In chapters 6 and 7, we look again at life inside the IS. Before that, we look at how it all began.

3   LIGHTING THE CANDLE

amnesty began life at the height of the Cold War, with John Kennedy in the White House, Nikita Khrushchev in the Kremlin, and the vast energy released by decolonization racing like wildfire through the politics of the south. In 1961, the UN went to war in the Congo (and UN Secretary-General Dag Hammarskjoeld was killed in a plane crash), the Bay of Pigs was an unmitigated disaster for the United States, and Paris waited for a threatened airborne invasion by rebel French army units from Algeria. And, of course, the Berlin Wall was built, the conflict between East and West now crowned by its most enduring symbol.

Although much has changed in the era of U.S. hegemony and the War on Terror, the 1960s also saw the emergence of organized responses to the impact of "globalizing modernity" that are much more familiar.[1] This undercurrent provided the sociological context for Amnesty. More specifically, secularization, understood not just as the decline of attendance at established—especially more traditional Protestant—churches, which was already well under way before the Second World War, but as the privatization of religion and the fact of religious pluralism. The church could no longer fulfil its classic function of providing overall social integration, its monopoly on public morality declining rapidly in the face of growing competition from functional specializations such as medicine, education, technology, and business. The massive trauma of 1939–1945 and the Holocaust only accelerated these tendencies. Religious leaders were forced to look harder at their performance and comparative advantage. It was this displacement, and the dislocation of those in search of a new integrative structure, that Benenson identified so acutely in trying to "re-kindle a fire in the minds of men."

There were both religious and nonreligious responses to globalization. In terms of the nonreligious, the 1960s saw the birth of so-called new social movements, based not around labor (as the classic social movements were) but on social, environmental, and identity issues that affected the growing middle class in the West. These movements were concerned with quality-of-life issues, not redistribution (even though many of those who joined were broadly of the Left).[2] Benenson was somewhat ahead of his time here, and if he had been more cautious, and less religious, one of these movements might have suited him very well even though (organized as they were around building blocks) they would not have been able to provide the renewed sense of total identification he desired.

Religiously, there were two main Christian responses to dislocation: liberal and conservative. The conservative option, most pronounced in the Christian Right and evangelism in the United States, was a reassertion of traditional biblical authority and personal salvation.[3] The liberal option, in contrast, was tolerant, universalist, and politically engaged. This ecumenicalism made common cause with other religions, new social movements, and universal human rights; and its diversity inevitably drew it away from doctrinal purity and toward a different justification for its importance—its political and social role in advancing universal goals.

For Peter Beyer, both religion and the new social movements found their niche dealing with the contradictions of globalization. Whereas conservative Christians stressed the private, liberal Christians and new social movements were united in their concern to provide a public response. This meant, in practical terms, working to make global values a reality through "fuller inclusion of all people in the benefits of this global community."[4]

Thus, Amnesty's first faltering steps were taken alongside religious and social organizations seeking answers to similar questions: Who are we, what are our values, and what should we do now? Although Amnesty sought a renewal of authority, it also shared the aim of full inclusion. Indeed, it took the most marginal figures—isolated individuals, forsaken within their own societies—and sought to rescue them in the name of humanity as a whole.

The initial target against which the task of sustaining authority was counterposed was therefore the state rather than discriminatory social structures on a global scale. Amnesty had a virtual monopoly, as a non-governmental authority speaking the language of universal human rights, at least until the Watch Committees were set up (beginning with Helsinki Watch in 1979), and probably until the early 1990s and the end of the Cold War. Through the long years of U.S. combat in Vietnam and apartheid, from CIA involvement in Latin America to the 1968 Prague Spring in Czechoslovakia to the partition of Pakistan, Amnesty kept the flame burning. As Benenson had said, "My work consists of trying to hand on the spark in many different shapes, in altered ways, to divers [sic] people."[5] This spark is the subject of the next section. We then expand on the argument that Amnesty was a quasi-religious response to globalization. Finally, we introduce the work culture that emerged from these beginnings and revisit Durkheim.

The Spark

We begin with Peter Benenson, who provided the moral and emotional energy required to start Amnesty. It is often the case with radical reform societies and dissenting religious groups that their founders have a "charismatic authority" to which "the governed submit because of their belief in the extraordinary quality of the specific person."[6] Benenson was no exception. An early collaborator described him as "an evangelist with a divine spark."[7] His zeal lay behind everything. Unsurprisingly, perhaps, within just six years he had clashed so badly with the evolving organization that a painful separation ensued, this messy departure almost destroying what he had so laboriously created. Relations had improved by the 1980s, and his name now adorns the IS building in Easton Street (his picture is still proudly on display in the audiovisual archive). He is regularly invoked, like a touchstone, in Amnesty discussions, and all the secretaries general have visited him, including Pierre Sané and Irene Khan. When he died at age 83 in February 2005 after many years of ill health, the obituaries were as fulsome in their praise as they were circumspect about the less wholesome events of 1966 and 1967 (further evidence of Amnesty's status as a sacred institution).[8]

Born in 1921, Benenson was the Jewish son of a Russian émigré mother from Baku. His hugely wealthy grandfather, Grigori, had left his gold concessions in Russia in 1914 and eventually moved to the United States, via Germany and London, where he lost his fortune in 1931 after having survived the Wall Street Crash.[9] Benenson's parents had what he himself described as "an unsuitable marriage." His Jewish father, a British army officer named Harold Solomon, was paralyzed from the waist down after a riding accident while serving in what was then Palestine. He died when his son was nine. Benenson's mother, Flora, remained a powerful figure throughout his life.[10] The Solomons were wealthy enough at first to have a butler, Flora receiving £1,000 a month from her father until his bankruptcy. The poet Wystan H. Auden was even Peter's personal tutor for a brief time. Benenson went to Eton and then Balliol (at Oxford) before serving during the Second World War at Bletchley Park, the government's principal code-breaking and intelligence center.

After the war, Benenson practiced as a barrister and stood four times, unsuccessfully, as a Labour Party candidate for election to Parliament. He was active in numerous organizations during the 1950s, including the Society of Labour Lawyers, and was most notably the driving force behind Justice, an all-party lawyers' grouping that sent observers to oversee the conduct of trials in other countries.[11] Before long, by his own admission, he was frustrated with the conservative nature of a lawyers' organization and, after a sojourn abroad in Sicily due to illness in 1960 and his conversion to Catholicism, he returned to London and (according to his own version of events) was so angered after reading about two Portuguese students imprisoned for drinking a toast to liberty that he put his formidable energy into the Appeal for Amnesty, launched by an *Observer* newspaper article, "The Forgotten Prisoners," in May 1961. Neither Tom Buchanan nor the Amnesty leadership was able to find any trace of the story about the two students, however, and they did not become POCs.[12]

The Appeal for Amnesty, syndicated worldwide, provoked a large response and was effectively transformed into a permanent organization from December 1961.[13] The first paragraph of the article read:

Open your newspaper any day of the week and you will find a report from somewhere in the world of someone being imprisoned, tortured or executed because his opinions or religion are unacceptable to his government. There are several million such people in prison—by no means all of them behind the Iron and Bamboo

Curtains—and their numbers are growing. The newspaper reader feels a sickening sense of impotence. Yet if these feelings of disgust all over the world could be united into common action, something effective could be done.

Benenson's social conscience went deep. The causes that motivated him—the Spanish Civil War, Nazi persecution—always led to action, often instigated by him but also drawing in a circle of friends. At the age of fifteen, while still at Eton, he undertook what he called his "first political act" by adopting financial responsibility for a Basque orphan, as did other friends at Eton, the Republican struggle in the Spanish Civil War making a permanent impression on them.[14] This was followed by a scheme to adopt Jewish teenagers from Germany and educate them in England.[15]

Although well-connected with lawyers in the liberal wing of the Labour Party, who would after 1964 be in government, Benenson nevertheless displayed three characteristics found in many of those who became enthused by the Amnesty idea. First, his social position, although secure, remained somewhat set apart, his Jewish-Russian background, conversion to Catholicism, and left-wing sympathies placing him on the margins of the establishment.[16] This was a kind of liminality, an existence nearer to the entry/exit boundaries between social classes than to the center. The second characteristic, which reinforced the first, was internationalism. Through family connections, but also inclination, Benenson's interest was drawn overseas, and throughout his life he conceived of Amnesty as an international organization. He made strenuous efforts to foster sections in countries outside Britain, especially in France, to prevent Amnesty being "a wholly Anglo-Saxon organization."[17] Finally, his was also a spiritual journey, one in search of a deeper meaning. In writing a 1989 dedication for the AI Oral History, he said that immediately after reading about the students he went straight into St. Martin's-in-the-Fields church in London.

It was then and there that what I have always envisaged to be a collective concern with the suffering of those who strive for change in the world was dedicated to Our Lady, *Mater Mundi*. Some who read this history may already or come to share my belief that the growth and influence of *Amnesty International* is due to the dedication, conscious or unconscious, to the benevolent influence of a universal, uniting, indomitable power usually referred to as compassion. This is the power and influence that I believe is symbolized in the concept of *Mater Mundi*, which I have endeavored to paint in the picture which I hope may be regarded as one man's striving to convey a concept which so very many have since conveyed by their own dedication to this great concern.[18]

These three features—marginality, internationalism, spirituality—were to be found in many early supporters. They were on the same wavelength, one that found an outlet in the idea of rights, a freely available and symbolically useful tool for practical prisoner work. When Benenson explained what he thought Amnesty might become, however, he described "a permanent international civil liberties organization."[19] Indeed, he later said, "I'm very strong on 'civil liberties.' I still use it. I much prefer it to 'human rights.'"[20] He understood that the Appeal would attract precisely those *not* united by interests, identities, philosophy, or a god. These lost souls were searching for hope in the world of globalizing modernity, and generating collective moral action among them was as important as freeing prisoners. The Amnesty movement was to be a spiritual awakening that would stimulate moral change in members' own societies as well.[21]

So who did respond? The most detailed accounts come from those who were, to all intents and purposes, the central staff (the IS) after May 1961, the people who dealt with the influx of letters, money, and material on prisoners. The AI Oral History interviewed many of them. These people shared, at least in terms of background, some elements of the three features.

The barrister Peter Archer, for example, who in 1966 became a Labour MP, knew Benenson well and had discussed the Amnesty idea with him before the Appeal. He served on Amnesty's policy committee in the early years and was a practicing Methodist and lay preacher who described himself in a written contribution to the oral history as a "convinced internationalist." He chaired the British Section of Amnesty in the early 1970s and recalled that a lot of the force of the British Amnesty groups came from either Unitarians or Quakers.[22] Andrew Blane and Priscilla Ellsworth also interviewed two British Section members for the Amnesty

International Oral History who had established local Amnesty groups, Dorothy Warner and Diana Redhouse (who is credited with drawing the original candle-in-barbed-wire symbol). Warner was German with a Catholic mother and a Protestant-Jewish father; Redhouse (secretary of the pioneering Hampstead Amnesty group) was from a Russian-Jewish background and had gone to a convent school.[23] Tom Sargant, who was involved with Benenson in Justice and Amnesty, was raised a strict Methodist by his parents, his father reminding him that the origin of the Sargant name was "servant."[24] Christel Marsh, a central figure in Amnesty's institutional development, was German and had been arrested by the Gestapo in 1939 before marrying her British husband and coming to England.[25]

Sean MacBride, the one early Amnesty figure with a reputation and charisma to rival Benenson's, ex-Irish foreign minister, winner of the Nobel Peace Prize, and leading member of the International Commission of Jurists (ICJ), was the son of parents who had organized resistance against the British in Ireland; his father was executed in 1916 and his mother, Maud Gonne, was imprisoned. MacBride himself was sentenced to death during the Irish civil war. Another barrister, who introduced Benenson to David Astor, the editor and publisher of *The Observer*, was Louis Blom-Cooper, who came from a middle-class Anglo-Jewish background.[26] Peggy Crane, an "active socialist" who worked in the very early years in the central staff, had come to Britain from South Africa in 1938 when she was twenty.[27] Marlys Deeds, another early staff member (whose brother Benenson had helped flee from Germany), was Jewish and from Cologne, whereas Keith Siviter, who co-ran the British section for many years and was heavily involved in Amnesty's development, had wanted to be a missionary and had trained at a Congregational theological college (and was a conscientious objector during World War II).[28] Eric Baker, highly influential through the 1960s, was a committed Quaker who had also been a conscientious objector and had spent time in India with his wife Joyce doing missionary work.[29]

These pioneers were not establishment figures. Their religious background, if they had any, tended to be other than the established Anglican church (they were Catholic, Free Church, or Jewish); they often had some overseas experience and a natural sympathy with the idea of their moral obligations not stopping at national boundaries (several being émigrés themselves).[30] It was Benenson, with his contacts via Eton, Oxford, the law, and the Labour Party, who provided the necessary connections.

Amnesty's ethos and working principles—conscience, individual responsibility, practicality, and self-effacement—found their most fertile ground in the soil of northern European Protestantism, at first in Britain, Sweden, and Germany and then in Norway, the Netherlands, and Denmark, (followed by Austria, Belgium, and France). Although the Irish section was influential, through MacBride, it was small. Of the other countries where sections were established at first, most were part of the Anglo-Saxon Protestant empire: Australia, New Zealand, the United States, and Canada. In Switzerland and Italy, Benenson found interest mainly in the expatriate community. In terms of membership within Amnesty, this list is identical today. In fact, Amnesty has failed to secure any significant membership or income from countries outside the West.

There was an ambivalence about its initial orientation. On the one hand, many founding members (and current IS members) were and are on the Left. On the other, Amnesty concentrated on freedom of expression (a classic civil and political right), characterizing human rights as non-political (as Benenson had with Justice) and emphasizing the personal nature of the work (individuals writing letters on behalf of other individuals). This put Amnesty closer to the Free Churches than to the social movements. In Peter Archer's words: "We were working for people, not ideologies or anything else, and it was people who were going to work for them. So it was people working for people."[31] This meant action not ascetic worship, but action centered on individual conscience not collective protest and social mobilization.

Claiming detachment from politics anchored Amnesty's reputation for independence during the Cold War, especially with a receptive Western audience. Yet it also meant a corresponding failure to attract membership in the south. This parallels Latin America's experience with a liberation theology that stressed local circumstances, the preference of God for the poor, and the prospect of earthly salvation.[32] This was more attractive than the established church's universal rules, tactical rigidity, cross-class solidarity, and individualism, along with its promise of only heavenly salvation.[33] Amnesty could have been more like the former, mixing natural sympathy with the Left and practical work on social justice. What it became was more like the latter.

Why did bearing witness become so important? Amnesty's lack of building blocks—its social and geographical separation from any specific national social class or group—created an initial detachment. Its growing symbolic role as a universal flame-bearer then edged it toward rules, procedures, and finally doctrine that maintained moral authority by elevating the idea of impartiality to an organizational imperative. It sought to construct in practical terms the kind of space—above, beyond, outside the world—in which the idea of objective morality, of a kind of universal truth, could be anchored.

One crucial decision in this respect was related to nonconformist religion—the principle that Amnesty would not work for prisoners who had used or advocated violence. This was central to Eric Baker's Quaker philosophy.[34] Baker, after Benenson, was the key figure in terms of early Amnesty practice; it is worth noting his comment that, whereas Benenson was the inspiration, he was the engineer.[35] The ban on violent prisoners ensured that those whose cases were adopted possessed the virtue that went with principled suffering. Indeed, Baker wrote, as acting director general, in a 1967 memo that Amnesty's principal aim was "to help those who are suffering *unjustly* and cannot help themselves."[36] These prisoners were innocent in a more profound sense, part of a tradition that included Jesus, Gandhi, and Martin Luther King. They all were nonviolent, led by personal example, and paid the ultimate price.

The long-term institutional effect of these initial decisions was far from predictable. At first, founders described Amnesty's aims in a variety of ways. MacBride wrote of "an international movement dedicated to the preservation of liberty," whereas Benenson spoke of "the freedom and dignity of the human mind."[37] The call to free those imprisoned for their opinions mentioned religious and political beliefs, but the first edition of *Amnesty* (June 27, 1961) focused only on religious toleration (Benenson was optimistic that "Christian oecumenicalism" would triumph on the basis of the "highest common denominator . . . revealed truth"). Of the six men featured as forgotten prisoners in Benenson's original article, three were religious and three political (an early example of the idea of balance, although not in gender terms).[38]

What Durkheim called necessary theorization began with staffers asking members what it was they actually believed. On July 25, 1961, *Amnesty* asked its readers, "what is the widest area of individual liberty that is practicable in a democratic polity"; and a questionnaire included on September 6, entitled "boundaries of freedom," asked subscribers to write in with answers to the questions:

What rights should an individual have in a society?
What limits can a society impose on an individual?
What circumstances should permit an individual to leave his country and go to another one?

Prepared for an abortive Amnesty conference, this questionnaire had been designed to find "the highest common factor of agreement."[39] It demonstrates perfectly the absence of building blocks—the central staffers were trying to find out what the members' values actually were; all that could be presumed was a willingness to write letters for POCs. It also shows the content of natural rights was far from self-evident as one moved beyond faith.

Read forty-five years later, the results of this questionnaire allowed remarkable latitude to the state in restricting freedom of speech during the Cold War (grounds included secrets, a state of emergency, and breach of the peace) and, in terms of refugees and asylum, affirmed that a state's first duty is to its own citizens. But natural rights intuitions are also in evidence, legitimizing dissent and affirming that individuals must follow their conscience while trying when possible to obey the law.[40] It is a core principle of natural rights that government infringements of those rights may legitimize citizens breaking the law and even using violence. Amnesty's foundational aversion to adopting violent POCs closed off this avenue for direct action, however.[41]

Nonviolence was one core principle, but Benenson was also adamant from the first that Amnesty—to generate his ideal of a world conscience—had to see itself as apolitical. This was implemented through the Threes: when an Amnesty group was formed, the central staff (squeezed into Benenson's chambers) would send out three cases on which group members could write letters and raise money—one from the West, one from the East, and one from the south. Amnesty was to be nonpolitical in two ways. First, it was international and thus not located, in theory at least, under the authority of any one political system. Second, it rejected political questions as appropriate questions for Amnesty. The stress on individuals, evident in the original article, separated the prisoner from the reasons for his or her imprisonment.

Amnesty's foundational practice was therefore to bear witness to the private suffering of nonviolent innocents, to demand their release on the sole ground that such suffering was unjust, and, it was hoped, to generate a collective sense of purpose among those on the same wavelength. This is as much as can be said about Amnesty's theoretical origins. It was a hybrid, culturally and by inclination Christian but allied to universal rights that were successful precisely because of their secularity.

Religionless Christianity

One of the founder members of Amnesty's Eltham group in London in 1961 was the bishop of Woolwich, John Robinson. He gave the first £1 donation and was a lifelong member. Already known for his liberal views, Robinson in 1963 published a hugely influential book, *Honest to God*, in which he assessed the choice between conservative and liberal responses to globalization. The first he called "a restating of traditional orthodoxy in modern terms," the other "worldly holiness." He even mused on whether the church should "give up using the word 'God' for a genera-tion."[42] His argument drew on the work of three theologians: Rudolf Bultmann, Paul Tillich, and, most of all, Dietrich Bonhoeffer. Their attrac-tion, he said, was that "they so evidently spoke not only to intelligent non-theologians but to those in closest touch with the unchurched masses of our modern urban and industrial civilization."[43]

Bonhoeffer was a German Lutheran pastor and theologian. Actively involved in resistance efforts to assassinate Hitler, he was imprisoned in 1944 and hanged by the SS a week before Hitler's suicide. Benenson had wanted to name the Amnesty library the Bonhoeffer Library and to have Bonhoeffer's bust on display. He said, "To me he's the archetypal, apart from Jesus Christ himself, he's the archetypal prisoner of conscience. . . . He didn't mean much to many other people in those days, if they weren't involved in Christian theology."[44] This observation is remarkable given that, as Keith Siviter pointed out, having advocated violence against Hitler, Bonhoeffer could not have been an Amnesty POC.[45] Siviter, who recalled the library idea as being that of an early Amnesty member called

Irmgard Payne, described himself as being at one time a Bonhoeffer disciple (having been on exchange visits with Lutheran pastors in Germany), and Dorothy Warner named Bonhoeffer as one of her idols.[46]

Bonhoeffer's life and theology illuminate Amnesty's ethos acutely because he combined the kind of religionless Christianity out of which Amnesty was born with the courage and suffering that went with it.[47] Stephen R. Haynes, writing in 2004, even refers to him as a "prisoner of conscience" (without mentioning Amnesty).[48]

Writing from prison in 1944, Bonhoeffer saw precisely the threat functional specialization posed to traditional religion. "People have learned to deal with themselves in all questions of importance without recourse to the 'working hypothesis' called 'God'. In questions of science, art, and ethics this has become an understood thing at which one now hardly dares to tilt. But for the last hundred years or so it has also become increasingly true of religious questions; it is becoming evident that everything gets along without 'God'—and, in fact, just as well as before."[49] Christianity had a "credibility problem."[50] *Letters and Papers from Prison*, written passionately and without undue theological exegesis while he faced the prospect of his own death, consolidated Bonhoeffer's reputation as a "Protestant Saint."[51]

His question was: "Who is Jesus Christ today for a world of adults who no longer believe in Angels?"[52] His complex answer involved personally following Jesus's example as "the man for others" living "unreservedly in life's duties, problems, successes and failures, experiences and perplexities."[53] In times of danger, the church had three options: to press the state on a law's legitimacy; to "aid the victims of state action [because] the church has an unconditional obligation to the victims of any ordering of society, even if they do not belong to the Christian community"; and to "not just bind the victims of the wheel, but to put a spoke in the wheel itself," engaging in "direct political action."[54] These were Amnesty's choices. It did the first, half-did the second (for POCs only), and has argued ever since about the third.

For Bonhoeffer, practical moral action could coexist with skepticism about traditional authority. Keith Siviter, an ordained Congregational minister, linked Robinson's *Honest to God*, and its message that "we're not being bullied by a white whiskered man up there," with the 1961 Amnesty Appeal as follows: "I think it's a sense of freedom. We were beginning to challenge authority. I thought that I really ought to become an anarchist. The nature of authority, what law is. I think it's very hard to think through it nowadays, to remember. But we were challenging the whole business of authority."[55] Suffering, embodied in Christ on the cross, was vital. For Bonhoeffer, "There remains an experience of incomparable value. We have for once learned to see the great events of world history from below, from the perspective of the outcast, the suspects, the maltreated, the powerless, the oppressed, the reviled—in short, from the perspective of those who suffer."[56] This echoes the liberal response to globalization in its mission for full inclusion and affirms that the place of the Christian is with those who suffer. In a letter to his godson in 1944, Bonhoeffer foresees the decline of the established church because it "is incapable of taking the word of reconciliation and redemption to humankind." He then predicts the rise of something like the human rights movement (as a new way to "utter the word of God"): "It will be a new language, perhaps quite nonreligious, but liberating and redeeming—as was Jesus' language; it will shock people and yet overcome them by its power; it will be the language of a new righteousness and truth, proclaiming God's peace with people and the coming of God's kingdom."[57]

Bonhoeffer was hanged with five other members of the resistance at Flossenbürg concentration camp on April 9, 1945. Their bodies were then burned. In his last letter he wrote, "This is the end, for me the beginning of life. I believe in universal Christian brotherhood which rises above national interests and I believe that our victory is certain."[58]

Amnesty was, in practical but secular terms, this universal Christian brotherhood, a kind of moral solidarity, and the adopted language of universal human rights fitted it perfectly. The founders shared the spirit, if not the explicit beliefs, of Bonhoeffer's vision. For example, when Norman Marsh, Christel Marsh's husband, was asked about the possible influence of religious ideas, he said, "Oh, in a non-denominational way, although Christel was a Lutheran, and I was conventionally a member of the Church of England. In a non-denominational way I should say that in both our cases religious ideas have been very strong. But quite non-denominational. I should say that they have been very strong indeed. In my case, certainly [it was] in a non-denominational way, because I reacted very violently against the, as I felt, very narrow evangelical framework in which I was brought up at school."[59] There are many more obvious ways in which the varied religious beliefs of the founders were evident: the candle, of course; the inclusion in an *Amnesty* issue in 1961 of a prayer; and the commemoration of Human Rights Day (December 10) in churches such as St. Martin's-in-the-Field and St. Paul's Cathedral. Benenson deliberately chose to launch the Appeal for Amnesty on Trinity Sunday, this threefold division of the Father–Son–Holy Ghost reflecting, for him, a world divided into three that needed to be made whole. Thus, the Threes—a POC from each Cold War bloc.

Bearing witness and political agitation were both available strategies, but the crucial idea of conscience (rather than simple compassion), of the decisions about nonviolence and apoliticism, and the religious milieu in which the founders operated, with Benenson, a Catholic, and Baker, a Quaker, at the core, meant that Amnesty's sympathy with the Left was in effect suppressed. In 1967, Benenson wrote to Baker that he had always regarded Amnesty as part of the "Christian witness."[60] The tension was visible in Benenson's paradoxical thought and actions, a four-time candidate for the Labour Party and social activist of long standing who was convinced that political contest would achieve less than the "conversion" of individuals who would then change the "external framework" in favor of social justice.[61]

How It Worked

Amnesty was culturally Christian, but the key to its foundational method was practical solidarity. Operationally, the fledgling IS[62] collected and collated prisoner cases and sent the material to groups who raised money to send as relief to prisoners' families. Before long, the IS was also asked to provide sample letters. The original Appeal was reproduced by newspapers worldwide, and almost immediately correspondence began arriving offering both assistance and giving details of prisoners.[63] A rough follow-up plan existed in the minds of Benenson, Baker, and a handful of others who had been involved in pre-Appeal discussions (often recorded on napkins over a lunch at the pub near Benenson's chambers, *The Swan*). The principal idea was to establish the Threes who would adopt the cases of a POC from each bloc.

In Benenson's cramped rooms, what was variously called the registry and the library became the center of operations, staffed largely by female volunteers.[64] This was the forerunner of the Research Department. In charge of this operation was Christel Marsh.[65] Benenson, she recalled, insisted it be called the library even though it had no books. He never interviewed anybody for skills: "Anybody with good will was taken on, and some very peculiar people were, I can tell you." She copied out the case material mainly from newspaper clippings, which made the need for experts to write background papers essential. "It all had to be worked out by trial and error," said Marsh. "It was very slow work." She remembered, "Gathering the information was the most difficult of all. Even if you got some you didn't know necessarily if it was reliable. . . . I remember from South Africa we once had some black visitors who told us about prisoners there. However sympathetic one feels, you couldn't be sure that they were prisoners of conscience, that they hadn't advocated violence. So this was always the greatest problem." The two central functions of the Research Department—background knowledge and investigating the veracity of POC claims—were identified almost immediately, in other words. Although the nonviolence clause was the source of endless problems, Marsh was adamant: "the line was always taken 'no', because that would spoil the whole case for Amnesty. I'm convinced of that, it wouldn't have got where it is now if it hadn't been so absolutely single-minded on that point." If the status of a case was unclear, she recalled, "We called them investigation cases. . . . In the beginning we would always give the information which we had, which sometimes was jolly little, so it was quite clear [that] in those cases they couldn't be absolutely sure. They had to try to find out."

The groups did not pay for this service—they received this information and traded it for anything they had discovered.[66] ("They got it all for free," said Marsh.) But the groups soon complained about a lack of case information. Even as the need to professionalize grew, amateurishness was still seen by some as a virtue. Louis Blom-Cooper said of Amnesty that he "adored it in the days when it was really small and amateurish": "I mean when . . . there were just a handful of people who were doing splendid work. But very disorganized in a way, and very under-funded. In a sense I like the idea of operating within a system whereby the people involved have a commitment, a personal commitment, in which you are not paid for what you do and everything is done in a fairly sort of nonprofessional way, I mean in a sense one becomes fairly professional simply by force of circumstances."[67]

Peggy Crane, whom Benenson had known from his Labour Party days, was recruited in October 1961 as a kind of executive officer. She described the Mitre Court offices when she arrived: "There were people everywhere, with literature and all else, anything and everywhere. Everywhere masses of people coming in and out, and everywhere congestion. And he said we should perhaps try and make some executive sense [of it]."[68] For Keith Siviter, who was a volunteer at Mitre Court and subsequently Crane Court (he was paid from 1966), the amateurishness and the lack of money combined in a positive way: "It was very good fun. One of the things was, when you had Peter around, you never had . . . a closed door. Whatever was going on, it would be an open office, very much so." He went on to describe library meetings when "All the staff, volunteer and paid, met on Friday lunchtimes. If there was a problem over a prisoner or a group, that was the place it was discussed. By everybody including the telephonists. You know, if you'd got a contribution [to make], you could make it. That's what I mean. There was no sense of a hierarchy and a structure and authority, and all those things. Just a job to be done. That's what we were there to do."[69]

Others recalled the working environment less fondly. The burden carried at the outset by volunteers and staff, especially women, was heavy and largely unacknowledged. Benenson's relentless energy and constant demands dominated every aspect of organizational life. All the early staff members gave full credit to Benenson for his achievement and spoke without reserve of his inspirational leadership, boundless enthusiasm, constant creativity, and extraordinary work rate. They also described his flaws in equal measure. These included an utter lack of administrative ability or sympathy for bureaucracy, a tendency to make weak staff appointments, no appreciation of the limits of time ("Time was nothing", said Peggy Crane) or of the existence of anyone's private life outside Amnesty (acute for those with children), an inability to devolve responsibility, and a sense of frustration with those who would not keep up the pace. Benenson made his view of management clear, for example, in May 1963: "Those who support the AMNESTY movement in its efforts to secure the release of prisoners are not generally concerned with points of order, and all the formality of stuffy meetings."[70] Management versus activism, bureaucracy versus autonomy—Goran C.O. Claesson and Cornelis van der Vlies saw the damage this heroic individualism had already done in their 1967 report. The two sides of Benenson's personality—inspiration and impetuosity—went hand in hand. Marlys Deeds recalled, "He often had so many ideas, all at the same time, he'd give directions to everybody to get on with it because he felt the inner urgency that it must be done at that very moment. Not tomorrow."[71] Benenson's tendency to use people reflected his sense, she said, that "the suffering of a prisoner of conscience was more important than the comfort of one of his office staff."[72] Eventually, of course, the same logic sank Benenson as well.

There was inevitably a mismatch between those who led the movement and those who did the everyday work. Benenson, himself a man of ideas and inspiration, tended to talk about the movement in terms of the public figures who were Amnesty's face in the wider world. He described the initial responders as "writers, composers, journalists, lawyers and preachers." These were almost all men doing classic public-sphere things—representation, action, decision making (the policy committee was all male), speaking—while, implicitly at least, the women were doing much of the day-to-day work in, almost literally, the private quarters (Benenson's own cramped rooms or the kitchen where his wife Margaret Benenson provided food for a stream of visitors). It was, said Benenson, "essential to keep the movement one of ideals," emphasizing its visionary quality and higher purpose rather than the daily efforts of backroom staff.

Much of his energy went into developing the movement. The first international meeting was held in July 1961 at the Café Carrefour in Luxembourg. Representatives of national sections came from Belgium, Ireland, France, Germany, Switzerland, Britain, and the United States (lack of money restricted more from coming). The question on the agenda, according to the news sheet *Amnesty*, was "international and impartial control of the Amnesty movement."[73] MacBride was the key figure here; a future ICJ secretary general and chair of Amnesty's IEC, he later handled Benenson's departure in 1967. MacBride shared Benenson's view of a nonpolitical prisoner movement: "A humanitarian organization that would do for political prisoners what the Red Cross did for prisoners of war."[74] Even though its founding principle was need, without qualification, Eric Baker also claimed the Red Cross was the best analogy for Amnesty, an organization with, as he described it, a humanitarian not a political purpose, acting "in the name of humanity itself."[75]

At Luxembourg, MacBride took the chair and, according to Benenson, "by the end of two sessions, on Saturday and Sunday, we had agreed an outline plan for an international organization, each country committing itself to form a National Section before the next International meeting."[76] This meant creating a British Section, separate in terms of budget from the staff of the international movement (Benenson estimated thirty groups existed in Britain by the end of 1961, by which time national groups and fledgling national sections existed in as many as twenty countries).[77]

Amnesty International was formally so-named from 1962 onward, the national sections having their own constitutions, fixing their members' subscriptions, and submitting resolutions to international meetings. The next major stage came in 1963 (at Konigswinter) when the policy committee, composed of men known as "the godfathers," gave way to a five-man International Executive with each member elected to represent a language-speaking area (English, Scandinavian, German, Flemish-Dutch, and French). MacBride was elected as chair, and Benenson was named honorary secretary. In addition, two further decisions were made. First, according to Egon Larsen, because Amnesty now had 2,800 case files from eighty-three countries a decision was made to turn the registry/library into a more formal Research Department. This department would prepare background papers and check case details—through an Investigation Department—before sending them to groups for adoption. Second, there had already been talk of a constitution for Amnesty—a statement of identity—even though Benenson's attitude to such formalities was skeptical. At Konigswinter, it was formalized as a Code of Conduct towards Prisoners of Conscience.[78] This was a forerunner of what would become in 1968 Amnesty's Statute, giving rise to the single most influential piece of lore within Amnesty—the mandate. Lionel Elvin, a key member of the policy committee, described the outcome of Konigswinter as Amnesty "beginning to become what we wish to be, the Ombudsman of the imprisoned conscience everywhere."[79]

This was impossible without money, which was in short supply. Most central staff members were unpaid volunteers. A few of the women could afford to work at Mitre Court because of their husbands' salaries, whereas Benenson himself still had enough private means to cease being a barrister (he had to leave his chambers as a result). In *Amnesty* newssheet no. 2 of July 11, 1961, the Central Office asked for £5,000 to expand its casework. A financial appeal was launched again in October 1961 to fund the POC library when it moved to Essex Court (nearby in London) and to pay for Amnesty to make representations to various financial bodies. The first annual report, 1961–1962, listed just over £7,859 as the amount raised in the first year. The struggle for money would be constant, largely because as the number of cases and members grew so did the need for staffers, who eventually began to be paid.

In managing the funding, especially the absence of a reliable source of regular income, Amnesty was confronted by British charity laws that classified it, despite legal challenges and its strongly held self-image, as a political organization. The establishment of the British Section's Prisoners of Conscience Fund was a way to get around this problem. The management of money at the time was, to say the least, creative, with POC money regularly being used to pay administrative expenses, including for the IS (to fund Research Department work, for example).[80] By 1967, Amnesty's amateur approach to funding would see it nearly bankrupt.[81]

This was but one problem. Benenson's exit cast an unflattering light on Amnesty because he publicly alleged, from late 1966 onward, that the British government had infiltrated AI through the then secretary general, another Catholic old Etonian, Robert Swann.[82] Newspaper stories also claimed, rightly as it turned out, that Benenson and Swann had arranged clandestine British government funding for Amnesty work in Rhodesia (without the knowledge of Amnesty's IEC). U.S. press claims about CIA covert funding for the ICJ (of which Sean MacBride, the IEC chair, was also secretary general) reinforced Benenson's fears, and he demanded that the IS be moved out of Britain to a neutral country.[83]

An investigation found largely in favor of Swann while revealing that he had indeed worked for British intelligence. The IEC backed him (he resigned within months) and kept the IS in London. Benenson was considered to have resigned. Until Martin Ennals became secretary general in 1968, Eric Baker assumed executive control. The oral history interviewers, Blane and Ellsworth, were steered away from this story, unfortunately. What the interviews do contain are largely suggestions that

Benenson was ill, even mentally unbalanced. In the words of Joyce Baker: "It wasn't too surprising that Peter burnt himself out for a bit. I'm delighted when I've seen him since to realize it was only a temporary thing, but he really had done himself a sort of harm with this."[84]

Amnesty as a Secular Religion

Amnesty was neither a new social movement nor a traditional religion. In its diversity it resembled the former; in its concern with authority it reflected the latter. Without building blocks, it could not cohere as a movement dedicated to its own interests; its foundational principle was the opposite, advancing the interests of humanity (the interests of all, by definition the interests of none). We have seen how central Christianity was, as a fertile cultural and social soil. Amnesty's structure and working methods are difficult to understand, as are its initial symbolism and imagery, without it. In Benenson's case, his written dedication to the oral history shows just how much active faith was at work. For these reasons, Amnesty is best understood as a kind of Free Church, an ecumenical gathering concerned with the earthly relations between human beings rather than between an individual and a god.

Yet Durkheim's argument says much more than this. For Durkheim, collective purpose comes first, religion second. Making the case that Amnesty was already in some sense a religious community is to focus on the effect rather than the cause. Just as it would be inadequate to see proscriptions such as those against adopting violent POCs as purely functional rather than rooted in the existing beliefs of founders such as Baker, so it would be misleading to see Amnesty as the evolution of already manifest faith.

Durkheim would say that we are making the case for Amnesty as part of the liberal Protestant response to globalization, alongside Bonhoeffer and Robinson, and there is plenty of theory to deal with that. But once Amnesty is up and running, the IS elaborating both its identity and working practice, Durkheim's insights take hold. Amnesty *became* a kind of religious organization through practice, a manifestation of the very collective spirit for which Benenson had hoped. Through this secular practice, embodied in institutional culture, a kind of religiosity evolved. When combined with the example of POCs—whose existential suffering gave Amnesty its fuel—this growing store of moral authority placed a greater and greater premium on purity, coherence, and integrity. The debacle of 1967 only intensified this, threatened as Amnesty was with the taint of scandal. It became vital to protect Amnesty as a symbolic moral authority, and this made detachment from any threatened pollution not just attractive but increasingly essential.

4 TELLING THE TRUTH ABOUT SUFFERING

"wounds on the body [are the] authentic authority of Amnesty." These perceptive words are those of a senior director in May 2003. Prisoners of conscience, torture victims, these are Amnesty's moral bedrock. If words are required to tell their story, they serve only as a transmission mechanism. They themselves must be devoid of moral content because the use of emotive words is redolent of persuasion, and persuasion is a signal that authority does not exist. Human rights—as international covenants, as customary law, as rhetorical demands for behavioral change—are an argument and, as such, rely ultimately on persuasion. Their meaning is not self-evident. Amnesty has more power than this: it can open the prison door and show you the prisoners' faces and wounds, so you can see and feel for yourself, so your conscience can be touched. For Richard Wilson, as we have seen, "unflinching realism" is simply a way to create "the aura of objectivity and neutrality by wiping the stain of subjectivity off the surface of the text."[1] Thus, "Once it is recognized that all narratives are the result of artifice and design, then rather than hide any reference to this process, it might be preferable to place the interpretative filter in the foreground of the account, to convey something of the conditions in which knowledge is formulated and represented."[2] I argue in chapter 8 for the existence of something like moral facts. But Wilson's account is naïve about moral truths more generally, whether manufactured or discovered. Even as socially constructed, such truths can be established at such a profound level of deep culture over time—the level at which they assume the mantle of authority—so as to be to all intents and purposes objectively true. They are culture become nature. Contesting them is not a simple matter of advancing alternatives because one is truth and the other opinion. They may be, in a fundamental sense, ideology, but this just confirms how potent ideology is once it has become seemingly common sense.

What is beyond question in Amnesty's case is that moral authority was accumulated and that this authority relied heavily on detachment. In this chapter, we look at how that detachment extended not just to the facts of prisoner cases, but also to Amnesty International as it slowly became a source in itself.

The Ethos in Practice

In bearing witness, researchers functioned like investigative journalists. Their role was not to be indignant or self-righteous or to articulate Amnesty's natural rights philosophy. This approach is beautifully captured in the words of a current senior researcher: "It's not for us to draw the limits of the right to life and sell that. But I see us being much more pragmatic and saying, look, whatever you think about abortion, this woman in Nepal, she's been locked up for twenty years . . . and this is the background of her case. And something instinctive I hope would kick in to the average reasonable human rights defending person to say, well that's not on. You know. She shouldn't be locked up. Whatever you think about the right to life."

Consider, for example, the aversion to using emotive phrases (and contrast it with the world of spin and public relations, the children of fractured authority). Efforts at the manipulation of sentiment were likely to deter sympathizers (whether or not they were an audience conditioned to objectivity). By the 1966 ICM in Copenhagen it was resolved that AI literature should "avoid emotive or abusive expressions."[3] A veteran IS staffer who started work in the early 1990s remarked that "another thing we rarely allowed ourselves [was] the luxury of using adjectives or adverbs." Or consider the following contrast: the first statement is from a 1999 Amnesty report on honor killings in Pakistan, the second from the campaigning version of the same material.

Every year in Pakistan hundreds of women, of all ages and in all parts of the country, are reported killed in the name of honor. Many more cases go unreported. Almost all go unpunished. The lives of millions of women in Pakistan are circumscribed by traditions which enforce extreme seclusion and submission to men, many of whom impose their virtually proprietorial control over women with violence.

Women in Pakistan live in fear. They face death by shooting, burning or killing with axes if they are deemed to have brought shame on the family. They are killed for their supposed "illicit" relationships, for marrying men of their choice, for divorcing abusive husbands. They are even murdered by their kin if they are raped as they are thereby deemed to have brought shame on their family. The truth of the suspicion does not matter—merely the allegation is enough to bring dishonor on the family and therefore justifies the slaying.

The fifty-seven-page report is titled *Pakistan: Violence against Women in the Name of Honor*; the sixteen-page campaign document is called *Pakistan: Honor Killings of Girls and Women*.[4] The second version is designed to grab the attention like a tabloid headline. The style of the first, needless to say, is the epitome of the researchers' craft.

Here is another example. From the 1990s onward, under the stewardship of Pierre Sané, Amnesty came under increasing pressure to undertake crisis response. It was pressed to comment as a moral authority quickly and continuously on what was happening first in Bosnia and then in Rwanda. This is how the ethos dealt with such situations, in the words of a veteran researcher:

Now when I first started, Amnesty had a very clear response which was, we're not doing anything about it. Because we didn't react to crises. We didn't do anything for the first six weeks or so, until the dust had settled. And then Amnesty would see whether there were Amnesty type concerns to be addressed. But a war wasn't an Amnesty concern. . . . Amnesty researchers were protected from having to produce immediate reactions. . . . They were expected to take their time. And to get things right. That was what they were expected to do, not to talk off the top of their heads.

This is the essence of quiet persistence.[5] The very detachment at the core of moral authority made it hard to use practically because it risked undermining its own foundations. It had an either/or relationship with political authority. The veteran ex-researcher who made the previous comment described herself as "still imbued" with the foundational spirit: "[Amnesty] started off to work for forgotten prisoners. . . . the idea was to shine a light on things that people didn't know about." Or as another interviewee put it: "The candle actually doesn't show up where the spotlight already is. That's an irony." This view has been overtaken by the media's insistent question about crises: What is Amnesty doing about it? Rwanda presented the IS with a real test of its historical culture. Could saying "we're not doing anything" be a legitimate response? One researcher involved in discussions about what to say when the UN vacated Rwanda in 1994 ahead of the genocide recalls a sense of outrage at being told by a long-serving colleague in a heated exchange, "we have to remain dispassionate and objective." "I remember the words," the researcher said. "That's the only time I've ever walked out in the middle of a meeting. It was that meeting. It was. I can remember it very well. And I think somebody, I can't remember if it was me or somebody else, said, well, yes we have to be objective. Of course that's the nature of what we do. But we don't have to be dispassionate. In fact, we should not be dispassionate. We should be passionate. Because that's what we're, what we're for."

These are examples of the ethos-in-action (as research) and of the case for reform. As Amnesty bore witness to and helped to free thousands of prisoners and as it took on the issues of the death penalty, torture, and disappearances, a shift occurred, recognized explicitly (and augmented hugely) by the award in 1977 of the Nobel Peace Prize. Amnesty's own authority was inexorably growing, a transfer of moral energy from the POCs to their champions. This meant Amnesty could speak, in its own voice, for those basic principles of humanity to which Benenson had referred. Soon it would face a temptation—to spend its own moral capital (to cash it in, morally and financially).[6] Globalization has only increased that capital's value.

The Research Department

Developing membership was the founders' principal concern. Eric Baker even proposed that research be hived off from the core IS functions of administration, publicity, and fund-raising.[7] He suggested the investigation function become an "Autonomous organization to which Amnesty sections in effect subscribe and to whose research work, in fact, other organizations e.g. press associations (as well as charitable trusts) might subscribe in return for information in which they are interested." The International Secretariat would then deal with Amnesty's main work, "Bringing pressure to bear on behalf of Prisoners of Conscience in ways which might be broadly described as 'political.'" For Baker, the role of the IS was to help national sections carry out the purposes of the movement in an international spirit, and this gave the IS its edge. Field operations, for example, had to be conducted in a way that "the Central Office feels is in keeping with the spirit and purpose of the movement." Baker warned, "National sections must, therefore, be willing to resist the temptation to act entirely independently. They must be willing to consult the Central Office before undertaking a project and to accept the advice of the office as partners in a joint undertaking the policy for which has already been agreed upon. . . . A spirit of mutual trust and confidence of this kind, based on a willingness in the last resort, to subordinate the part to the whole is essential to Amnesty." By 1983, Secretary General Thomas Hammarberg would be able to say, "We have a strikingly centralized approach on who can say what for AI. There are good reasons for this. . . . The *one voice principle* is not only important, it is essential."[8]

Amnesty's founders did not fully appreciate the implications of their own organizational form, in other words. The lack of any building blocks created a vacuum that the permanent, full-time staff filled. If the IS occupied this role in the movement, the researchers occupied it within the IS.[9] Claesson and van der Vlies wrote in their first report of the 1967 crisis, "The subject matter of Amnesty International and the tasks this movement has undertaken require considered judgement based on elaborate knowledge and qualified interpretation of news, material and experience. This stresses the importance of permanence and expertise. . . . The Central Secretariat is indispensable to *all* groups and *all* national sections."[10]

In March 1966, the Research Department had only two paid staff (one half-time) and several volunteers providing nearly four hundred groups with three different cases each.[11] As we know, political geography structured the work. The limits to this approach were already clear to Claesson and van der Vlies: "As the reliability of our information is essential we must have the guts to confess that we cannot manage everything and to stop a token covering of many areas." Yet the proto-researchers sought deeper and wider coverage. In an unsigned document for the October 1967 IEC meeting, the Investigation Bureau made its case for retaining at least three full-time investigators by claiming that, with adoptions in sixty-four countries, Amnesty needed country knowledge and a wide enough geographical scope to be able to demonstrate impartiality.[12] Reducing the number of investigators to fewer than three would damage the movement: "Too great work-loads could cause investigators to make decisions on countries of which they knew little, and had not time to learn, while essential contacts with area-experts would necessarily lapse." Fearing mistaken adoptions, the Bureau linked its own operations and Amnesty's external authority: "Inadequate briefing of observers, the press officer or the Director General so that Amnesty's reputation for informed judgement—rather than random protest—might suffer, thus reducing its power to influence governments, the press, and the public." The Bureau's opposition to decentralizing research is worth reproducing in detail:

> Decentralization would detract from the unity of the Amnesty movement. It would also have many practical disadvantages. The taking up of cases, sending observers, special campaigns, etc, need to be undertaken in an international framework so that proper priorities can be established. It is difficult to do this if all the information is not centralized at any given moment. The distribution of adoptions also requires to be done centrally, from a vantage point where the work of the movement—groups and sections can be seen as a whole and correlated with the political susceptibilities of the governments by whom prisoners are held. . . . The International Secretariat must be able to answer authoritatively for the movements [sic] actions and attitudes to any given problem. Failure in communication or action without consultation could cause serious embarrassment. . . . Continuing work by any one Section or group in a particular area could lead to partisanship or lack of perspective because of ignorance of problems in other areas. Criticism from such a source might be believed by observers to be partisan even if it were not. The international character of the work is one of

Amnesty's most important assets which it cannot afford to lose. . . . Sections should be encouraged by the International Executive to undertake research; but this should only be done under correct supervision from the Investigation Bureau, taking the form of special projects rather than continuing responsibility for work on a particular area.

This was ethos manifest in research. Nothing in the tendencies inherent in Amnesty's founding principles, religious milieu, or the theory of human rights dictated that this was how practice would necessarily unfold. Puzzling through the gaps between structure and action is where what Amnesty understood as human rights acquired meaning.

Martin Ennals became secretary general in 1968, and as finances improved the number of researchers and research-related staffers grew. By May 1970, of six full-time senior IS staff members (plus Ennals), five formed the Research Department, the number of groups now at 832 (a 63 percent rise in eighteen months). There were also three part-time paid staff (working on the USSR and Greece), four secretaries, and volunteers doing 150 hours in total a week (with 2,500 prisoners now adopted or under investigation).[13]

Researchers investigated cases for adoption, briefed mission delegates, and soon undertook missions themselves.[14] The level of expertise required of researchers was high. The head of the Investigation Department, Stella Joyce, wrote in June 1967, "The Investigators are responsible, like desk officers at any foreign office, for the collection and assessment of information about their area; the political, legal and social background of the countries concerned, the number and nature of political prisoners and their conditions of imprisonment, and the most effective channels of pressure to be used in order to influence governments to release prisoners of conscience, improve conditions, alter legislation and official attitudes."[15] Judging whether someone was a POC required "political, legal and personal knowledge of the source and situation in the area," and a single case took an average of three days of full-time work to compile. Despite a decision by the IEC to allow double adoptions (the same prisoner going to more than one group), pressure for more cases increased. The IS tried to restrict the demand to meet the supply, arguing in May 1970 that a ceiling should be placed on new groups, and national associations formed that did not have the workload associated with being in a group.[16] As the management consultancy McKinsey & Co. noted succinctly, "At the simplest extremes, those responsible for formulating policy will have to determine whether Amnesty should continue to pursue growth in the group organization or whether the Secretariat should consolidate its position and seek to develop techniques that have the greatest impact on the release of prisoners of conscience throughout the world."[17]

In July 1970, a full-time head of research, a Czech academic named Zbynek Zeman, was appointed. The proposed IS budget for the year 1971–1972 was £63,500, of which £40,000 was for salaries. Zeman outlined in detail what was required to make Amnesty research of high professional quality: "The hard core of the research department should consist of people with high academic qualifications, who are good linguists and who specialize in a particular subject in their area. They should, however, be flexible enough to be able to address themselves to any problem that may arise in their area, and they should also be able to attract the right kind of volunteer. We should perhaps rely less on volunteers than we are doing now."[18]

Research Takes Control

By 1971, two key questions were already being asked: What would the membership's relations with the centralized IS be like, and how could the limitations of casework as a form of activism be overcome? A Long Range Planning Committee (LRPC), which described the IS as the central nervous system of the Amnesty body, recommended new forms of action beyond prisoner adoption (e.g., mass campaigns) and suggested efforts be made to attract individual members who might only give money (and therefore not need cases). Being a member of an Amnesty group was a more serious commitment, of course, and the report argued that through selection and training "the quality of groups should be improved."[19]

One of the report's key suggestions was to separate the research and action functions in each of the five regional areas that had been established by this time (Africa, Americas, Asia and Far East, Europe, and Middle East). Researchers would be "concerned with research, and with research *only*,"[20] concentrating on collecting important country-based information, monitoring human rights observance, and selecting prisoners for adoption or investigation. Policy planning was also added as a secondary function. Lower priority was to be given to countries that had good human rights records or that were small, the report went on, and external groups of expert volunteers would be kept on hand to deal with urgent violations of UDHR articles 5, 8, 18, and 19. The report, however, called for a general move to increase the number of countries on which in-depth research was conducted. The action group would take this research and run follow-up actions, communicate with groups and sections, plan missions, and undertake international contacts.

The LRPC addressed identity, suggesting that beyond northwest Europe, "the public is confused regarding the image of Amnesty International." It went on: "It must be possible to define Amnesty International aims and objectives within one phrase easily understood by everyone without 'ifs', 'whens' and 'provided'." This was the vacuum that research practice filled. Identity had to come from within because, without building blocks, Amnesty did not have one of its own. Even the term *prisoner of conscience* was confusing, the German Section abandoning it in favor of "political prisoners who have not used or advocated violence." The influential Swedish section read the LRPC report as a manifesto for greater centralization and feared the IS would absorb more and more resources, thereby dominating Amnesty's development.[21] They considered calling for the disbandment of the IS, emphasizing Amnesty's core strength as "personal contacts of groups with and work for individual prisoners." The ethos was just as strong in the founding members and sections, in other words. And yet the IS grew—adding a legal officer, permanent representation in New York, a new fast-response technique called Urgent Action, and from 1972 launching a Campaign Against Torture (CAT) that eventually became the Campaigns Department. This also reflected a concern that Amnesty techniques such as adoption and letter writing were not effective outside the West, a growing problem because most new POC cases were from the south and the East.

The CAT was a first effort at a theme campaign in that it addressed torture as a systemic issue, albeit still based around casework.[22] Those responsible for it argued that action belonged on the same footing as research. Sherman Carroll, of the CAT Department, sent a memo to Martin Ennals in 1976 insisting that "*utilization* of information" was as important as the "*gathering* of information."[23] Using information was the priority, he

argued, research having had its day in "building the organization's reputation for accuracy and reliability." As he concluded, "We are a text book
case of a lopsided organization, high on production and low on marketing. Despite the thousands of potential AI 'salesmen', we under-use
them and produce far more than can now be adequately consumed. The
time has come for the management to bring marketing in line with production so that the high quality of our product is not spoilt in the
stock-piling."[24]

Little has changed. In evaluating the third major Amnesty torture
campaign, run from 2000 to 2002, entitled Take a Step to Stamp Out
Torture, external consultants wrote that quality research was only one
component of the "portfolio of approaches within AI's campaigning programme." The evaluation recommended giving campaigners more authority and holding researchers more accountable, a sentiment captured in
the words: "The logic of the campaign drives the research programme
not the other way around."[25]

Writing in 1978, Dick Oosting, in the CAT Department at that time and
later deputy secretary general and candidate for secretary general, echoed
Claesson and van der Vlies's observation that staff resisted devolving
authority and more efficient management by citing "the uniqueness of
this organization," one of the reasons he had been given for "why it would
be terribly difficult to improve the running of this office."[26] In another
memo, he wrote, "There is a great deal of uncertainty and insecurity
about who takes decisions on what, which leads to exaggerated attempts
to take decisions by committee and by consensus but this only gives a
false sense of democracy and security, because decisions by individuals,
groups or committees are as easily reversed as anything." "Too often the
buck stops nowhere," he said, and "chaos" ensues.[27]

These years, under Ennals's leadership, saw extraordinary success in
terms of consolidating Amnesty as the world's foremost human rights
organization. Its work on disappearances, as well as its lobbying efforts
for advances in international law, were recognized in awards such as the
Nobel Prize, while membership and income grew inexorably. At the
beginning of the decade, IS staff members numbered in the single digits,
but by the end there were well over one hundred and rising. A three-day
Cambridge Crash Committee (CCC) was convened in June 1977 to try to
deal with this continuous expansion, participants including Hammarberg,

Ennals, Oosting, Whitney Ellsworth (of AIUSA; and later the IEC) and Bo Lindblom (of the Swedish Section). The CCC was an early recognition that what Amnesty did was decided and implemented on a daily basis by its permanent professional staff, dominated by the Research Department. The issue was not the ethos. Both sections and the IS agreed that at Amnesty's core was long-term work on individual prisoners. Indeed, the Swedish section was often zealous in protecting the ethos from what it feared was the willingness of the IS to compromise. The problem was the number of cases. Researchers could not meet demand; some new groups got just one prisoner to work on.

The trend of declining case sheet production is clear. In 1974, 2,458 cases were produced. In the following four years, the numbers were 1975 (2,015), 1976 (1,948), 1977 (2,275), and 1978 (1,888). This was despite a quota set by the movement for 1978 of 2,500. The June 1979 total was only 832.[28] The main reason for this deficit was a swelling movement that outstripped the capacity of its central staff to support a labor-intensive basic technique and meet increasing new demands. And yet the pivotal role of the IS as the voice for Amnesty prevented devolution. Thus, the Research Department tried again to reduce demand. In a memo on "Research Department Planning" for the April 1979 IEC, headed "consolidation," it argued for "A policy that will reduce the demands until they equal the resources. From the many diverse calls on the Research Department, the movement must choose those which it considers most important. It must also clearly state those which it expects the Research Department to refuse or give lowest priority. Most important, it must be realized that the Research Department's fundamental task is to do the necessary research to ensure high quality in all AI's work."[29] The CCC was already wary of the potential drawbacks of an increasing membership, especially of those members who might pay to join but not be active.[30] It stressed the need to attract, and train, better-quality members, arguing that comprehensive knowledge of the organization, the techniques applied, and the reasons behind strategies were a must if members were to be effective both inside and outside Amnesty.

Restricting access through quality control thereby maintained scarcity—such a distinction enhancing the sense of sacredness—and increased commitment by deterring free-riders (members who wanted to join but not be active).[31] The CCC proposed more training for members, section staff, and even for IS employees, with the seat of the training function to be, inevitably, at the IS; this occurred as the CCC also sought limits to the IS's "rapid and hungry growth." It feared that a permanent gap with national sections was evolving. The IS budget for 1978–1979 was predicted to be £1.3 million for a putative staff of 160. After underlining the importance of groups and work for individual prisoners, the CCC advocated an enhanced capacity for national sections, the political arm of the movement, to take action and service their own groups. It also created a research outpost in Paris. The CCC saw the potential dangers: "Decentralization will necessitate a strict observance of AI principles and procedures in order to ensure that a single AI identity is preserved and that AI speaks with one voice on all levels of the organization in all parts of the world, instead of with as many different voices as there are national sections." Although policing this identity seemed to be a charter for expanded central control, the CCC also wanted a permanent cap on the size of the IS at around 170 to 180 staff members (in 1981, membership stood at 326,000). Hammarberg thought even this was too high. His solution was to cut IS programs, improve administration, and decentralize. "When we cannot cope, we just have to lower our ambitions," he said.[32] He soon faced this issue from the other side of the table, as secretary general.

The Whitney Committee Report

The Committee on Administrative Structure of 1980, convened by the treasurer of AIUSA, A. Whitney Ellsworth, was an IEC initiative to address movement concerns about the IS and to deal with the aftermath of unrest among IS staff members over a wage claim, the staff having been unionized since the early 1970s.[33] Ellsworth, who had been a CCC member, perfectly captured the core tension over ownership of the Amnesty ethos. There were, he said, two competing formulations: "*IS staff help members to help prisoners*" and "*Members help IS staff to help prisoners*." Compare this with the view of an Americas researcher in 2003: "You've got the push and pull. You've got the members who pay for you to work for Amnesty International, who think that they pay therefore you should do what they say. That's a very basic way of saying it. And then you've got the other view which is that you have people who pay to join Amnesty International because they believe in what Amnesty International does.

And what Amnesty International does is decided by other people within the movement."

Although the classic ethos was widely shared in 1980, the question was where Amnesty International's members fitted into the relationship between researchers and prisoners. Were the researchers in any moral sense the employees of the members, a profane formulation? Weren't they in service to an ideal and only incidentally funded by the membership?

Based on extensive interviews with IS staff and senior movement members, the Whitney committee report was the most detailed account yet produced of the IS-Amnesty relationship. Although Ellsworth identified the rapid growth in the size of the IS staff (from 53 in 1973 to 146 in 1979) as the root cause of organizational problems, after conducting more than forty 45-minute interviews with IS staff in October 1979[34] he wrote to the IEC in the following terms: "What emerged very clearly, even overwhelmingly, from the interviews was deep concern over the lack of a clear decision-making process and allocation of authority." He went on:

> There is unease, confusion, or criticism from virtually all members of staff interviewed concerning the difficulties of establishing or identifying clear lines of authority and decision-making. Associated with this are the problems of lack of proper consultation in some cases or, conversely, the time consumed in consultation and shepherding a decision through the IS structure. Staff members—both those who expressed a preference for looser, "democratic" decision-making processes and those who prefer more conventional, hierarchical structures—universally urged that there be clearer lines of decision-making authority and a less cumbersome process of consultation. In my opinion, the interviews thus established the major problems to be addressed in any recommendations as to changes in the current structure.[35]

This proved to be the major finding of the final report, along with concerns about lack of trust between departments, long-term staff "leap-frogging" others to take issues to the secretary general, and problems with the five-department structure as a whole.[36] Of these five departments, only the Research Department was left untouched in the report's recommendations (as well as in the IEC and IS response to them). This was despite Ellsworth's acute recognition of how moral authority worked inside the IS. Researchers were, he said, an "expanding star":

> A researcher has little ongoing contact with the administrative and support services within the IS and is not particularly aware of their problems and priorities. Then the researcher has a report or a press release or whatever which he or she wants to come out on a specific date of importance. This date conflicts with other work scheduled and the Press and Publications unit and/or the postroom insist on delay. The matter quickly goes to the SGO [secretary general's office] and the researcher, because of the unquestioned moral and intellectual authority attributable to having responsibility for prisoner work in that country, becomes an "expanding star" in terms of power. The priorities and practical arguments of the administrative and service staff have little chance of contradict- ing the expanding star's power. . . . Once the matter is resolved the star contracts and the researcher goes back to work, probably mum- bling about the lack of flexibility and the removal from core issues of the administrative staff. On their part, the administrative and support staff feel bruised because their priorities and planning can be so easily overturned. . . . The hypothesis is exaggerated but it points up the special nature of many posts within the IS. Looking at an organizational chart it is not apparent that posts such as researchers have as much power as they can occasionally command.

Ellsworth feared that if staffers listened only to their own expertise and knowledge, Amnesty would lose members, and then "would we not risk losing our ability to sway public opinion and to lobby at the highest levels of government . . .?" Neatly identified, therefore, is the dilemma: the way researchers built and protected moral authority risked, in the long term, denuding Amnesty of its political authority.

As the 1980s dawned, Ennals moved on to be replaced by Hammarberg, who knew Amnesty as well as anyone. He was a secretary general with a strong sense of the ethos.[37] He also had a thorough understanding of the tensions inherent in amateur professionalism, writing that the work "tends to attract *committed people,* those who want to contribute to an important cause. This has brought a *volunteer* tendency to the office which sometimes clashes with the *professionalism* that has been stimulated during recent years."[38]

The IS was in its "cellular interior" at Easton Street from 1983 onward, with one-half of the now 160-strong paid staff members in the Research Department, helped by 30–40 volunteers. The head of research for most of the 1980s was a Canadian, Clayton Yeo, who had been the USSR researcher. In a memo from March 1980, with Ennals still at his post, this hugely influential research chief warned that researchers "have repeatedly expressed concern that they do not have sufficient time to do research as such on their countries." The view of the Research Department was that "Much of researchers' time should be spent in basic research to keep them informed on all the countries for which they are responsible. Not enough time is available now for this and researchers are concerned that the quality of their work is affected. Researchers complain that there is rarely time to think critically about the work on any country."[39] Researchers feared, said Yeo, that contact work (the crucial means of information gathering) was becoming harder to do with all the other pressures (from campaigns and membership) on researchers' time. Yet the demand for good information was only growing. Researchers had "increasingly less possibility to assess, advise on and react to many developments affecting their work." "The consequences are obvious: compromise of AI's one voice principle; lack of thorough planning even on important countries; frustrated incomprehension among the membership as to what our strategies are (or the considerations behind the strategies); risk of loss of credibility for AI." The Research Department needed more staff, he said. In a further document for the IEC in July 1980, Yeo dealt with quality of research and established the aspirations of the Research Department for the coming decade, beginning with the claim that "it would be accurate to say that the quality of RD [Research Department] work now is higher than ever before."[40]

This memo is a definitive description of the fusion between ethos and research at the zenith of Amnesty's symbolic moral authority, establishing ten pillars that supported it. Under, "Foundations of 'Quality of Research,'" the memo says:

The structural arrangement which makes it possible for the RD to undertake high quality research is the organization of the RD as a separate department, add [sic] within it the assignment of responsibility for research on specific countries to a particular researcher and two people working with him or her. Each person in this three person team is a specialist, both vis-à-vis the others in the team (with regard to the particular tasks each carries out) and vis-à-vis the organization (in that they have a unique responsibility for AI's work on the particular countries they work on). The organization has traditionally respected the unique expertise of these RD people. *To the extent that their authority and competence are challenged from within the movement, problems are likely to arise.*[41]

Thus, the first pillar is that Amnesty's authority lies in its research and the movement should remember that. The memo goes on:

Also essential to quality of research is recognition that a researcher cannot deal with all cases, countries, situations at once. This ought to be obvious, but every researcher is under pressure for having the common-sense to set priorities among his or her countries so as to have time to do work of high quality.

AI's tradition of focussing its work on individual prisoners (and, when describing general situations, using individual cases as illustrations) is important both in providing discipline as regards factual accuracy and in strengthening the presentation of our concerns. . . . Other AI traditions are important: for example, the recognized emphasis on factual, sober reporting at the expense of newspaper "scoops".

Thus, three further pillars: researchers ought to set priorities, work on individuals is now traditional, and "unflinching realism" is paramount. The memo continues:

Many RD staff risk becoming over-specialized in one particular facet (human rights) of the country/regional expertise which brought them to AI. There appears to be a common dilemma as to whether to stay in AI and risk falling behind in other facets of one's expertise. While the intellectual content of AI's work is in some respects enviably rich, in other respects AI imposes severe constraints on its employees' and members' work as regards the scope of research and the content of writing, and means of compensation for this should be sought, if only in the interest of "quality of research".

Pillars five, six, and seven: regional expertise, not human rights, is the key for researchers; the work's intellectual content is a main attraction; and research is an end in itself for researchers from which, while they are there, AI benefits but for which researchers make sacrifices. In referring to movement input to research and campaigning, the memo goes on:

> Difficult to sum up, but significant, is the input from the AI membership which in a disjointed way helps by supplying information of one sort or another on adoption cases, government responses to AI campaigns, contacts, etc. This is obviously more significant the more the membership are involved in country-related work (case sheets, campaigns, etc). Unfortunately its overall benign effect is sometimes negated when members accompany the information they obtained with strident demands for immediate action.

An "overall benign effect"? There is no doubt where the Research Department stands on Whitney Ellsworth's dilemma. Little wonder that sections—led by the United States—would soon demand the IEC represent their interests and not those of the IS.

The memo had more. Under "Quality control," pillar eight was the approvals process. This was (and is) most evident in the Annual Report, still a touchstone for researchers.[42] Here's the procedure from 1984 for writing an entry on just one country:

1. First draft prepared by specialist researcher.

2. Draft read and commented upon by head of region (responsible for quality control at the regional level).

3. Second draft prepared by researcher, taking head of region's comments into account.

4. Draft submitted to Head of Research Office for next stage of quality control—all texts checked bearing in mind mandate questions, application of AI policy and consistency of presentation.

5. Third draft may be needed at this stage, taking Head of Research Office's comments into account.

6. Text sent to the Legal Office and Secretary General's Office for next stage of scrutiny and comment.

7. Some text edited in Press and Publications Department, aiming at clarity, consistency, uniformity of tone and style, also taking into account the comments received from the Legal Office and Secretary General's Office.

8. The edited text, after discussions with the researcher, is sent to the member of the IEC nominated to read full text of the report.

9. The final text is approved by the Secretary General.[43]

No wonder the principle of "one voice" was maintained for so long. Approvals were required for news releases, external papers, newsletter articles, government and intergovernmental organization (IGO) submissions, AI reports, Urgent Actions, and more. This meant a tightly controlled message, a severe bottleneck at the top of the IS, and a tendency toward conservatism (as the 1980 memo accepts): "The person approving will look especially critically at statements that stand out either from the rest of the material or from normal AI practice and experience."[44] The lore was by now self-perpetuating and self-authorizing.

The 1980 memo concludes with two final pillars. The ninth stresses how the use of external expertise must be treated with caution. Amnesty researchers were often the recognized experts on human rights violations in their countries, it said, knowing far more than they could fit into Amnesty documents. Furthermore, "the independence of AI's research establishment is essential," the impartiality of external researchers a concern that makes them more appropriate as "sources rather than authorities." One researcher who worked in the IS during this time recalled this as follows: "The researchers were the key figures. They were the heart of the organization. The whole organization depended on them. . . . Amnesty was only as good as its information was. And it had no, no other sort of influence than sort of moral influence. And nobody would listen to it unless, you know, it was able to establish over a period of time that it got things right." "You can't do all the rest without the information," she said, adding, "But then I'm probably speaking old speak." A relatively new Amnesty researcher put it similarly: "Working on the country that I do, where human rights is so instrumentalized . . . Amnesty's name is so important. Amnesty's rules are so important. The quality of the research, its impartiality, its independence, being accurate, these are all issues from which Amnesty gains its strength."

The final pillar is about socializing keepers of the flame. The memo advocates more time be spent with new researchers for "going over their work." Indeed, in a reflection of the experiences of established researchers mentioned in chapter 2, the nature of this demanding culture is clear in the recommendation made by one researcher that "It would be quite useful if quite early on in the researcher's time here s/he voluntarily (or forcibly) submitted him or herself to a grilling on the value of any proposed action."[45] This sounds like an interrogation and serves as a powerful indicator of how the research culture provided a strong incentive for conformity among the researchers, of whom at this stage there were still just over twenty. One of the current staff members talked about this "culture of excellence," still intense in the early 1990s, where "every comma counted," adding, "If you had a typo in your paper, you would be shaking in shame." Another recalled how a veteran researcher stood in disbelief when her work was returned to her after the disbanding, in 1994, of the HORO without reams of fabled green ink scribbled all over it or the words *let's discuss* in the margin. This intellectually demanding atmosphere was dominated at the time by powerful men, one of whom described the process of working through the country strategy (how each separate country should be tackled) as being "like an exam," one country at a time for an hour and a half each week.

A researcher had to summarize what was going on for the moment and give suggestions on what to do next. Sort of strategic steps. Whether to involve the membership, whether to go public with a report or a press release . . . go there, or whatever . . . and these became the kind of the high point in the week. I think it elevated the status of the research department. . . . other people came in from the campaign and membership and listened and perhaps asked questions, but it really was the research department which dominated that. But it was fun. And I think it was good that these researchers had a challenge. They had to think strategically all the time.

And having said all of this, we still have the two strongest mechanisms by which the ethos was operationalized to consider: the mandate and impartiality. Through these mechanisms, the boundaries of Amnesty's identity were monitored and controlled from London.

The Mandate

Oh, the mandate was on our lips every moment of the day. And in fact that was central to, you know, everything we did. I mean, as a researcher, I get a piece of information and my first question was: is it within the mandate? Before I even bothered to find out whether it was worth pursuing . . . The mandate was absolutely the most important thing in our lives. . . whether something was inside or outside the mandate was, you know, the big question.

So said one legendary ex-researcher. Another described the formidable Clayton Yeo, head of research, as "like Moses with the mandate under his arm."[46] In a 1983 memo entitled "AI's identity in the late 'eighties," Thomas Hammarberg even argued that the "present mandate should be seen as permanent."[47] For him, Amnesty's success was based on the focused mandate, impartiality, and factual information. "We are independent and non-corrupt," he argued, making it "easier to convince journalists (and others) that we are genuinely impartial." His warning about endangering this reputation is stark: "It would be close to suicidal for AI to change or drop any of these basic principles in its work. The ambition should rather be to protect and safeguard them. This basic approach, however, should not prevent us from analyzing in depth the major choices we now confront relating to our mandate and policies."

The mandate evolved out of the 1968 Statute as working rules for selecting adoption cases. The formal content of the Statute, and therefore the parameters of the mandate, was a question for members at ICMs. Its interpretation on a case-by-case basis was the preserve of the Research Department unless the case was difficult enough to be referred to the suggestively titled Borderline Committee (also formed in 1968), which included senior members from the movement. The IS would, however, try to resolve borderline cases before they went to the committee. The first formal Mandate Committee, established by the Cambridge ICM in September 1977, met at the IS in 1978. It included several legendary Amnesty figures.[48] This meeting differentiated the mandate from the Statute as follows: "It was recognized that an area of concern may be within AI's statute but that AI is not *obliged* to work on it. Mandate, however, defines the primary objectives of AI, the generally accepted emphases in the philosophy behind our statutory concerns."[49] This elevated practice, rather than theory, to preeminence, creating doctrine in the process. The mandate was the set of filtering rules that turned the wider concerns of the Statute into operational principles. The Mandate Committee considered, for example, whether the nonviolence rule could be relaxed in the case of political prisoners (i.e., by definition, for Amnesty, those who had committed violence). It concluded:

It was suggested that AI should distinguish between political prisoners working against oppressive regimes and for human rights and those using quite unjustifiable violence. It was pointed out that such a policy would lead to accusations of one-sidedness and would also be against AI's policy of political impartiality, whereby AI does not criticize systems of government as such, only the actual repression under such systems. . . . If AI says that a person is not a POC it generally means that s/he has or may have used violence and AI cannot then ask for their release but only for a fair trial, sentence and decent prison conditions. However, in practice AI only involves itself in the trials of political prisoners if there is a question of death penalty or torture, or if it is thought that a person is being unfairly treated because of his/her race or language and that this is representative of a general pattern in a country.

This was not a definition from first principles but from established practice. Hammarberg recognized as much: "There is nothing sacred about our present mandate; it is not even logical in all its elements. One could add or subtract from our present tasks and get a 'mandate' which would make as much sense as the present one. Still, it is striking how *relevant* the present combination of tasks has turned out to be. . . . My own opinion is that AI should stick to its present mandate and actually decide that its cornerstones are *permanent.*"[50] The mandate was in reality increasingly sacred, as Durkheim would have predicted. A senior IS director urged me to get hold of a leaflet (it turned out to be more of a wall chart) entitled "Is it a case for Amnesty International?" It was almost "Jesuitical" in its complexity, he told me. Its centerpiece is a tree diagram that enables one to answer the question whether or not a prisoner qualified as an Amnesty case. This intricate diagram gives a clear message—adopting a POC requires expert judgment. Only one route through the maze leads to the result, written on the chart in bold: "This is a prisoner of conscience, imprisoned in violation of the Universal Declaration of Human Rights. Amnesty International works for the immediate and unconditional release of *all* prisoners of conscience."

For the first question in the leaflet ("Is the person a prisoner?"), there are three answers (yes, no, and has the person disappeared?). No leads to four options, whereas yes leads to a set of further questions with yes/no answers including "Is the person a political prisoner?" and "Is the prisoner facing the death penalty?" These, in turn, have further yes/no branches attached. This is all derived from the mandate of Amnesty.

One young researcher, who joined in the early 1990s and worked briefly on mandate issues, described the chart as an "anachronism," left over from a simpler time when Amnesty's issues were few. He said:

> One of the things that made me quickly realize that the mandate was an artificial construct . . . was that chart. . . . I just thought it was laughable. And we did a joke about it. And we said: Imagine trying to update this, you know, make it more reflective of reality. But the problem is that that chart is a very good emblematic symbol. . . . A lot of people had that mentality when I was working on the mandate. And I saw that I couldn't go along with that

mentality. . . . Why was I trying to make people in the IS adhere to standards I myself thought were artificial constructs that didn't work? And my answer to that was, well the standards that I'm really keeping in mind are international human rights norms. Which I think we really should adhere to.

The mandate was such that researchers no longer needed to refer to the prisoner; they could refer to the mandate. And they interpreted it. The mandate became the source of researcher authority, and while it retained its grip on the movement little could change. Growing dissatisfaction with this situation—stoked by a new generation of AIUSA staffers and members who had replaced the Whitney Ellsworth–Andrew Blane generation—led to the establishment in 1988 of a Mandate Review Committee (MRC) to conduct a far wider review. In a memo for the MRC, Clayton Yeo described the mandate as follows, "The mandate is the authority the movement has given to the component parts of AI to work on a particular body of subject matter. No part of the movement is authorized to state that AI as an organization takes a position on any matter that is 'outside the mandate'. So while the mandate is positive in its conception, it is usually evoked in a negative way, in the decision whether or not a particular matter can be the subject of AI's work."[51] Yeo looked for the sources of the mandate as a lawyer might argue for the source of law. He located them first and foremost in Statute Article 1 (although the word *mandate* did not appear) and in subsequent careful elaborations of Amnesty's object arising from there. The mandate was a codification of actual practice. The ICM was supreme in changing the Statute, but this major step was rarely taken on substantive issues because a two-thirds majority was required. Much more important were the guidelines, issued by the IS, of course, about how the mandate ought to be interpreted. These authoritative statements were kept in the Mandate Dossier. In Yeo's words, "There is also a permanent process of clarifying, or interpreting, or fleshing out AI's policy as adopted by the ICM. The IS is constantly engaged in this· process. It reports on such matters to the IEC and to the membership. Sometimes this too results in the adoption of guidelines or similar written materials suitable for general reference."

Yeo drew a tight connection between the mandate and Amnesty's authority through both consistency in application and strict impartiality about political matters (he noted how difficult this made issues such as apartheid for Amnesty).

> The requirement of impartiality has the most intimate relationship with AI's mandate. We must apply the same standards to every country. If AI takes an issue into its mandate with a view to one country (be this by way of an ICM decision or an interpretation of the mandate in the IS routine) we must henceforth be ready to take up the same issue in any other country where it appears. . . . So with rare exceptions the AI movement has made much effort to get a picture of the global effects of its decisions before making changes to the mandate. . . . And the IS aims on a day to day basis to apply the mandate consistently. This is not always easy. It often requires careful reading and editing of texts prepared for publications or submission to a government. There is a natural tendency to interpret and apply the mandate liberally so as to bring victims of human rights violations within AI's field of work. While AI's mandate on a particular issue may be expressed in fairly straightforward terms, "reality is messy" . . . and AI's "jurisprudence" and past decisions may not supply the answer to an issue in a particular country context. Researchers and others in AI are quick to pick up new possibilities for AI action. And the result is a creeping growth of the AI mandate. This may in general be a good thing and corresponds to what the AI membership seem to want. However it can amount to unplanned growth and create an image at least of inconsistency.

The scale of change in the 1990s is evident from the fact that since 2001—after an ICM in Dakar, Senegal—Amnesty has replaced the mandate with a word and concept that would have meant plenty to the founders, *mission*. This was the final act of a process begun ten years earlier in Yokohama. In 1994, for example, the Head of Research Office, which Yeo and then his deputy Malcolm Smart had presided over for more than a decade, was disbanded by Pierre Sané. This was the culmination of an internal struggle that had seen the first head of a regional program to become secretary general, Ian Martin, resign from the organization.

Impartiality

Impartiality was a further mechanism for enshrining detachment and preserving moral authority. As a 1985 IEC subcommittee phrased it, "Impartiality is a principle. It means that, within its mandate, AI should work for victims of human rights violations regardless of the ideologies of government or the views of victims."[52] We might add—as Yeo did, quoted in the previous section—that Amnesty also had to be prepared to take up an issue in every country where it manifested itself, an indication of the commitment to global coverage. From this principle, a series of more specific rules were derived. One was the Work On Own Country rule (WOOC). Once you joined Amnesty you stopped being able to work—in Amnesty's name, at least—on local or even national human rights concerns. If you were a member of the IS staff, you could not work on your own country and you might not be able to work on the country of your spouse or partner either. On the face of it, this had a functional rationale, protecting Amnesty groups from the state in countries where they might be at risk, allowing Amnesty researchers access to prisoners, and enabling researchers to deflect allegations of bias. In the words of a researcher on Africa:

> I've frequently come across situations where I've just been really thankful for that own country rule. You know . . . the way that governments will of course always accuse Amnesty of being biased . . . and they may, you know, sometimes they get really personal with those things and say that because so and so is from X country that proves he or she is partisan, or whatever it is. And it's actually great to be able to turn around and say, well actually no. . . . Precisely because that person lives in that country, they're not allowed to work on it.

If states could point to anyone involved with a piece of research who had a relevant national link, they could reintroduce the specter of an interest and thereby dent Amnesty's moral authority. The governments of Israel (over reports on the Occupied Territories) or of the United Kingdom (over Northern Ireland), among many others, would go over reports line by line looking for a hint of bias and would demand to know which staff members had been involved in the work and where they came from.

The WOOC rules evolved "In a period of rapid growth of the movement, as a means of ensuring that all new sections developed in a way consistent with the fundamental principles that had characterized AI since its foundation: impartiality, independence and international solidarity. These principles had given AI credibility and it was important that they be reflected in any AI section."[53] The rule was comprehensible in the Cold War world of the 1970s and 1980s. Beneath its functionality, however, the rule was a way of detaching Amnesty from the business of political agitation, and thereby reinforcing its own sense of a separate, distinct, and sacred identity. As a result, it robbed Amnesty of political authority, making it hard to generate membership outside the West and in turn recasting the colonial dynamic of largely white middle-class Westerners working as experts on behalf of largely nonwhite non-Westerners. One African IS staff member from the 1990s was even more blunt about WOOC:

> I think it's utterly rubbish. . . . You can't come back and say own country rule. It's bullshit. And again for me, as an African, who has worked in my own country, it is a misunderstanding of what human rights is. Human rights in the south is domestic. Human rights in the north is foreign policy. You've gotta decide where you're going to be. If you're going to be a real human rights organization, it's gotta be domestic issues.

WOOC meant that people attracted to set up Amnesty sections in the south were precisely *not* grassroots activists. A senior IS staffer from the 1980s talked about his mystification that so many members liked the WOOC rule: "That rule was their protection. What kind of people were joining Amnesty International? If you couldn't work on your own country? Well, the least politically exciting people in the country. Anybody who cared about Zambia was going to be fighting for democracy in Zambia. They weren't going to be joining an organization that told them why you can't fight for democracy in Zambia. You have to trust that somebody in some other country will fight." This has severely hampered Amnesty's growth outside the West, and non-Western section after non-Western section has stagnated, collapsed, or imploded. The whole idea of replicating identikit Amnesty sections outside its core Western base is now being abandoned, as we will see, and since the ICM of 2001 the WOOC rule has effectively been scrapped.

A related question is about representation and authority within the IS. Many nonwhite or non-Western staff members feel constrained by a culture that they think implicitly discriminates against them because they do not fit the mold of Amnesty researcher, the legendary figures who were experts on vast, complex countries thousands of miles away whose language or languages some of them, especially in Asia and Africa, were (and are) unable even to speak.[54] As one non-Western staff member from the 1990s explained it:

> The use of the word expert was always something that was really annoying to me. When somebody says I'm an expert on Burundi. What do you mean by expert on Burundi? Well maybe you have lived in that country for six months or were there as an expatriate. But do we have an expert on France here? No, we don't have an expert on France. So for me this "expert on certain countries" was a remnant of a colonial way of thinking; that you would have, in London, people who would be experts, but we didn't have an expert on Britain. We had somebody who was working on Britain, but he was not an expert on Britain. So therefore you are not an expert on Burundi. Maybe you know Burundi legislation, you have good contacts in Burundi, maybe even you speak the language, you've been there several times. But you are a human rights researcher on Burundi. Don't call it expert.

And yet this attachment to the notion of expertise, even of mastery, is still strong. Here are the words of one young researcher who was avidly reading all he could on the historical background of his new brief because "you have to be prepared to answer anything."

> I think being the master of the country that you're working on is absolutely essential. You have to be able to understand that country in order to be able to do the job that you do. You can have certain skills that will help you develop that mastery of the subject area.

But you need to develop it at some stage. But it's something that takes years and years. I think that a lot of people that work here are experts on their countries. I think it's a good thing that there is an academic slant. At least with the researchers. Because that is actually good for the whole. It's the raw material. For the campaigning work. It's a good title, research. The stuff that we do is research. And then campaigners in collaboration with the researchers put that research into action. It's a wonderful combination. But you can't have one without the other. I mean, just having research would just turn us into a research institute.

The WOOC rule protected the prevailing ethos by reinforcing a culture of expertise that delegitimized those whose expertise came from experience (the expertise of those most active in human rights struggles in their own countries). The effect of this was to treat the south and the fringes of Europe (Russia and Turkey) as objects to be researched from outside.

Certain sections pressed in the 1990s to do their own projects exempt from WOOC, and by 2003 some simply did their own research and sent it to the IS afterward. A U.S. campaign in 1996, in which AIUSA was prominent, was a notable case of work on own country. Other sections, especially older established European ones, remained (and remain) committed to the IS as the source of research. Drafting was also underway in 2004 on replacing WOOC within the IS with a Conflict of Interest Policy (the IS having been advised that its WOOC rules might contravene the European Convention on Human Rights, even under the Freedom of Expression article).

A second practical example of impartiality was the idea of balance. The Threes were based on this principle, as was Amnesty's refusal in Annual Reports to rank countries in terms of their human rights performance (implicitly, of course, the ranking was unavoidable). From the graphics for campaigns to the length of Annual Report entries to the posters sections displayed, the need for balance was considered. So-called "closed countries," those to which Amnesty could not get access or that it could not research properly, were a great concern because they increased the number of cases from countries that were more open.[55] Being closed was a way to avoid scrutiny, in other words. Balance also meant trying to denounce human rights abuses wherever they occurred, and this lay behind the importance researchers attached to universal coverage, known from 1993 on as Minimum Adequate Coverage (MAC).

The International Secretariat at Its Zenith

Through approvals, the mandate, balance, WOOC, and "one voice," the IS had by the mid-1980s established Amnesty as a moral spokesperson for the interests of humanity. And Thomas Hammarberg was its appropriate champion. In an IS archive file composed of reminiscences about him for his leaving present in 1986, an unsigned sheet of paper (by someone who clearly knew him well) described his passions as clarity and anonymity. The text is an exemplary account of self-disciplined persistence:

> [His] obscurity has been deliberate. God help the IEC member, IS staffer or section volunteer who got themselves featured in a newspaper, strayed from the party line or gave a hint that they were riding to glory on the back of AI. "No one shall have the right to hijack this movement," he once hissed in Biblical Swedish. The vehemence is tactical but the conviction is unshakeable. He knows there is no glory in this business. He has put his name to countless urgent telegrams and talked to innumerable politicians and bureaucrats. He can name some prisoners whose lives AI has saved. But he knows he has stood in the waves like King Canute while thousands the world over have been silenced, tortured and killed. The crown has meant nothing.

Hammarberg presided over the full realization of Amnesty's symbolic moral authority and helped consolidate the parameters of its identity. Thus, three things came together—ethos, research, and authority—and Amnesty was the synthesis. In his leaving speech, Hammarberg saw the twin spheres of the sacred and profane very clearly:

> My final recommendation . . . is about the spirit inside the movement. We are growing, we are getting more money, we make many more travels than before, we are more important than ever. This is fine. But let us not be carried away by that, and let's not be cor-

rupted by it. Corruption is not a big nasty beast, sleeping outside the air-lock here. Something that you can easily identify and you could protect yourself against—keep outside. Corruption is invisible, corruption is creepy, corruption is very contagious. It often starts with friendship relationships but it spreads very easily. Money of course is one aspect but only one aspect. We work on money that people have given us on trust, those who give Amnesty International money, who finance our work, our salaries here, they give it because they believe that that very power is going to the business of the release of prisoners. That means that we must maintain a moral here to be careful of money. . . . But there are other things than money, I don't think we should go to unnecessary conferences and mingle too much with the false diplomatic world. I don't think that we should allow ourselves to begin to personalize our work, because we are only representatives. We should stay amateurs, that's what it is about.[56]

This was Amnesty circa 1986. It was seductive even for those who came with more radical views. One senior IS staff member who worked at the IS for more than fifteen years recalled, "The organization had its own momentum. It had its own ethos. I doubt I was the only person who came to it with, at worst, a political axe to grind and at best as a haven from harming something I believed in politically. But somehow there was an ethos about the place that forced you into that basic respect for the other and those underpinnings. The inarticulate native premises of what human rights are about." There were tensions and pressures, of course. The line always had to be held. In the 1980s, for example, Amnesty began working on ending impunity for perpetrators of human rights abuses, especially in Latin America and Southeast Asia, presenting a challenge to those—led by Clayton Yeo—who insisted that Amnesty's purpose was to keep people out of prison (as its very name suggests; it has also been an ardent and influential supporter of the International Criminal Court). Amnesty reports did not deal with the past and did not provide context—they presented the facts of imprisonment and demanded unconditional release for POCs (this lack of context lies behind Richard Wilson's critique). Despite these faint intimations of change, by the 1980s Amnesty was firmly anchored as an institution apart.[57]

In 1982, for example, in a report called "An International Personality," Amnesty took stock of its public identity.[58] Much of the foundational spirit was strongly in evidence. Natural rights, for example, appeared under the label "internationalism," AI taking "as its starting point certain principles that transcend the divisions of nationality, race, culture, religion and politics." "These principles are themselves part of the heritage of the world's cultures. Even if the particular legal codes and procedural frameworks with which AI is so often concerned vary from country to country and culture to culture, certain fundamental ideas remain common—the enduring values of justice, fairness, compassion and humanity." The report accepts that the ethos was seen by some as "too cold," its "somewhat anonymous" style "emotionally restrained—letting the facts speak for themselves." This meant suppressing "the sense of outrage and tragedy that can motivate people to respond to our appeals." But it adds, "AI does not claim credit and should adopt a modest tone. We do not know all the factors that lead to the release of a prisoner of conscience and our experience inevitably leads us to be modest when we compare the scale of political imprisonment, torture and the death penalty throughout the world with even our best efforts." The movement's role was vital but circumscribed, the report once again referring to the quality and training of members and the need for them to be responsible; to maintaining editorial standards; to making sure AI's mandate is described precisely in letterheads, reports, and so on; and to ensuring that internal rules were followed. The report concluded:

> Defining in this way the essential elements of an effective public image does not impose a straitjacket on the movement. It establishes the minimum core of values and principles that all must respect, but does not prescribe how those should be communicated in each country or culture. This is where the creativity of the movement must be tapped to adopt [sic] AI to national and regional cultures, in the words of a long-standing AI member, and "to use our diversity as the positive force that it can really be".

There is a chronic ambiguity here. Amnesty was a highly centralized and rule-bound organization in which the only scope left to members was communication, and even this was carefully managed. The final quotation in the report is the description of AI by someone who called it "an effective popular movement of well-meaning stubborn people who will not go away or shut up—backed up by impartial, authoritative research." This does not sound much like the reality of "one voice." Amnesty was, in fact, a dedicated and professional research operation backed up by members whose commitment to action was channeled by the central institutions to maintain a clear and consistent message. Maintaining external authority required maintaining internal authority. Diversity, spontaneity, and individuality had all to be constrained in the service of moral authority. All that was about to change.

5 POLITICS AND DEMOCRATIC AUTHORITY

robert frost, the american poet, said that a liberal was someone who could not take his own side in an argument.[1] This is the essence of liberalism's claim not to be just another sectarian doctrine but to be a kind of "higher-order impartiality."[2] It is grounded in the kind of morality we have been considering—one that claims its stance is detached, objective, and universal (i.e., disinterested). This was Amnesty's position: we express no opinion on the argument, but we stand for the principle that no one should be imprisoned, tortured, or killed just for engaging in it.

This form of theoretical authority combines claims about what to believe and what to do. It is moral in that it doesn't appeal to our own interests in making these claims. But what of claims to authority that rely neither on formal authority (the state), nor theoretical authority (truth, expertise)? These are the claims of those who are neither already powerful, nor aiming to speak for either the truth or the whole. They are claims anchored in the identity and interests of a specific social group or class. To represent such a claim entails a delicate balance—one must try to build authority with those whom one seeks to influence while at the same time maintaining authority with those one represents. This is what I have characterized as small "p" political authority. This takes us closer to persuasion and opinion. It is ethical action in the "first person," for a category of persons, whether women, children, the poor, minorities, the nonheterosexual, or the disabled, and so on. Whoever represents them always speaks, in some sense, in their name.

To be a representative, as single-issue groups are, requires a certain kind of authority. This can be loaned through a formal process such as an election or through a contract to an outsider. But being a representative usually requires a less substitutable qualification—belonging. This is certainly true if you are to *be* representative; you must be part of the community of fate. In most cases, there can be no meaningful global democratic poll of the whole, and so those who volunteer themselves as speakers must possess validation that is personal and/or bestows the appropriate (and usually visible) markers—gender, sexuality, color, ethnicity, or religion—of community membership. One way to think about this is as a question of trust. You trust a moral authority because *it* does not have an interest; you trust a political authority because *he* or *she* does. Moral authority is genderless and colorless; political authority always has both (and more besides).

Against this, the univocal detachment of classic moral authority appears alienating and inflexible. It is like the established church versus liberation theology. Most of all it lacks political relevance. When the issue is the systemic and systematic maltreatment of a class of people in the here and now, appeals to good conscience—in the face of dictatorship, violence against women, slavery, and torture—lack conviction. To secure change you need to mobilize social power—to get people in movement, whether through the political process or on the streets. As in the call to arms of Emmeline Pankhurst, suffragette leader, you need "deeds not words." There has to be more voice and less paper, more placards and fewer reports. There has to be more political struggle rooted in what Amnesty reformers called "a theory of social change." "I can only see human rights as an overwhelming thing that invades your personal sphere as well as the political sphere. It's about radical structural changes. In the way societies are governed . . . and also the way you live your life," said one reformist researcher. Human rights were not, he said, just "a badge." According to another (ex-IS) reformer, "You can't be profoundly neutral in issues of life and death. You just can't. You've gotta choose life. If you're gonna save people, you know, be on the side of life or the side of death. We used to call it in [country deleted] the area between good and evil. You're either with god or with the devil. And President [name deleted] is the devil. So you choose where you are. You can't stand and say, I don't choose any side. You've got to be on a side."

Amnesty's store of moral authority—its moral capital—was a substantial resource, and it attracted those who wanted to fight more political battles. This did not decenter the need for research, but it threatened to decenter the researchers because political authority places more emphasis on pragmatism in message and method. If moral authority was no longer an end in itself, then Amnesty research—hitherto synonymous with the ethos—would have to be more instrumental. For the keepers of the flame, this risked eroding the core of what made Amnesty special and sacred. As one veteran researcher put it, "Just because Amnesty says something is wrong, the world is [not] going to sit and listen indefinitely. If it can't back it up with facts. And less and less research is actually being done. Less and less facts are being established or checked. Sections, new people in sections, think that simply denouncing something and Amnesty denouncing it is enough. But governments won't listen to that."

Even before the Cold War's unifying stimulus was removed and the Berlin Wall came down, there were visible signs of wear and tear in the pillars of the ethos. Of these, the first was the growth of AIUSA, with new members, who joined in the era of the Reaganite New Right, seeking political change, not the preservation of hope. On the U.S. political Left, many of the AIUSA members are graduates of the fight for civil rights, civil liberties, and the anti–Vietnam War protests (with conscientious objectors a key early concern for AIUSA).[3] A second sign was intensified pressure to take up newer rights issues that directly challenged Amnesty's authority to try to fix the meaning of universal human rights.[4] Because these new rights were more questions of "us against them," the social identity of the movement increasingly began to matter. And a third sign was competition. In a more dynamic environment, the POC came to seem somewhat isolated and irrelevant—a tiny symbol of hope in a fast-moving world where old certainties were gone and murder happened on a vast scale.

Amnesty was also forced to address the logic of the market. Its moral authority, precisely what money could not buy, could be recast as a powerful brand. It was this world Hammarberg warned against in his leaving speech. One well-publicized aspect of Amnesty's claim to impartiality has been a rejection of government funds for its core work, and in the 1970s this extended to foundations as well, the IS and IEC refusing funds from the Ford Foundation because of fears about its alleged links with the CIA (and trying, and failing, to stop AIUSA from taking them). By the 1990s, however, with the mass media now transformed into something extraordinary, where speed, clarity, brevity, and punch were essential, Amnesty found itself confronted by a more agile competitor for publicity and money: Human Rights Watch (HRW). Reinforcing the role of AIUSA in the movement was the fact that it directly faced this new challenger on its home turf.

The Rise of Amnesty International USA

Compared with its western European counterparts, AIUSA, founded in Washington, DC in 1961, made a faltering start to its Amnesty career. It had little influence inside the movement and what relations there were appear to have been fraught.[5] Some of these tensions centered on divergent attitudes toward the money–membership relationship. AIUSA saw individuals, as well as groups, as an important constituency for Amnesty, quickly distinguishing donors from members and experimenting with fundraising techniques like direct mail. According to the AIUSA executive director in 1967, Paul Lyons, for example, in the United States: "There seems to be a feeling among most of those willing [to] write letters that others should provide the financing (and definitely a corresponding feeling among our most generous contributors that others should do the letter-writing and other leg work)."[6] This approach not only clashed with the classic ethos, and the significance of groups within it, it also failed to generate income or members, and by the late 1960s the IEC saw the U.S. section as moribund, going as far as setting up a rival not-for-profit, Amnesty International Development Inc., to try to circumvent AIUSA.[7]

After this inauspicious start, a surviving combined group, centered around Columbia University in New York, took over the section and, after amalgamation with a semi-autonomous San Francisco office in the mid-1970s, AIUSA—and its profile within the movement—began to expand.[8] While the U.S. section retained its distinction between active members— who worked for POC release, for example—and donors, who gave money, it was the donor base that grew sharply. Through improved direct mail, for example, AIUSA's contribution to the international movement went from $1,000 in 1972 to $1 million in 1981. This emphasis on income rather than members was in part explained by IEC (and AIUSA) fears that substantial growth in active American membership might overwhelm AI's internal political processes.

The distinction between active members (who mostly gave time) and donors (who mostly gave money) was, of course, an ambiguity Amnesty's internal culture did nothing to resolve. We have already read of IEC concerns in the late 1970s about the quality of "members." National sections had different criteria for who counted as an Amnesty member, and not all of them even filed membership returns. Even the aggregate figures the IS received were divided between active and passive members. As late as 1995, estimated membership figures of 900,000 fee-paying members listed only 100,000 who were considered "active."

Nevertheless, as AIUSA grew in the 1980s, its headline membership figure comprised all those who paid their dues, active (in the classic sense) or not. Thus, by 1991, the German Section registered 600 groups comprising a mere 12,100 members while the U.S. section registered just 416 groups but a membership of 341,000.[9] (See tables 5.1 and 5.2) In the sphere of democratic public politics within the United States, numbers count, and the impact of 12,100 intensely committed active members did not compare with that of 341,000 individuals irrespective of their level of commitment. This did not, necessarily, translate into power within internal Amnesty structures, of course, where authority politics were not about size. But it is pertinent that Amnesty as a whole now works out its

TABLE 5.1
Amnesty International Local Groups Registered with the International Secretariat, 1965–1991[a]

	AI (total)	Western Europe	AIUSA	US (%)
1965	376	347	1	0.3
1970	931	874	6	0.7
1975	1,573	1,398	85	5.4
1980	2,464	2,103	203	8.2
1981	2,628	2,186	230	8.8
1982	2,895	2,371	260	9.0
1983	3,179	2,552	281	8.8
1984	3,392	2,686	288	8.5
1985	3,624	2,828	306	8.4
1986	3,739	2,918	319	8.5
1987	3,844	2,959	343	8.9
1988	3,963	3,000	370	9.3
1989	4,124	3,046	418	10.1
1990	4,159	3,045	413	9.9
1991	4,191	3,041	416	9.9

[a] From "AI Membership Statistics" (AI Index ORG 40/02/96).

TABLE 5.2
Fee-Paying Registered Individual Members in Amnesty International Sections, 1983–1991[a]

	Western Europe	AIUSA	AI (total)	US (%)
1983	287,642	222,400	571,439	39
1984	254,263	130,000	—	—
1985	261,510	140,000	—	—
1986	306,230	170,000	527,257	32
1987	302,625	308,000	670,000	46
1988	347,550	402,000	—	—
1989	388,392	375,300	—	—
1990	421,920	386,000	876,719	44
1991	464,140	341,000	(898,565)	38

[a] From "AI membership statistics" (AI Index ORG 40/02/96). No total individual membership figures were listed for some of these years because the information on Latin America, Africa, the Middle East, Maghreb, and Eastern Europe was considered too unreliable. Many of the U.S. figures are clearly rounded estimates. I have added in total membership estimates where they can be found in membership reports, and thus the percentages must be considered highly conditional. The total for 1991 is actually for 1992.

membership in terms of a figure based on individuals, the whole idea of the group seeming somewhat anachronistic in today's world.[10]

As we see, by the mid 1980s, AIUSA's "membership"—a composite of all contributors—had passed that of the established European sections. The picture is different today, the United States having the largest individual section (as of 2002) with 320,000 members, but with the other European sections—now recording a composite definition of members too—combining to a much higher figure; France, the Netherlands, and the UK total 670,000 between them.

If growth in U.S. membership was monitored in the 1970s, the 1983 election for AIUSA executive director challenged this approach. One member of the board at the time described it as a choice between an "internationalist perspective" and a more "aggressively U.S. centric position." After much debate, the board split over a choice between ex-IS deputy secretary general Dick Oosting and an Irish American former priest from Pittsburgh named Jack Healey whose connection with AI had been minimal. The board finally chose Healey. In a sense, it was in microcosm the kind of choice AI as a whole has been wrestling with ever since. Healey, an outsider to AI, brought a campaigning style into Amnesty that was about as different from quiet persistence as one could get.

Healey's outlook resembled liberation theology—that human rights work was about connecting with the poor and oppressed. He was certainly a radical departure from what one AIUSA staffer called "the rich New Yorkers" who had hitherto been influential in the development of AIUSA and the IEC (although they remained influential on the board). Under Healey and board chairman James David Barber the drive to increase the number of individual members, not groups, continued, as did direct mail campaigns to increase funds. As one AIUSA staffer of the time put it, the groups were "eating money," whereas donors actually gave it. Healey aimed to increase membership, especially among the young; raise income; and expand Amnesty's mandate to cover all the articles of the UDHR. His preferred vehicle for this was to stage rock tours to publicize Amnesty and its work. The first was a domestic U.S. affair in 1986, the Conspiracy of Hope tour, involving acts such as U2, Sting, Lou Reed, and Joan Baez (an early AIUSA member). The spike in AIUSA membership—from 170,000 in 1986 to 308,000 in 1987—is testament to the success of this tour in raising the profile of AIUSA in the United States. In 1988, therefore, to coincide with the fortieth anniversary of the UDHR, Healey proposed a worldwide rock tour to highlight Amnesty's global role.

The Human Rights Now! tour, involving artists Bruce Springsteen, Youssou N'Dour, Sting, Peter Gabriel, and Tracy Chapman, was an extraordinary undertaking. On two chartered DC-10s, two hundred people flew a six-hour concert around the world for six weeks, playing twenty tour concerts to 1 million people, half of whom signed the UDHR. An estimated 1 billion people saw the broadcasts on television. The emotional high points were many, topped off by Sting singing his song for the disappeared, "They Dance Alone," with twenty-five relatives of the disappeared on stage in Mendoza, Argentina. It is hard to imagine that there has ever been a comparably ambitious high-profile traveling road show; few organizations dare to dream of such global publicity for their message. But Amnesty's reputation was enough to make it happen. It comes as no surprise, however, that this tour placed an intolerable strain on an organization structured for "one voice."

After undergoing a background ethics check, Reebok was enlisted to underwrite any tour losses ($3 million in the end on sales of $23 million and costs of $26 million), and it provided a $2 million advance to enable the concerts to go ahead. But Amnesty's fears of the profane—of corporate money, of losing control, of liability—meant that a foundation, Human

Rights Now! (headed by Healey), was set up to run the tour. Yet it *was* an Amnesty International tour and endless quarreling followed as the organization tried to get operational control, sometimes allowing the logo to be used and other times not (confusing Reebok, for example, about with whom it was dealing).

The tour presented numerous dilemmas: how to deal with speeches from governments, how much tickets should cost, and what the artists would say on stage (and would it be within the mandate?). The IEC supported the tour, but the IS, including its Campaign and Membership Department, concerned about logistics and venues, was opposed (most sections were in favor). At a management (Group of Sixteen) meeting in April 1987, the regional programs set out their objections.[11]

The Middle East region thought rock music was not "an appropriate vehicle for promoting AI in the Middle East, since it could reinforce the image of AI as being a decadent Western organization"; the Europe region was slightly more positive than the Middle East, but was concerned that rock music was not the best way to introduce AI in eastern Europe. The Africa region was "not opposed to using rock music in some form at some future time, for example for membership development, [but] the current proposal was felt to be inappropriate," whereas the Asia region worried that events outside "Westernized places" such as Hong Kong and Japan might be "exploited in the wrong way." Researchers in Asia were also concerned whether "the anniversary of the Universal Declaration of Human Rights was more important than the music or vice-versa." Finally, "Discussion in the Americas Region had . . . produced a feeling of suspicion and hostility to the idea. Rock music was seen as being associated with the wealthy elite and therefore a tour of this kind would be bad for AI's image."

Secretary General Ian Martin was not persuaded by these objections, and the IEC made the decision to go ahead. The negotiations with individual sections left performers and their agents bemused when decisions about where best to promote human rights were engulfed in section politics about who would get a concert. As a tour organizer put it, "The fundamental question raised by our experience was how can AI make decisions as a movement in a way that works realistically for an international project?" This is the core question for a genuinely transnational organization. Amnesty had national sections, but all of these shared in a brand that was globally managed. If Amnesty got a bad name in one country or through an international mistake, all sections would be affected, however well they ran their own affairs and however high their national reputations. As one organizer explained, "Primarily the issues revolved around territoriality, the sense of control that each section felt it had over the name and image of AI in its country, which control was threatened by a need for international consistency and single, universal decisions about what AI would do with respect to the tour worldwide." For example, Reebok was given an exclusive license to sell Human Rights Now! T-shirts, but soon national AI sections said they intended to produce their own Human Rights Now! T-shirts as well. Then AI wanted to control which countries Reebok could advertise in and what they could say about human rights when, at the same time, it was a condition of the deal that the names *Amnesty International* and *Reebok* would never appear together. This helped scupper a suggestion that Reebok might buy half the advertising time for the 1988 Olympic Games to promote human rights, including promoting Amnesty. As the concerts approached, of course, national sections began pushing for more and more association between Amnesty and these high-profile events. The issue, always, was control.

For a global organization committed to universal ethical ideals, Amnesty has some peculiar institutional arrangements. For example, in two countries, Belgium and Canada, there are different section branches based on language (Belgium Francophone and Flemish, Canada English-speaking and French-speaking). As a tour organizer put it, music industry professionals thought it was incomprehensible that concerts were planned in both Toronto and Montreal. The familiar idea of balance was a consideration when it came to how many concerts could be staged in Western Europe and the United States where the audiences, and certainly the prospect of increased income, were larger. The most tense negotiation of all was over a concert in India, sponsored by the *Times of India* on the condition that there be no official AI representation at the venue.

Control of AI's image did not cease with the tour. A *Rolling Stone* journalist, Jim Henke, wrote an official behind-the-scenes account of the tour that Amnesty tried to recall after it had been printed and distributed to bookstores because it was unhappy about remarks made by tour producer and AIUSA publicist and fundraiser Mary Daly. She said, "We had seen this amazing success from the Conspiracy tour, but other Amnesty sections around the world were stagnating in a kind of bureaucratic quagmire. The European sections were decreasing in membership and weren't raising much money. The developing sections weren't developing. The whole movement seemed to be on the decline."[12] We know AI does not handle internal dissent well, but at a cost of $500,000 it is remarkable that the recall was ever considered.[13]

To this day, in the AIUSA Washington office there is a Human Rights Now! poster on the wall bearing the legend "One movement, one message, many voices." This shift from the language of "one voice" was the result of a major internal reform undertaken by a Committee on Long-Range Organizational Development (CLOD), formed in 1985 to address whether "the IS was too large, the IEC too weak and the movement too poor," according to IS deputy Secretary General (and former AIUSA staffer) Larry Cox.[14] One senior staff member when reminded of this committee put his head in his hands, groaned, "Oh God," and then laughed:

> It was an attempt to recognize that you couldn't have a world that brought everyone together. That you had to start developing sort of regional mechanisms. But . . . the whole starting premise was wrong. I mean, look at the name. The committee for long range organizational development. It was about Amnesty. It was about building Amnesty. It was about internal debates. I mean, it didn't say, you know, the committee for more effective strategy for ending human rights violations. Or the committee to adapt our organization to new trends in human rights.

Much of the drive behind CLOD was provided by AIUSA, a prominent member of which, David Hinkley, was its chair. The final report, submitted to the 1987 Brazil ICM, said:

> If the movement embraces the considerations and recommendations contained in these chapters, it must radically transform both the way AI functions internally and the way we interact with the rest of the human rights movement. The slogan **"one movement, one voice"** will be replaced by one which emphasizes openness to change, flexibility, diversity and innovation: **"One movement, one message, many voices."** And beyond symbols and attitudes, the

movement will be embracing a vision of the future characterized by **horizontal** rather than exclusively vertical relationships: collaboration, cooperation and interaction in planning, in program and in the exercise of democracy.[15]

The aim was more internal democracy and a greater openness to the human rights movement as a whole. A year earlier, two CLOD members who interviewed IS staff for the report wrote, "Decision-making is as hopeless as in the past. Eighty percent of our findings can be found in the Whitney report of 1980. Although hardly anybody in the IS does not have a good understanding of the problems, solutions will not easyly [sic] be implemented. Traditions and the attitude of a super-democratic organization often result in: no decision at all, bureaucratic solutions, really undemocratic decision-making." "Management is the word that becomes a miracle," they went on. "What we need is a way out of the vicious circle: Crisis—review—recommendations—*no* implementation, crisis on a new level—review—. . . ." The answers were ready, they said. The IS must learn "TO GET THINGS DONE!"[16]

The final report hardly mentions the IS. Its focus is on movement growth, especially outside the West. Despite AI's efforts, it concludes, "Few if any sections have attracted people from a broad, heterogeneous mixture of social and cultural backgrounds to their membership or leadership. If a profile of the 'average' AI member were drawn, the person would be white, middle-class, well-educated and have at least a passive knowledge of English or French, living in Western Europe." This hampered membership development and undermined Amnesty's political authority.

Would an Amnesty International with a richer proportion of members, activists and leaders from Africa, Asia, the Americas and the Middle East not be better able to develop suitable strategies and approaches to pressuring the wide range of governments AI must engage? Would our interventions not carry more credibility and moral force, not only by virtue of the heterogeneity of our voices but by the nuances and sophistication such a range of new minds, traditions and experience could be expected to bring to the work?

To preserve what has been seen as the essence of AI, in the last decade especially, a plethora of sometimes rigid guidelines has been developed. Expressed by the slogan "One movement, one voice," the motivation for these guidelines has been to guarantee at least a minimum level of consistency in the working methods and priorities of AI throughout the world. But the effect, though never intended, is to limit severely the accessibility, flexibility, dynamism, therefore the diversity and effectiveness of the whole organization.

To overcome these impediments to wider, non-Western membership, the report sought a "partial transformation of AI's approach, beginning by throwing out the mentality which regards established AI practice as sacrosanct." I have argued that Amnesty was, in effect, its practice—it was what it did. What else made it cohere? Overthrowing practice would be far from straightforward as a result.

Sexual Orientation and the Mandate

Concern with identity rights was prominent in the new social movements of the 1960s and 1970s. As an issue for Amnesty, gay rights dated back to 1974.[17] The question was: Could someone imprisoned for being gay be a POC? This had a subtle alternative: Could someone imprisoned for advocating gay rights, rather than for being gay as such, be a POC? By 1977, the ICM had passed a resolution saying that sexual orientation and behavior between consenting adults were legitimate grounds for POC status, and it amended the Statute to add "sex" to "ethnic origin, color or language." This did not put sexual orientation in the mandate, of course. By the time of the 1978 Mandate Committee, it was accepted that those persecuted for advocating homosexual equality could be taken up as POCs but that, in the majority's opinion, a person imprisoned "for sexual offences alone does not fall within the AI terms of reference." As the Luxembourg section made clear in criticizing this conclusion, the Mandate Committee located its conclusion in AI's terms of reference, but then went on to say substantive things about sexual conduct that were more evaluative, claiming that homosexual behavior was genetic, for example, and not related either "to a point of view" or "a question of choice." This takes us back to the principled nature of POC status and the idea of conscience as a question of choosing right over wrong.

A 1986 study by Dutch member George Siemensma aimed to document actual cases in which someone had been imprisoned because of his or her homosexuality. This study spent time working through causes as well, making a distinction between "homosexual inclination" and "homosexual conduct." Siemensma pointed out inconsistencies in the AI mandate and argued that rights to homosexual inclination and conduct were fundamental and should be considered "as a combination of someone's personal and essential features and someone's conviction." This was enough to ground POC status, he said, believing that few cases would result.[18]

The Research Department had reservations. It pointed out that in the fourteen cases that Siemensma identified none concerned anyone "charged and imprisoned simply for homosexual acts between consenting adults in private (which is the basic model type of case)." There would be mandate problems over national differences in ages of consent and rules for heterosexual sexual behavior. There was little international legal support for the proposed position, and fact finding would be hard. And AI's image might suffer. The Research Department pointed out, "For AI to get into the field of sexual behavior would be to enter into matters so different from those we work on now that it will make people question all our activities."[19]

From all of this, a mandate interpretation evolved that enabled work on those imprisoned for advocating homosexual equality under the rubric "freedom of expression." But the pressure continued. The MRC of 1988, which took three years to produce its final report, saw its one-time chairman, Michael Schelew, resign from the committee claiming the IS was trying to stop the mandate from expanding to take in sexual orientation. In his resignation letter, he wrote that IS management was "continually expressing their own private views" and trying to persuade the MRC to accept them. The greater knowledge that the IS staff members possessed enabled them to use undue influence, he went on, adding, "Their strong intervention for no change in the mandate during the debate on homosexuality is but one example of their lack of neutrality." Schelew had earlier resigned as chairman because other members had not, he said, supported his efforts to restrict IS attendance and modify its role away from advocacy toward neutral advice.[20] AIUSA had already expressed its concern about the functioning of the MRC, unhappy that it did not include anyone from the larger sections, for example.[21] It was also unhappy that procedural questions were not to be discussed, such as the functioning of the Borderline Committee. In a letter to IEC Chair Franca Sciuto, Paul Hoffman, chair of the AIUSA board (and in 2003 chair of the IEC), wrote, "Our board believes that the practice of having mandate interpretation questions decided solely by the Head of Research, without the involvement of the Borderline Committee, raises important questions of process which deserve serious attention by the Committee."[22]

The secretary of the MRC was, of course, Clayton Yeo, soon to retire as head of research. He produced a detailed document at the outset for the MRC entitled "Some general observations on the AI mandate" that, given his unrivalled knowledge of its workings and peculiarities, established a dauntingly complex set of questions revolving around how new issues might impact on the existing mandate and its operation. As the MRC pointed out in its final report, "few are the mandate 'experts' in the movement and most of them are IS staff."[23] AIUSA commented acerbically, "The statement that most mandate experts are members of the IS staff is not a positive one. In a democratic movement this should not be accepted and the movement should find a way of involving section volunteers in meaningful ways in this process."[24]

The MRC inadvertently recognized how the vagaries of political authority had become critical in areas such as sexual orientation where the classic, and "innocent," prisoner of conscience was absent. It was clear that in countries where there was widespread discrimination against homosexuality this was often with public approval, and some sections felt it would weaken Amnesty's reputation to take up such cases. On the other hand, in many Western states, not taking on cases of imprisoned homosexuals weakened Amnesty's authority as a champion of all human rights. Amnesty was being lobbied by gay rights groups looking for its support. As the MRC said,

A change of policy might strongly affect the harmony within the movement. On the other hand, those in favor of change will argue that this harmony will be harmed by *not* adopting the proposed changes. . . . Both those who favor change and those opposed to it consider AI's image of importance to its effectiveness. Those against change argue that this effectiveness will be harmed, because AI's credibility in some countries and with some governments will be undermined. Those in favor of change say that AI is being inconsistent by refusing to work for the release of one specific category of (non-violent) detainees, thereby harming its credibility and effectiveness.

Mediating fundamental clashes had been the role of the IS for nearly three decades, the mandate—practice made lore—settling matters that, if aired, were difficult to resolve. A divided MRC finally recommended that "The interpretation of the mandate should be extended so that 'advocacy of homosexual equality' would also cover expression of homosexual orientation." This covered cases in which people were arrested simply for being (or being suspected of being) gay. It was not intended to cover arrests involving "specific acts of sexual conduct proscribed by law." The MRC argued that its recommendation "Comes closest to meeting the demands of multiculturalism, as expressed in the divergent views on the subject within the movement as well as outside." This was the true challenge of sexual orientation—some members and sections did not think it should be part of Amnesty's mandate (one senior researcher at the time described the African, Middle Eastern, and Latin American sections as saying, "oh my God, no, you'll destroy us"). Nevertheless, within the movement at large there was a clear majority in favor of making the change.

The MRC forestalled mandate discussions for two ICMs (1987 and 1989), but decisions had to be made at Yokohama in 1991.[25] In the end, the ICM voted for a compromise that did not change the Statute but made it clear Amnesty would adopt people imprisoned because of homosexual acts or homosexual orientation as POCs. The method was interpretation of the word *sex* in the Statute (to be read as including sexual orientation). This was taken as a victory by those seeking change, but it put the onus squarely back on the IS and its researchers.[26] According to David Matas, getting this change was part of a deal struck with non-Western sections that wanted resolutions opposing forced exile, house destruction, deportation, and administrative detention, all issues of solidarity with the Palestinians. As Matas says, "The change in the mandate on homosexuality became the drive wheel for mandate change generally. Because the movement realized a change in mandate on homosexuality could not happen in isolation, and because a significant majority in the movement felt strongly that there should be a change in the mandate on homosexuality, a whole range of mandate changes became possible, and indeed, inevitable."[27]

The other major change was a decision to work on nongovernmental and quasi-governmental entities that were political (i.e., not criminal) such as guerrilla organizations. Amnesty would henceforth hold them to the same standards of human rights observance as states, although they would be guilty of "abuses" because only states with legal obligations could be guilty of "violations." The implications of this were profound—it opened the way for social and economic rights, allowing Amnesty to move its attention away from the state exclusively to take in corporations or the relations *between* individuals (e.g., men and women). This facilitated promotional work, the space where reformers could talk about and support, in Amnesty's name, the whole rights agenda, even while concrete work on this wider agenda remained prohibited by the mandate. Thus 1991 was a watershed, the moment when the assured grip of the keepers of the flame, the guardians of the Amnesty ethos, began to fail.

Indeed, the year 1991 probably ranked as Amnesty's worst since 1967. The IS had already suffered from the realization in early 1991 that it had made a terrible mistake—the most publicized error it has probably ever made—in wrongly alleging that Iraqi soldiers during the Gulf War left more than three-hundred babies to die after taking them out of their incubators. The origin of this story seems to have been an appearance before the U.S. Congress by the daughter of the Kuwaiti ambassador to Washington.[28] Amnesty published a report after doing further research and visiting the alleged mass graves of the babies. But by March 1991 it was forced to admit that the story "did not stand up."[29] Amnesty's report was used extensively before and after the Gulf War by President George Bush to justify the conflict. Inside Amnesty, things also reached a nadir, exemplified by an incident in which a member of the IEC was caught red-handed secretly taping a conversation with Malcolm Smart, the head of research, and Yvonne Terlingen, Asia researcher, in order, it appeared, to use it as evidence against them in a dispute over Amnesty's work in India. But most of all, the event that marked the declining IS fortunes was the resignation, before Yokohama, of Secretary General Ian Martin because of what he saw as the impossibility of staff members meeting movement demands due to inadequate resources and constant interference. For many researchers, he was the perfect chief; for many members, his resolute defense of the IS (i.e., of the ethos) was part of the problem.

Ian Martin's Resignation

Martin's resignation seemed to be a personality clash between two strong-minded Englishmen, Martin, on the one hand, and Peter Duffy, barrister and IEC chairman, on the other. During a sabbatical from the law, Duffy moved into an office in Easton Street to be more involved in the day-to-day running of Amnesty. This provided an immediate cause; Duffy's intervention in a personnel matter being dealt with by Martin's deputy proved the last straw. But it was also a symptom of a deeper shift in power toward the movement.[30]

In his resignation letter to Peter Duffy, Ian Martin described his time at Amnesty as "an immense privilege," but said he felt the loss of IEC support since 1989 had made the secretary general's job "untenable for anyone." He wrote:

I have come to conclude that—despite the sincere commitment and extraordinary hard work of many people in leadership positions—there is a crisis of voluntary leadership in Amnesty International at the international level, as well as in some cases at the national level. . . . The commitment, professionalism, integrity, skills and experience of so many staff at the International Secretariat constitute one of Amnesty International's greatest assets. The movement has however passed on to its secretariat the burden of growing expectations, while often being impatient both with the message that greater resources are required to meet those demands, and with the lost opportunities which are inevitable when these resources are not available.

Martin concluded:

I recognize that the International Executive Committee has taken and is taking the message on resources and arguing it with the movement, but I think the International Executive Committee has shared in the lack of realism regarding what can be done, how fast, with existing resources. I very much hope the International Executive Committee and the sections will find ways to convey better to the staff of the International Secretariat appreciation of their extraordinary work for human rights, and will retain their commitment and experience. Working alongside those staff has been my greatest privilege.[31]

Peter Duffy's short reply made no attempt to change Martin's mind (acknowledging his "hard work, commitment and exceptional contribution"), saying that "there is much in your letter of resignation which does not accord with IEC members' perceptions."[32] A review of the fraught secretary general–IEC relationship found things had been awkward from the moment Duffy became IEC chair in 1989, when Martin expressed concern about having two British citizens at the top. Tensions grew, and in January 1991 Duffy sent a letter to sections saying that IEC confidence in IS management was "qualified." Martin resigned soon after, feeling, as one observer put it, that he was seen as "the leader of the IS as an interest group rather than the secretary general [who was] the lynchpin of the movement as a whole."

Martin's praise in his letter for IS staff met with an equally heartfelt response. A petition collected 232 signatures (out of nearly 280 established IS posts in February 1991) urging the IEC to reconsider. Senior staff wrote separately, calling the decision to accept Martin's resignation "devastating." They saw the problem as an ill-defined division of responsibilities between the IEC and the IS (the movement's "cohesive leadership," they said—the sections were notably absent). The IEC was shaken and convened a special meeting on Sunday, February 24 with Martin and with ICM chair Dick Oosting, who had been a candidate for secretary general in 1986.

Oosting wrote a brief report of this meeting, noting that "there is no high moral ground here."[33] He drew attention to the problems caused by growth in the number of members and the amount of money, a Norwegian telethon having contributed large sums to Amnesty from 1984 onward. The 1989 Dublin ICM, unhappy with CLOD, had commissioned external consultants to report on decision making in Amnesty. Called Participlan, this study had greatly angered senior IS staff members, who felt "exposed and unprotected" now that the IEC had taken unto itself the role of holding the permanent staff to account. Oosting's phrase was "the scales had tipped." Despite a "brilliant record of committed high-quality work," "The IS as the most powerful body in this movement is at the same time powerless when it comes to having [a] part in the evolution of that movement through its democratic processes."

The Participlan Report, presented to the Yokohama ICM, was thought by IS staff to undervalue effectiveness in favor of "democratic decision making" (the original brief had been just "decision making"). One senior Research Department member was still visibly angry when recalling Participlan, even in 2003. The consultants issued two discussion documents, "Making Hard Choices" and "Concerns and Issues as Seen through the Eyes of Members and Staff," in advance of the full report. The first of these noted the high regard AI members had for staffers—quoting praise from sections for the "super professionals" of the IS. The report said, "From our observation and discussions, we believe that IS staff is a dedicated group of people who are committed to what they do. They seem to approach their work with a serious social commitment. They want to do the best job possible." In the margin of the copy of "Making Hard Choices" that I read, a senior IS staffer had written "no kidding!" in pencil. The IS "dominated" Amnesty, the documents went on, and was "conservative, defensive, unresponsive," and "insensitive," even resisting the implementation of some IEC and ICM decisions. The IS was the only centralized structure, it had ever-more tasks, and it did all the research in a research-dependent organization. One paragraph in "Making Hard Choices" says:

The emergence of such concentration of control and dominance gave the IS a great sense of its importance in the organization; it may even now feel that it is the key to the effectiveness, image and reputation of Amnesty. As it gained central control and dominance, the IS seems to perform the role of **"guardian" of AI**. It tends to protect AI's image and reputation in the world and resist any apparent threat to that image and reputation. It sees itself as neutral vis-à-vis the political interests of sections and leading members. This role forces it to be defensive and resistant to change. Even more important, the IS, in particular the research department, sees itself as the guardian of the mandate to ensure adherence and conformity. It has also taken on the role of interpreter of decisions, arbiter of some conflicts and enforcer of rules and procedures.

In the margin of my copy, the same IS staffer as before wrote, "What's strange with that?" The final Participlan Report was openly critical of IS engagement with the process, and IS staff members were openly critical of the report's methodology, which they feared merely confirmed conclusions that Amnesty's leadership had already reached. The Participlan Report was forthright:

> IS staff and managers didn't see decision-making as the problem. They saw the main issue as effectiveness; resources and a capable membership being necessary to realize effectiveness. . . . In fact, one of the more challenging aspects of this project has been (to us) a puzzling lack of enthusiasm on the part of many staff members at the IS, particularly senior managers and researchers, in wanting to engage with the issue of decision-making. Many said to us that prisoner work is the priority, things are going well, being concerned with decision making is in-ward looking. Many couldn't understand why the study was needed. They would point to AI's success in doing things—the accomplishments, the output; research gets done, new members join, campaigns run, credibility is high, AI is building good relationships with important governments.[34]

Participlan sought activism, a more diverse global membership, more intersection communication, deconcentration, and decentralization. The main problem achieving these was the gap between the IS and the movement, resulting in "a **vicious circle** locking the membership and the IS in a **dance of control and mistrust**."[35]

The IS management's response to Participlan noted that the "IS as guardian" role had been bequeathed to it by the movement—as institutional memory and as "experienced professionals with an overview of the movement who are in a good position to make judgements about the application of AI principles and the development of strategy."[36] Sometimes, IS managers wrote, the movement was apt to "shoot the messenger," although they agreed that a need existed for more responsiveness and accountability.

Participlan was the context for Martin's resignation. In the weeks following, his deputy also resigned. A Review Committee appointed to make some sense of this raised, as subtext, the possibility that there was not a single vision of Amnesty shared by the professional and voluntary parts of the movement. The report was sympathetic to the professionals. As it noted:

> Several IS staff expressed the fear that there seemed to be a conflict between the values of staff and volunteers which at times of tension can appear to be exploited. In this context the work of volunteers is regarded as being of greater moral worth.... At times there appears to be a strange perception that real activism is only undertaken by the volunteer segment of the movement. Given the composition of IS staff the RC [Review Committee] finds it difficult to understand how such a perception can rationally be sustained.[37]

Nothing could better illustrate contested authority. Who owned the candle? The now million-strong membership or the permanent paid staff, some of whom had been in the IS since the 1960s and who had built up the symbolic moral authority that these new members now wanted to use to change the world?

Ian Martin remained in his post for more than a year after his resignation so that a new secretary general could be chosen. Peter Duffy retired at Yokohama after six years on the IEC.[38] When a new secretary general arrived, he was in almost every way except gender the antithesis of the Western white men who had hitherto dominated Amnesty. Pierre Sané, a black African development specialist from Senegal, arrived at the IS in autumn 1992 with an agenda for change from the IEC and the major sections.[39]

Pierre Sané as Secretary General

Pierre Sané read copiously before starting work to familiarize himself with Amnesty's internal lore. With the end of the Cold War, things had changed dramatically and his job was to help AI with an inevitably painful adaptation. He believed its main impact came through concerted action by members worldwide. In a discussion paper for the 1993 Boston ICM, he wrote, "AI has the potential today to become a truly global actor, able to use its moral authority, professional expertise and mobilization potential to influence not only specific situations but also events at global level."[40] Echoing the CLOD findings (the need for dynamic action, universal presence, and efficient organization), Sané acknowledged that through the huge growth of the 1970s and 1980s Amnesty's identity had been maintained by means of the tightly defined mandate and complex decision-making process. Yet "The factors that made AI's strength conspired against the required flexibility to adapt to rapidly changing world challenges." Amnesty would have to learn to better handle crises and end its isolation from the "family" of like-minded movements (i.e., those seeking liberty, justice, peace, etc.) "to pursue a much needed collective strategy in the global human rights movement and build coalitions that will address at national and global levels the structural causes of violations and abuses of human rights."

"This could be done without AI losing its soul (i.e., independence and impartiality)," he added, seeing that Amnesty's isolation had fostered "self-awareness and a sense of belonging among its members." Amnesty had to widen and increase its membership, involve that membership more, and plan better, especially as work on nonstate actors and discrimination became central. It had to do preventive work as well as reactive work. A better division of labor was also necessary between the leadership (who should be visionary priority setters monitoring the results) and "AI professionals" who, once objectives and plans had been agreed, should be protected from "undue daily interference." The "vexing and recurring tension between volunteers and staff ought to be addressed resolutely," the report said.

Furthermore, as a "bearer of the human rights ideology," Amnesty should seek to influence the public in the "battle of ideas in which governments, social groups and various institutions participate to impose a vision of society, a vision of normative political and economic relations within countries and across the world." Was Amnesty in or above this battle? In conclusion, the report says that AI is to be at the center of "the global struggle for human dignity": "As we enter the 21st century we should seek to have AI's vision and values permeate societies all around us through information and action, through education and promotion. Tolerance and solidarity are the necessary pillars of any social and international order in which rights and freedoms set forth in the [UDHR] can be realized. Promoting these values locally and globally will ultimately depend on our continuous capacity to mobilize and grow everywhere in the world."

This vision required the IS to change. Sané and his supporters knew they needed to break the hold, which one called "the fortress of resistance," that the HORO had on the movement. Sané provoked researchers early by declaring at a staff meeting that Amnesty could "afford to make a few mistakes." This was a deliberate challenge to the research culture and therefore the ethos.

By the time of the 1993 Christmas Party, IS staff members led by the Americas Program, all wearing badges with Sané's face on them, were singing a satirical song to the tune of "Those Were the Days My Friend." Verses included:

Those were the days, my friend,
We thought they'd never end,
We strategized for ever and a day,
We lived the life we choose,
As research ruled the roost,
Oh we were pros, so keen to have our way.

But that was history,
We weren't empowered then,
In days before the vision lit our way,
Let's make the future great,
Let's all assimilate,
These are the days, oh yes, these are the days.

A thirty-five-page Research Review of 1993 had given this uneasiness form. It called for a campaigning, action-oriented style of report, with greater use of visual imagery, and for membership to be more involved in research. The Research Department needed to change, said the Review:

There appears to be a strong consensus within AI that AI must have a strong, professional, impartial and highly credible research operation that is organically linked to action. The starting point for the place of research in AI is that AI exists to take action to stop human rights violations. Research into those violations is necessary to provide the basis for effective action. . . . There is strong agreement in the indivisibility of AI research and action. We therefore propose that the movement replace the term "research" with "research/action" which we do in this report. We understand this terminology is also being taken into account in the reorganization discussions taking place at the IS. We recommend that, whatever the outcome of these discussions, the title of "Research Department" be changed to incorporate the action component.[41]

What happened was that the Research Department disappeared altogether. The head of research position was scrapped, and its occupant, Malcolm Smart, left Amnesty. His deputy, Michael McClintock, had gone a year earlier to help replicate for Human Rights Watch in New York quality control processes similar to those at work in HORO; Smart joined him later in the 1990s, as did other members of the IS research staff. Within the IS, the mandate and policy function was hived off into a separate unit called the Research and Mandate Program (RMP). The five regions became self-standing programs of their own. Within regional programs, several researchers were amalgamated into subregional (not country) teams with their executive assistants (now called campaigners). Secretaries disappeared, to be replaced in part by research and campaign assistants (RCAs).

But equalizing formal authority made it harder to deal with the informal authority that researchers had in abundance. Here is a view from one IS veteran:

The torture campaign [2000–2002] was dogged by a fundamental political disagreement that went on for four years, to my knowledge. . . . It may well have preceded that. But I know of four years of meetings that failed to resolve the central question of what Amnesty thought torture is. Between the progressives, who wanted to include kind of basically nonstate actors and therefore, you know, domestic violence, violence against women and all that sort of thing and the conservatives. . . . And I honestly believe that in the old structure, whoever was head of research would have made that decision. Rightly or wrongly. And that they would have proceeded. But that campaign was completely paralyzed because there was no one with the authority, either hierarchical or personal, to make that decision.[42]

Pierre Sané's vision put the accent on flexibility and action, not rigid structure. A succinct table outlined his aims under thirteen headings, including joint action with other NGOs, a less researcher-led division of labor, weakening WOOC, and more membership action. Of the other headings, three were:

MANDATE: **Current implementation**: Focused and carefully defined mandate interpreted primarily by IS professionals. **Change in emphasis**: Emphasis on all areas of the mandate, including new areas added at 1991 ICM; freer section/activist interpretation within full scope allowed by rules of action and campaigning; less reference to IS professionals for ruling on what is "in" or "out" of scope.

STAFFING STRATEGY: **Current implementation**: Long-term buildup of expertise, primacy of permanent IS staff; expectation that new demands will be met by permanent new resources. **Change in emphasis**: More generalized job descriptions or areas of expertise; more flexible reallocation on the basis of priorities within areas of expertise; more project/FTC [fixed-term contract] staff or use of outside resources.

DOCUMENT APPROVALS: **Current implementation**: Careful approval of external material; primacy of accuracy over timeliness. **Change in emphasis**: Approvals determined by use of document; timeliness or needs of end user may take precedence over improving quality.

Taken together, the proposals meant less casework, less new research, less emphasis on country expertise, and more campaigning, public relations, and crisis response.

Researchers fought back, and in a submission from thirty-eight staff members, mostly researchers (a core of whom are still in the IS), they asked the AI leadership to:

a) Confirm that AI's ultimate aim is to benefit victims of human rights violations, and that therefore all parts of AI must always operate in accordance with such aim;

b) Confirm that "reactive" and "preventive" action are complementary and should both be reinforced;

c) Confirm that AI is to continue to speak with one voice, and that therefore requires a centralized quality control and approval system;

d) Confirm that universal coverage (being able to intervene effectively anywhere in the world) remains a fundamental organizational aim;

e) Clarify the criteria for setting priorities on country work, including whether AI should give priority to countries and issues "forgotten" by international public opinion;

f) Clarify whether taking up individual cases should be the priority form of action or should be considered one among other equally important forms of action.[43]

Nearly thirty years after Christel Marsh emerged blinking into the sunlight, the ethos was so clear to these keepers of the flame that they wrote it out in a statement almost canonic in its purity. Their chief spokesperson distributed a photocopy about how the International Committee of the Red Cross (ICRC) "dealt with some of the issues we've been debating." The ICRC had, since 1965, been formally the "guardian of fundamental principles" that resembled Amnesty's (Humanity, Impartiality, Neutrality, Independence, Voluntary Service, Unity, and Universality). It was a role of which the IS could only dream.

At the core of the researchers' response to restructuring was a renewed emphasis on country expertise and universal coverage. This had always been implicit, but the role of research had never been questioned in such a way before. Now researchers had to rely on their own credentials (knowledge authority), not their Amnesty expertise (moral authority). The question became: Why does Amnesty need you? Sané was the first secretary general prepared to ask it. If Amnesty was not to be just about research, why did it need so many researchers? If it was to run more thematic campaigns, why did it need so many country experts? These were heretical questions. And researchers could no longer defend themselves just by defending the ethos. Greater membership, more money, and especially professional section staff—most of all in the United States— had opened the ethos to scrutiny. Amnesty did not belong to its researchers any more. Now they had to fall back on their own contribution in service terms—what they did for Amnesty.

Country expertise, researchers maintained, was not only vital, it needed to be "significantly reinforced" if "AI is to be able to predict some crises and take preventive action." It sought in this way to integrate the movement's new concern about crises with its traditional emphasis on specialist country knowledge (to enable early warnings). At the core should remain small teams with a country expert at the heart of each. A "geographical (possibly regional) criterion [should] be maintained in restructuring the research and campaign function," they said. In notes for this submission, some researchers were more forthright about the virtues of the established culture.[44] They disagreed that the wants of members ought to override informed analysis of the most appropriate action for a particular country; an "independent research base which is protected from marketing strategies" was a must.

"A more casual, publicity-seeking approach might result in the loss of significant sectors of the membership," wrote one researcher. Amnesty's combination of research and political analysis with membership action made it very different from solidarity organizations, on the one hand, and lobbying organization such as HRW and the Lawyers' Committee for Human Rights, on the other.[45] Country expertise was essential for undertaking effective action on countries with "highly complicated state, military or ideological structures." "Country experts know who politicians, military and police are related to and what their hidden vested interests are. They have long-standing relationships with human rights and other activists. There is a whole area of intuitive analysis which escapes the newcomer, however competent." As this researcher went on:

In the "country expertise" debate it has also been suggested that we do away with country knowledge altogether, replacing it with "research skills", drafting in researchers to write reports. This seems even less desirable. Who would these writers be? In the Philippines journalists are periodically flown in to monitor major political events. They are competent people but they do not know much about Filipino society—nor do they care because ultimately they are there to satisfy a readership located elsewhere, to write a good story. As a result their reports are often superficial; at worst they reinforce some of the more unacceptable and misleading stereotypes about Philippine politics and everyday life. Likewise journalists and social scientists visiting Indonesia have become entangled in ideological representations of Javanese culture and visions of a tolerant multi-religious society; all of which are attractive to Westerners in search of the exotic. In a society where the military has incited inter-religious violence in order to repress political dissent, such pitfalls are particularly dangerous.

Another researcher thought it essential for country experts to have knowledge of "the history of a country/region and of the legal, political, social, economic and cultural systems," in addition to speaking relevant languages; having hopefully lived in the country or region for an extended period; having multidisciplinary experience in areas such as political science, journalism, law, languages, and sociology; and having fact-finding and writing skills. AI researchers did not engage in "the 'mechanistic' collecting of information," wrote a third. "It is a very complex process which requires specialist knowledge and political judgment." It was "obvious," said another, that "country experts should retain main decision-making authority on country work in whatever structure we move in."

This expertise defense, as we have seen, particularly irked those supporting Sané. They countered by questioning how many researchers possessed all these skills. How many Asia researchers were even fluent in their priority country's main language, they asked? The tension was over whether regions (geography) or functions (campaigns) would structure AI's work.

But by 1994 HORO was gone. The IS was now to have three deputy secretaries general and that meant management. This created a different coalition of opposition, driven by the voluntaristic side of the ethos. An influential member of Campaigns, Brian Phillips, wrote in an Amnesty Weekly Summary of March 1994 that the language of Amnesty was coming to resemble that of pre-1989 Eastern Europe parodied in one of the plays of an Amnesty POC, Vaclav Havel. He wrote:

I joined this organization (like most of you) because it was about something eternal. I loved its devotion to the truth, to indepen-dence, to sometimes painfully critical thought and rigorously pre-pared action. Accuracy, honesty, integrity—these were the qualities that made this the best workplace I could imagine. It was the best because these were things not subject to fashion or the lure of the marketplace. . . . It is a question of *value*. Enduring *value* which it seems to me is now losing ground in a war of attrition with fash-ionable (and therefore temporary) management theory.

The proliferation of management speak was creating "tremendous un-happiness and fear that are demoralizing the building," he wrote. Staff were increasingly remote from a top management "lost in a cosmos of 'organigrams.'" He went on:

I don't need someone with a Stanford MBA Degree and a six figure salary to tell me that talking directly to your workforce in a place like this—taking a real, sustained interest in what they do and openly and sincerely communicating a sense of their value to them in simple conversation is a hell of a lot more motivating than sending them an indecipherable document insisting on manage-ment's commitment to "the development and implementation channels." . . . I am in no way defending the traditional financial incompetence or inefficiency of many voluntary organizations, but management of a human rights organization must surely by defini-tion be different from that in a margarine factory.[46]

Phillips's concern was that Amnesty's "eternal values" might be extin-guished by, "the use of a language which falls apart in your hands as soon as you try and pull apart its meaning." "During the past year or two, I feel I have been watching the fires go out in people here at the IS. I am talking about the fires of commitment, of passion, of trust on which the running of this building so entirely depends."

This impassioned plea drew a direct response from the secretary general, who denied that modern management techniques were contrary to effectiveness in AI's work but agreed that a gap had opened up between management and an anxious staff that had to be closed. This managerialism was part of the more general, globalization-inspired (I argue) infiltration of the mechanisms and ideas of capital into all areas of not-for-profit and private life, a development with which we are all too familiar now. It entailed a new conception of service, not as vocational obligation but as meeting the needs of the movement as consumers. This directly challenged the ethos. Researchers' control over priorities had once entailed various types of specialization comprising what Eliot Freidson calls working knowledge and formal knowledge, the former derived from on-the-job learning and often uncodified, the latter based on more theoretical and abstract knowledge.[47] Researchers' claims were founded on their Amnesty experience and their regional expertise. Things were bound to be tough when this "occupational control" as Freidson calls it, was challenged by both managers and consumers.

Under Pierre Sané, relations deteriorated so badly that IS staff members engaged in industrial action in April 1996. The walkout was caused by the distribution of letters to fourteen staffers informing them that their posts (and five vacant ones) were to be discontinued. With a worsening financial situation—the IS faced a shortfall in funding, the debt financed through a credit facility secured on Easton Street—the IEC had demanded that salaries be cut to the tune of around £750,000 (out of a budget that included about £18 million for salaries and related costs). This also reflected the IEC's determination that IS jobs should be related to movement priorities. More money for crisis response meant a transfer from other parts of the IS salary bill.

After the letters were distributed, without union consultation, about 150 staffers walked out (returning to work the following day after the letters were withdrawn). Weeks of intense negotiations followed, the union demanding a commitment to no compulsory redundancies. For some of this period, unionized staff members also worked to rule and in early August balloted for strike action. At a staff meeting in early May, the level of bitterness toward the management was so intense that some urged Sané to quit as secretary general. Through voluntary redundancy and redeployment, no IS employees involuntarily lost their jobs in the end. A complex and unwieldy procedure for job redefinition was then agreed on by a shaken management as the price for ending the threat of a longer strike.

Then, in 1998, a further shock came when management froze wages for the lowest grades and increased them for the highest. Relative equality in pay had always been a feature of Amnesty. In the 1970s, some senior staff even forwent pay rises. Yet, by 1988, a Coopers & Lybrand report for Amnesty claimed that IS salaries were more than 20 percent too high for grade As and more than 50 percent too low for grade Es (deputy secretaries general). The freezing of A- and B-grade pay was seen as an assault on the egalitarian nature of the ethos.

Pierre Sané's time in charge did not recover from these blows in the view of many of those interviewed. According to one senior IEC member at the time, by 2000, after an IS operational planning "fiasco" that had even forced an extra IEC meeting, the IEC compelled Sané to work with a deputy secretary general to improve IS management and so Kate Gilmore, formerly executive-director of AI Australia, was chosen to try to improve morale inside the IS. Here is how one veteran researcher described her feelings after 1994: "Restructuring didn't work, and the whole process of getting to it was so demoralizing. I suppose from then on, I've never really regained that sense of well-being that I'd had up to then. And a real sense of honor and pride and privilege. And, you know, salary didn't count. All those things didn't count because I felt so good about working here. And that really went more or less downhill from then."

And still the movement was not placated. In a letter to the IEC chair, Mahmoud Ben Romdhane, in April 2000, a group of sections dubbed by staff the Magnificent Seven launched a broadside against the IS, telling the IEC in no uncertain terms that it was responsible.[48] The group wrote, "The first area to be spot-lighted is the research capacity and output of the IS and related issues of quality control. We want to address what we consider to be substandard work in the area of research as highlighted by the recent campaign on Saudi Arabia and the forthcoming campaign on torture." This was followed by details of section allegations about late or poor research, inadequate preparedness and response to crises, and a failure by the IS to address section concerns in areas such as fundraising. The group continued, "Complaints or concerns of individual sections are often indicative of a broader experience of sections; some of us perceive our attempts to address these issues in a constructive and timely manner as being brushed off as the concerns and complaints of merely one or two sections not shared by the rest of the movement. The reason we are signing this letter jointly to the IEC is to counter that impression, and we believe that many more sections share our concerns as well."

Things had been so bad between the IS and AIUSA, for example, that in 1996 a special protocol had to be negotiated outlining the terms in which the two would treat one another so as to reduce the level of animosity. This tension centered on access to media space and whether, in the CNN-dominated 1990s, primary responsibility for dealing with U.S.-based global media lay with the IS or AIUSA. AIUSA, of course, now had a pressing reason for its concern—Human Rights Watch.

Competition

By the 1990s a decline in active members went hand in hand with membership growth as a whole. The figures for 1983, for example, listed total membership at 571,439 with active membership at 217,259. The figures for 1993, just ten years later, estimated total membership at 900,000 and active membership at 150,000, in other words a drop from just under 40 percent of members active in 1983 to just 16 percent in 1993.[49] This reflected much broader social changes, of course, greater personal and class mobility being effects of the very "globalizing modernity" that had framed Amnesty's evolution. By the 1990s, Benenson's hope for a new kind of community spirit was all but gone even as the organization he founded thrived. Amnesty could not resist globalization, as hard as it tried. A newly consolidated challenger to its global authority on human rights would see to that.

The Gulf War was the making of the satellite news channel CNN, and in the crises that followed, especially Bosnia and Rwanda, the speed and scale of abuses and the wall-to-wall media coverage found Amnesty ill-prepared compared with a new rival, a consolidation of the Watch

Committees called Human Rights Watch. One staffer, relatively new in 1991, recalled being handed a camera and cash and told: Just go to Bosnia and find out what you can (even though CNN and HRW already had a heavy presence on the ground). If Bosnia was difficult, Rwanda was something of a disaster; an evaluation of AI's response referred to "a great deal of reflection, soul-searching, anguish, even anger." It said, "Whereas some inside AI felt that parts of the response were acceptable, many more felt it was far from adequate. Some felt it to be AI's largest failure. Many felt that some of AI's actions probably had some effect but not on stopping of the killings. What we can say is that in our interviews in the IS we found a great sense of failure as we have never experienced on any occasion before."[50] Under the heading "Culture in the IS," the report was highly critical of the research ethos.

Professional staff by definition have a great deal of expertise, ownership in and concern about the areas they work on. While this helps lead the development and implementation of sound strategy, during the Rwanda crisis it at times led to a reluctance to incorporate ideas or suggestions from others; a reluctance to bring appropriate information or issues for decision to management for guidance or decision, or if brought, a reluctance to follow that guidance. Management direction or suggestions from other staff were sometimes interpreted as interference in judgement of staff with more professional knowledge or lack of respect of expertise.

The report's analysis of the competition AI faced in the post–Cold War world is worth quoting at length. It shows just what a watershed Rwanda was.

AI's conventional role has been to document specific violations and to act on that information as a means of exerting pressure on those responsible for abuses. AI has often been reluctant to act unless it has been able to do its own research. In earlier years, AI traveled where few others went, and gathered information no one else did. It often had facts unavailable elsewhere and was able to act on them according to its own timetable.

Today others—human rights groups (often indigenous ones), journalists, and others—are providing good human rights information. And they are often doing it faster and in more depth than AI has been able to, or may be able to even with an increased crisis orientation by AI. What should AI's role be when news organizations are out in the field covering a situation as a human rights story? Or when another human rights group produces before AI does a good, solid report on a situation? Does human rights information by professional journalists or others need independent verification by AI? Or is it appropriate as the basis for action even if AI cannot confirm some details? How can AI better balance the need to be timely with the need for accuracy?

In the Rwanda situation, the killings of course were no secret. They were all over television around the world. AI appeared to have little new information to contribute to that already in the public domain. Although materials were produced . . . for external distribution, these added little to existing coverage and received relatively little public attention.

Some have argued that there was no need for AI to document the massacres in order to show that they were happening. Instead, what was needed—what AI's special role should have been—was effective action by its membership to bring pressure to stop the killing.

Without mentioning Human Rights Watch or CNN by name, the implication is clear. Amnesty cannot compete on the old terms. It cannot do what membershipless HRW can, and it does not provide the kind of material that the global media wants.[51] The report refers to section unhappiness with low-profile, late, and uninteresting AI statements. The reasons?

The Review Team was told that the content and language of many media statements were often the result of "committee consensus" and lengthy interdepartmental discussions. Various actors had understandably differing notions about what AI should be saying. However, some staff complained that days or even weeks were lost as language would be hashed out among them, particularly when a statement dealt with complicated policy matters where opinions differed about what AI could or could not say on issues such as armed intervention or "genocide".[52]

Even in the report, genocide is still in quotation marks. The lore clogged up the Amnesty machinery, and HRW outflanked it. The report commends AI for contesting the notion that the Rwandan killings were "tribal," showing how they were a "government campaign of political murder." This insight is of historical importance, especially in undermining claims that so-called new wars are a throwback to the barbarian past of non-Western areas of the world. But it is a sophisticated, intellectual, subtle, and challenging point, a contribution to history. It is not the kind of observation that will attract members or concerned citizens engrossed with horror and disbelief at the scale of the killings, killings they can watch on TV. It is a perfect example of Amnesty's role as witness.

Compare this with the dream IEC chair Ross Daniels shared with the 1993 ICM in Boston (before Rwanda): "A vision of an Amnesty reporter—on Monday—sitting in a field near a refugee camp—typing vital information on a laptop computer—sending that information by disk and satellite to a project team—by Tuesday that project team has finished its strategy by email and electronic bulletin board—by Wednesday the information has been transformed into dynamic action that's being used throughout the world. Skilled research and dynamic action riding on the back of clever technology."

Amnesty's relationship with Human Rights Watch is ambiguous. For AIUSA, Amnesty's largest and most influential section, HRW is a constant competitor for money and publicity. For many at the IS, this competition is distasteful. Some reformers see a "good-natured battle" in the media with HRW; others see a serious competition for dollars. For example, the two groups interpreted differently Human Rights Watch's approach to AI after September 11 about combining its access to Congress with AI's public opinion pressure. Modernizers were clear: HRW wanted to strengthen its own hand at the expense of AIUSA. Yet, although at the organizational level there is competition for media attention and money, at the researcher level there are long-term relationships between quite a few AI and HRW staff (this cooperation on country strategies, research missions, and public statements is termed by some "co-opetition"). Some have worked for both organizations, sharing information and strategy that—through a strictly commercial lens—might be viewed as a kind of "intellectual property." This is one further facet of the tensions raised by the commodification of moral concern under globalization.

Human Rights Watch grew out of Helsinki Watch, founded in 1979 to monitor compliance with the 1975 Helsinki Accords. Based in New York, it has only more recently sought to build a membership base hitherto concentrating on researching and writing reports on a wide range of human rights concerns. Although Amnesty has been apt to ignore Human Rights Watch, HRW is only too aware of Amnesty.[53] Its website has a section headed "How is Human Rights Watch different from Amnesty International?" Although complimentary about a "healthy division of labor" between the two, HRW points out that AI's concerns are much narrower than its own, which have long included gay rights, women's rights, children's rights, and so on. The site pointedly states, "Amnesty International's headquarters is in London. Human Rights Watch's headquarters is in New York." This is somewhat disingenuous, of course. The competition for HRW is AIUSA, whose headquarters are a few blocks away in Manhattan. But the point, for any U.S. donors, has been made: we are the American human rights NGO. HRW usually describes itself as the largest U.S.-based human rights organization (although it has recently begun describing itself more frequently as "international").

In a widely circulated paper for a Carnegie Council seminar in 2002, HRW's executive director Ken Roth discussed the merits and drawbacks of having a large membership in reference to Amnesty's problems both in managing its constituency and making an impact politically with those members. (In a sense he was speaking the researchers' language.) AIUSA's executive director, Bill Schulz, then sent Roth an angry letter about what he perceived as public criticism of AI by HRW. Schulz wrote: "I am sure that you are asked as often as I am to distinguish the two organizations from one another and, whenever I am asked that question, I always respond with the highest of praise for HRW."[54] Schulz pointed out several examples in which AIUSA's 300,000 members had had "a pronounced effect" on human rights policy in areas such as sexual abuse of women in U.S. prisons and amending post–September 11 legislation. This went hand in hand with press work too. As Schulz pointed out, "Here are the press 'hits' Amnesty and HRW received in 2001, as of December 12 of that year: *The New York Times*: AI 53; HRW 47; *The Washington Post*: AI 125; HRW 115. Top fifty newspapers in the US: AI 10,775; HRW 4826. I'd say we were both doing pretty well in the use of the press to promote human rights issues." Schulz stressed that "shaming public officials"—HRW's preferred route—was only possible because people were watching. In a reply to this letter, Roth rejected most of Schulz's points and was at pains to make clear that Amnesty had options that no other human rights organization had precisely because of its success and size—it is, said Roth, quoting his original paper, "in a class by itself" as far as its resources are concerned. And it is competition for those resources that lies at the heart of the HRW-AIUSA relationship. AIUSA has one of the wealthiest donor bases in the United States, with at least 10,000 donors with assets of greater than $1 million. These are the very people Human Rights Watch also targets, especially in New York.

At a bilateral two-day IS-AIUSA meeting in London in May 2003, the links HRW is fostering with Amnesty via discussions with the secretary general that circumvent AIUSA were discussed. In terms of the U.S. intervention in Iraq, HRW sought an alliance with Amnesty in order, as one IS director put it, "to make the phones ring in the White House." For AIUSA delegates, HRW was "extraordinarily aggressive" in the media to attract New York donors but quick to ally itself with Amnesty to get over the credibility problem—the authority problem, perhaps—of having no constituency and of being seen as oversensitive to its main donors.[55]

A look at HRW's founding principles—"protecting the human rights of peoples around the world"—shows the flexibility it enjoys in interpreting areas of interest without the agonizing that attends the lore. It has no multinational membership to placate. It has, in a sense, grown in the widening gap that Amnesty has left in the field of international human rights by being slow to move into areas such as discrimination and crisis response. Even the reluctance of Amnesty to deal with major U.S. charitable foundations in the 1970s and 1980s contributed to their importance in developing HRW's funding base.[56]

Human Rights Watch found it much easier than Amnesty to respond to the media-driven agenda of the 1990s. It did not seek universal coverage, did not have the mandate, and had no qualms about raising money in the private sector. It was, in effect, the Research Department the modern Amnesty wishes it had—separate from the running of the organization and the membership, flexible and yet skilled in terms of country expertise and research. But HRW feels Amnesty's authority and is forced to be concerned about areas where Amnesty may pronounce before it does, such as social and economic rights, something with which both have struggled given the greater sympathy and relevance of civil and political rights to those in the West who can afford to fund and join human rights groups.

Under this kind of pressure, AIUSA has had little choice but to compete. This commercial approach is anathema to the keepers of the flame, of course. During the bilateral IS-AIUSA meeting, the delegates from New York showed a video of a major new advertising campaign titled Imagine. To the accompaniment of John Lennon's song "Imagine," the rights to which were given to AIUSA for two years by Yoko Ono, children from all over the world were featured singing the song.[57] At a meeting of Amnesty's senior staff and members in London where the video was played, one IS senior manager said, "there wasn't a dry eye at my table." When it was played at the IS, one staffer immediately asked if any Middle Eastern children were featured. Some were filmed, came the reply, but the answer for the final version was no.

Conclusion

What do AIUSA's 150 staff and similar number of volunteers bring to Amnesty? "The really smart political approach. It's people that know politics, aren't afraid of politics, and aren't afraid of using it. And that know that they can play clean. Just because it's political doesn't mean that you're going to lose your perspective or your moral compass. But it is a political equation that you're trying to shift. And you have to be political to get at that political equation," said a hugely experienced AIUSA manager. And what of the IS and its research? "As a senior member of AIUSA, I don't have a lot of respect for Amnesty's research. I don't think it's cutting edge. I don't think it's new. I don't think it helps us move agendas forward. Sometimes you can use it to a very good end and then it's really good. You can use it to get something to happen."

Perfectly encapsulated in these comments is the drive for more political authority (number of members and intensity of campaigns) and the sense that research is a service function not an end—bearing witness—in itself. Here is the view of a current senior campaigner at the IS: "I come from a place where people were committed to campaigning. Not to research for its own sake. We couldn't have imagined doing that. It seemed to me quite natural and self-evident that the way round things should be, and I expected them to be, was that we would determine what were our objectives, what we were going to campaign to change, and then we'd select the information to help buttress the case. And prove the case. And illustrate the case. And perhaps suggest alternatives."

Political authority requires a more intensive look at identity (whereas moral authority entails the opposite). This concerns both how representative Amnesty appears to be of the people for whom it aspires to speak, the focus of chapter 6, and also a recognition that, if shared practice is no longer the glue it once was, shared values need to be found to fall back on. Globalization in its current intense phase puts a considerable strain on the broad coalition within Amnesty. The U.S. vision of a campaigning Amnesty, of smart politics and commercial savvy, is much more sympathetic to harnessing globalization and the U.S. power that attends it than more radical Leftists. For many committed socialists within the IS, the absence of explicit attention to social and economic rights, and the focus on practical help for the victims of state repression, made working life easier because it did not trespass on their core beliefs about the role of class and capital in causing inequality and suffering. This made Amnesty, said one, a "classic united-front organization": "We disagree over almost everything, but we can unite in action around these various basic principles. Whatever field you're in. That's the advantage. I can see the advantage of the language of rights." Now, however, as another IS staffer firmly on the Left put it, "Human rights have been adopted by the powers of the world. They've usurped it. And so Amnesty is constantly battling against its work being used to justify imperialist wars. And it hasn't really got any defense against that. Because it isn't really neutral, or, it's a very Western view of the world, and Western view of human rights. And it's very, very linked to the United Nations. And the United Nations, for me personally, is an utterly corrupt body." Moving into the more political world—one of us (the powerless) against them (the powerful)—

narrows this space. Over the current war with Iraq, for example, some on the Left had begun to be uncomfortable with Amnesty's "no position-position" on war, U.S. hegemony for them being the biggest global threat to human rights even as the U.S. state talked the language of human rights itself.

The campaigners thus diverge from the modernizers. The core issue between them is money or, more accurately, capitalism. It is hardly a surprise that money should be the subject of such tension. Whether you were on the social-action or bearing-witness side, money was from the start a profanity, the inherent purity of purpose and innocence of will that supplied Amnesty's foundational energy sullied by the knowledge that in the end what made it all possible was money. As Durkheim says, to preserve sacredness, the break with the profane world has to be kept as clean as possible because, once the sacred is polluted, the ideal is lost.

Many interviewees referred to the IS culture as one of disdain for knowing how money is raised and spent, coupled with a deep aversion to accounting for that spending (a tradition that Benenson exemplified even while he was putting his hand in his own pocket). We have seen how powerfully Thomas Hammarberg warned Amnesty against the corrupting influence of capital. As one senior finance officer put it, "there's an anti-money ethos around the place [that] could be to do with the fact that there are too many academics in the governance systems of the movement": "They see it as being dirty. There's also an element that will not take money from anybody other than themselves. It's clean if it comes from within the organization, from the membership, but everything else is dirty because they don't trust business, they don't trust government. They don't trust anybody, basically."

This is where reformers split. Many of the campaigners are on the Left, and are as sympathetic to this aspect of traditional culture as are the keepers of the flame.[58] Both mistrust corporatism, whether in terms of money, branding, or management techniques. Capitalism is seen as a cause, not a remedy, of profound suffering. For AIUSA, of course, raising and spending money is an essential aspect of success for any NGO in the context of U.S. politics. It makes no sense in this environment to argue on principle against the utility of money. This is what it means to be politically smart—get the money for your side and use it. This pragmatism, I argue in chapter 8, is the essence of the U.S. approach to questions of practical morality. It presents a special kind of threat to the Amnesty ethos. As we will see, however, much still unites the reformers in their determination to change secretariat culture.

6

BEING AND DOING

witnessing built a large sum of symbolic capital for Amnesty. Yet, even as it was being amassed, the claim to anonymous detachment on which it depended was eroding. Under globalizing modernity, all established authorities—those that see no need to justify their presumption of authority—are vulnerable. Doubts about the existence of an enduring singular truth translate into a concern with who the speaker is on the basis that behind all claims to impartiality lie interests and identities. Who you are affects your authority as much as what you say in such a world. Character, as much as conduct, becomes an issue. The questions to ask of claimants to authority are therefore: Who are you? What or who is it that you represent?

Throughout Pierre Sané's discussion paper for the 1993 Boston ICM (see chap. 5), there is an ambiguity about whether human rights are part of a higher-order impartiality or of the struggle for justice. It seems, in the end, to be the latter. The phrase *human rights ideology* is even used, and ideologies are partial claims masquerading as impartial. If we view the idea of humanity as an ideology and accept that it puts the needs and interests of certain groups—the poor, the marginalized, and the physically victimized—first, then we enter the world of authority politics. Authority politics is the process of contestation, representation, struggle, and resistance within which the distribution of social resources, including things such as access to the law and access to jobs and services, takes place. Moral authority is based on difference; political authority is based on similarity and belonging. You must be, not just do.

Amnesty is, as it must be, embedded in structures of gender, race, and class (and more). This configuration makes some audiences receptive and some not. Just doing something avoided the need to ask such questions at the beginning. Despite their commitment to humanity, Benenson and Baker were, not surprisingly, unreflective about their social identity. They were doers, men of faith. And because the identity of the witnessers did not matter, Amnesty's monoculture escaped scrutiny from one generation to the next. Thus, a white and masculine working culture was consolidated (meaning, given the majority of women in the IS, that we must divorce masculinity from men).

Moral and political authority make uneasy companions. If Amnesty is in politics, its struggle will be about sociological realities, about finding a way, by instrumentalizing research, to promote social justice. If it is in politics, it must belong. We can see in the following sections on gender and multiculturalism how far it still has to go and why moral authority—and its protection through detachment—continually tries to pull it in the other direction.

Gender

Late in my fieldwork I conducted two interviews with women—neither from the research side of the organization—who had strong opinions about gender. The first said:

> I would describe the environmental movement as a very female movement. It you had to give it a gender you would say it was feminine. Human rights is very male. [The environmental movement] is more optimistic. It is intrinsically more flexible. It's very proactive. It's just much more optimistic, emotional. . . that's the other thing. It's very emotional. People cried when the good things happened. And here, people don't even cry when the bad things happen. And it's just very male. It feels very male.

"They're just brutalized by it I suppose," she went on, seeing it as largely a self-defense mechanism: "Without wanting to generalize horribly about men but, you know, I tend to think one of men's biggest problems is that they're not allowed to show emotion about anything. . . . And I think Amnesty's the same. We just have to find ways of allowing ourselves to feel what's awful and to celebrate what's good in order that we can retain the passion. . . . If you're not emotional about it, what are you doing here?"

In the second interview, with another senior manager, I suggested there were many powerful women in the IS. "Now," she corrected me. She continued, "We have some of the most anti-feminist women that I have ever had the honor to work with. I've never seen anything like it. And that tells me that it's a reminder of the power of organizational culture and the non-biological nature of these characteristics. "Short of violence," she said, the IS culture was a masculine one of "heroicism and self denial and nothing touches me and I'll break at nothing." "I shall be right. I shall produce. I am correct in the face of all onslaught. And I will never show vulnerability either intellectually or emotionally." One of the shocks for these women was the difficulty they found generating enthusiasm among the female staff in the regional programs for the SVAW campaign.[1]

That women predominate among the IS staff is a fact. As one female researcher in the Asia Program remarked, "Sometimes I sit around the table and think, gosh, all women today. Or just one man has turned up. I mean it's probably far worse for the one man involved. It's very interesting that you say it because I've never even thought about, you know, gosh, the poor guy, on his own. It must be quite intimidating, I think, some of the women there, including myself, we're a fairly intimidating bunch anyway."[2]

In a document from 1973, the forty-two staff members in the Research Department and secretary general's office were split thirty female and twelve male –67 to 33 percent.[3] The ratio was remarkably similar in early 2002, according to an HRP report, with 62 percent female to 38 percent male (out of a total of 422 staff members). Table 6.1 shows more detailed figures (covering most of 2002, with the total staff now 430) for gender in the regional programs.[4] The total employed by these five programs is 195. If we take from these figures just those labeled either researcher or program and deputy program directors (usually ex-researchers), we obtain the figures in table 6.2. The ratio is 53:47, women to men, with the Middle East included and 58:42 when it is taken out. Most of Amnesty's research is done by these researchers and by the regional program campaigners who work with them. Those listed in the HRP data from 2002 as regional campaigners (and campaign coordinators) and RCAs are as

TABLE 6.1
Gender in regional programs, 2002[a]

	Total staff	Female	Male
Africa	47	24 (51%)	23 (49%)
Americas	38	25 (66%)	13 (34%)
Asia	44	33 (75%)	11 (25%)
Europe	37	25 (68%)	12 (32%)
Middle East	29	12 (41%)	17 (59%)

[a] *This analysis is based on HRP data for the year 2002.*

TABLE 6.2
Gender and Researchers/Research Managers, 2002

	Total researchers and PDs[a]	Female	Male
Africa[b]	18	9 (50%)	9 (50%)
Americas	13	8 (62%)	5 (38%)
Asia[c]	18	11 (61%)	7 (39%)
Europe[d]	15	9 (60%)	6 (40%)
Middle East	9	2 (22%)	7 (78%)

[a] *PDs, program directors, and deputy program directors.*
[b] *Figures include a field and thematic researcher, a field researcher, and a researcher (east Africa).*
[c] *Figures include a field presence research coordinator.*
[d] *Figures include a Russia campaign researcher.*

listed in table 6.3. The percentage of staff members who are female rises as we move away from researchers and program directors. If we add them all together (program management, researchers, campaigners, and RCAs), we get 63 : 37, women to men. This mirrors the pattern across the IS as a whole. Although just over 60 percent of the IS staff is female, a disproportionate number, as of December 2002, were in the lower of the five grades (A–E), as table 6.4 shows.

In many nonprofit organizations, women are the majority of staff. The reasons for this include work-hour flexibility (allowing for family life) and the nature of the work (caring and direct contact with people).[5] On the other hand, discrimination in favor of men for higher-paid and higher-status jobs may drive educated women into jobs for which they are overqualified. Stress at Amnesty is high—understood in terms of the chaotic nature of the work—and, although one or two interviewees said they found Amnesty a good working environment in which to have a child,

TABLE 6.3
Gender and Campaigners/Research and Campaign
Assistants

	Campaigners + RCAs	Female	Male
Africa	18	10 (56%)	8 (44%)
Americas	21	15 (71%)	6 (29%)
Asia	19	18 (95%)	1 (5%)
Europe	17	11 (65%)	6 (35%)
Middle East	13	8 (62%)	5 (38%)

[a] *This table does not include staff working on membership. It does include campaign coordinators.*

TABLE 6.4
Gender and Grading, 2002[a]

Grade	Female	Male	Total
A	15.1%	5%	20.1%
B	24.2%	12.1%	36.3%
C	18.5%	15.9%	34.4%
D	1.9%	2.4%	4.3%
E	2.1%	1.4%	3.5%

[a] *The percentages have been rounded slightly and do not include the senior directors or the secretary general and her deputy (hence, the total is not 100%).*

others said that in order to have more than one they would have to leave.

One female researcher from the 1980s recalled informing her male program director she was pregnant and being told, "That's why I don't hire women researchers." She had been equally shocked when she discovered that Amnesty was sending a man to a major UN women's conference in Nairobi. She was told by a very senior manager, "We wouldn't send a doctor to a doctor's conference, we wouldn't send a lawyer to a lawyer's conference, why should we send a woman to a women's conference?" This position made sense for Amnesty, of course, because impartiality implied the same degree of detachment was possible from your gender as your profession. But could Amnesty be taken seriously (then, let alone now) sending a man to a women's conference? Could he speak with authority? Are there some kinds of knowledge you can only have if you share the subjective identity? Or can you gain the same insights through observation and abstraction?

There is nothing unusual in the presumption that you can. The whole edifice of positivist social science—the value-neutral observation of an object—is based on this premise. And claims to impartial morality inevitably lead us there too. There are no relevant qualities (gender, race, sexuality) for such a morality, only human beings in their essence, identically equal. Universal human rights must accept, logically, the same principle. But in a political struggle, value neutrality is not an option. If research does not further the cause, if it is too abstract or too contentious, it will be discarded or ignored. The struggle is not about what but about how. It would be as if feminist activists, finding there were conceptual ambiguities in women's rights, packed up their things and went home. Such a picture is absurd.

A reformist IS senior manager told a staff meeting on the SVAW campaign, for example, that international human rights law and "academic musing" had not done much for women, despite their other achievements, and that Amnesty needed to find a "black line of consequence" between theoretical work and real change in women's lives. Human rights, she said, were a "knowledge based project" (i.e., not grounded in some other-worldly authority but in the all-too-human battle of ideas), a claim she knew was "somewhat heretical in Amnesty's tradition." The UDHR was not a "sacred text," the human rights project "unfinished and incomplete" in terms of its "higher goal" of improvements in the "human condition." Amnesty was on "a journey to know more about the nature, extent and implications of violence against women," and would have to "have a higher level conversation than has been our tradition." This is just the kind of first-principles conversation practice avoided.

The SVAW campaign is thematic, with cases chosen for illustrative purposes, and it takes Amnesty onto more political terrain and into contact with existing and sophisticated women's groups that, far from being awed, have often been critical of Amnesty's failure to engage with the women's movement. It is therefore a challenge to the ethos and its working culture. Consider the ambivalence of one experienced female researcher:

I never thought that you need to prioritize women's rights over men's rights. I mean, I think you treat them equally, and I think that there are ways into both. So I actually have a problem. I mean, we've had one female prisoner of conscience—I think two now— but one, really, in the last ten years, whose case has been used again and again and again. And she's not representative of prisoners of conscience in . . . [country name deleted]. That is also true of most of the victims of the classic Amnesty human rights violations. I think where . . . they're right is, you know, things like domestic violence. . . . They're particularly high in the conflict regions, or post conflict. And there was a . . . very clear connection between state violations and then violence in the private domain. And I think that probably could be really explored.[6]

Amnesty's work on women's rights has been increasing slowly since the mid-1980s. AIUSA was one of the first sections to press the IEC and IS on the lack of systematic attention to women in Amnesty's human rights work, pointing out that in 1987, of the thirty-three prisoner cases carried in Amnesty's International Newsletter, only three were women and, of the eleven cases initially highlighted in 1988 as part of the Human Rights Now! Tour, only one was a woman.[7] For the UN's Fourth World Conference on Women, held in Beijing in 1995, Amnesty was better prepared, launching its own global theme campaign, Women and Human Rights, although it remained focused on its traditional issues—torture, state violence, abuses during armed conflict, and disappearances—as they affected women. It did not take on issues such as domestic violence.

High-visibility reports on abuses against women were produced on many countries after 1995, but by 2001, at the Dakar ICM, an experienced researcher was still able to say there were too few, as well as too few cases of women in reports on torture and the death penalty. She challenged the view of "research teams who will tell you that they have 'real' problems such as POCs or torture and that women have no specific problems in their region." Systematic institutional support to replace the existing sporadic campaigns and efforts by individuals was needed, she said (and a Gender Unit now exists).[8]

After consultations, IS senior managers recommended to the IEC that Violence Against Women (VAW or SVAW) should be a global theme campaign for 2003. It had "the best combination of wide positive support, low actual opposition and the lowest perception of being difficult for the IS teams to deliver."[9] The advice from managers recognized that "AI has a significant role to play in the work against VAW in that we work on the subject within a framework of international law/human rights. This is often a different approach to work on VAW to other 'frontline' organizations (e.g. refuges for women leaving violent partners)." By 2002, however, as the campaign unfolded, one of its two central themes had become domestic, or family, violence; the other was women in armed conflict. For the first time, the IS had women in its two top positions, one of whom, Deputy Secretary General Kate Gilmore, had been part of an all-female delegation to an ICM when she was director of the Australian section. For the ICM in 1999, AI Australia did a gender audit, pointing out that men made up 60 percent of delegates, 70 percent of delegation leaders, and 80 percent of IEC candidates.[10] "There is no private space that is Amnesty International that is demarcated," a senior manager told an IS staff meeting on the SVAW campaign; another added, "we must be ready to change ourselves," accepting that there was even "a possibility of perpetrators among the ranks" when it came to domestic violence. Without exposing itself to the gender lens, Amnesty could have no hope of political authority with the women's movement.

For example, Roxanna Carillo, human rights adviser for the UN Development Fund for Women (UNIFEM), told an IS staff forum in May 2002 that it had to overcome the "general perception from the women's movement about AI . . . always going solo . . . which could hamper AI's credibility as a voice for women's human rights." Charlotte Bunch, director of the Center for Women's Global Leadership at Rutgers University, told the same meeting that seeing violence against women as a human rights issue meant seeing how it had been "sidelined ever since the conceptualization of human rights."[11]

Recall the torture evaluation: the campaign should drive the research. In theory, the Campaigns Program with policy input would conceptualize the SVAW campaign and the researchers would then produce cases to illustrate its themes. That this might not be straightforward was already recognized by the Campaigns Program, whose manager pointed out that in existing research work there was an "uneven distribution" among countries, regions, and categories and "major gaps between research and action such as domestic violence and rape outside armed conflict." He added, "The real barrier[s] for researchers are workload, prioritization, new mandate, lack of expertise, training required for dealing with VAW and support needed to people working on VAW. . . . There is a lack of established methodology, unfamiliarity with the concepts and language. Also, work on non-state actors is relatively new."[12] The Campaigns Program circulated its strategy in December 2002. The main themes were "VAW in the family" and "VAW in conflict and post-conflict situations." It said, "We should expect **AI to be held to the same standards on gender** as those we advocate in the campaign so it is likely to throw up **challenges for the organization** to overcome."[13] To achieve this, the campaign was to be launched within Amnesty at the Mexico ICM. Amnesty had to confront its own gender blindness, filling in the gaps in the way it had dealt with women's rights in order to maintain "our credibility in the eyes of the public, our allies and most importantly, the victims and survivors that this campaign will represent." The word *victims* is old Amnesty, whereas *survivors* is new. The radical nature of the challenge Amnesty faced was clear from the opening paragraph of a campaign project idea on "domestic violence and legal reforms":

> The family remains one of the most contested sites for progress on women's rights. Contrary to being a retreat, a place where individuals are able to find security and shelter . . . research points to the fact that the family "may be a cradle of violence" and where women and children (and in many situations, the elderly) are at risk of violence. It is important to accompany any work on VAW in the family with an interrogation of the definition of "family" and not take for granted the traditional power relations and prescribed roles within the family as factors that could facilitate gender-based violence in this so-called "private sphere".

This was new terrain for most researchers. They needed advice on policy issues (such as abortion, rape as torture, criminalization of sexual conduct, and the definition of violence against women) and on what kinds of cases the campaigners envisaged using. As Wilson noted in chapter 1, researchers have to make a case—one that fits the definition of the abuse or violation in question. Violence against women is complex; violence takes many forms, has many justifications and excuses, and is politically fraught locally and contentious globally. What would a simple illustrative case be? An abortion rights organization would know—one that helped increase the legal availability of abortions. But Amnesty aims to speak for women everywhere in the name of universal human rights. What case can it choose that truly reflects the core intuition, the very spirit, of universal rights? The founders, Benenson in particular, had found one: the prisoner of conscience. That Amnesty identified with humanity as a whole—genderless, colorless, without sexuality—had been its virtue. The SVAW campaign thus is a challenge to Amnesty, and Amnesty cannot continue to be what it has been as a result.

By February 2003, as war in Iraq loomed, senior management (SMF)[14] worried that the campaign had no momentum. This came to the surface at a weekly meeting, held on this occasion in Irene Khan's small office on the second floor of No. 1 Easton Street. Given the subject matter, it was notable that we sat crammed around a table overshadowed by an iconic image of male violence, of heroic brutal masculinity, emblazoned on a powerful AIUSA wall poster protesting against the use of 50,000-volt stun belts. The image was a black-and-white photo of a young Muhammad Ali, muscular and bare-chested, standing with glove poised over the prostrate figure of Sonny Liston battered to the canvas.[15] Watched by Ali, the SMF was told that the SVAW campaign was faltering. It lacked "vibrance or leadership and no great enthusiasm [was] evident in the IS for it." Staff feared, for example, that adequate funding would not be found. The sections, in contrast, were keen, led by the Swiss, the Dutch, and the Americans. Directors agreed they needed to "keep selling it to our own people," making sure IS programs were "quite clear VAW is still a priority . . . not an option."

Operational matters—campaign strategy and research, and which came first—were often described in chicken-and-egg terms. As a senior campaigner conceded bluntly, the IS had to break the vicious cycle whereby researchers needed strategy and guidelines to research cases and campaigners needed cases to provide strategy and guidance. Problems included prioritization and regional balance. Most Western societies have reasonable legislation to deal with violence against women, even if the implementation is poor, whereas outside the West there were more openly prejudicial laws. Then there was the fact that, in countries such as Brazil, nine out of ten murders were against boys and men. Amnesty thus needed "a clear argument for why VAW in the family should be more a priority for governments than other violence," in one senior director's words. In addition, Amnesty's term *nonstate actors* needed to be "unpacked" because it did not distinguish among husbands, the Roman Catholic Church, tribal councils in Pakistan, and so on. This made appropriate targets for activism difficult to identify.[16]

The next day, the SVAW campaign organizers and senior managers roused the staff. This meeting showed acutely the difficulties the IS faced. First, there were the financial constraints. The fifty or so, mainly female, staffers were told by a (reformist) senior manager not to worry about money: "I don't think money has ever stopped Amnesty from doing what it wants to do. . . . if we have good work there'll be no shortage of funds." Thus, the constraints of the profane are rendered instantly irrelevant. Second, there was the need to make the broad goals of the campaign more tangible. Researchers and policy and legal staff monopolize intellectual authority within the IS. But research is usually empiricist, practical, and closely related to the lore, whereas policy and legal work concentrates on problem solving intra-Amnesty or intra-human rights issues. It is the campaigns staff, enlarged in the early 1990s, who are responsible for drawing up and driving strategy for global campaigns. But they lack the internal authority for all the reasons we have seen. Because Amnesty research has rarely been concept driven, focusing on named individuals and their cases, thematic campaigns are a challenge to the ethos from the start.

A series of policy questions added to these operational difficulties. Policy meant to "draw the line somewhere" (as more than one senior director put it). Unlike an academic analysis, in which the logical implications of a concept are pushed to its limits, policy in an activist framework is problem solving to facilitate operational progress. Thus, a line has to be drawn, meaning that a strategic goal such as "challenge discrimination against women by affirming the principles of universality, indivisibility and inter-dependence of human rights" has to be turned into a workstream. When one campaigner talked about addressing the question of universalism head on, she added that she knew such questions "put you all to sleep." Researchers could not move forward with general goals and concepts. They needed tangibility—a campaign launch report setting out

Amnesty's argument, guidelines and policy advice, and training in gender issues.

The search for policy coherence continued at a meeting with the consultant hired to write the launch report (at which no researchers were present). The use of outsiders to write such reports has a checkered history, several staff members recalling how the material that consultants produced for various campaign launch documents often had to be scrapped and a last-minute replacement written hastily by an internal team that understood, of course, exactly what Amnesty required. Yet, as the Spanish section pointed out at the Mexico ICM, a widely admired SVAW report they had produced (without IS approval) was so refreshing precisely because their consultant knew nothing about Amnesty.

Policy staff told the consultant that the report's central message should be about calling violence against women "a human rights issue and therefore an international issue and therefore a moral issue." The question was how to make violence against women a human rights question, that is (in Amnesty terms) a moral issue rather than an issue of the criminal law. The answer was scope, the suggestion being that the extent of the abuse—covering half the world's population—made it a moral or ethical question. The meeting agreed, "The moral case is grounded in the scope." Added to the moral and legal arguments were the economic costs of violence against women, although, as someone noted, "if there weren't costs we'd still be against it."

This answer floats above a theoretical investigation of a question such as: Is the scope of a social practice necessarily relevant to its moral status? If the answer is no, does that matter? Not if you want to end violence against women. The scale of the injustice provides the moral energy in this case, whereas in other cases it might be something else. What matters is finding a way to act. "Asserting a right," said one participant, was about making a "claim"—something more moral, in other words, than just a personal want. The theoretical case is unimportant. Women are not, in liberal theory at least, discriminated against. The discrimination is social, in practice, and that is where it must be fought.

The ethical concepts used in this fight need not be human rights, which are just a means, albeit a means with an aura of moral authority to which Amnesty has greatly added. Human rights are a formalized version of the claim: I don't want it to happen. We could argue that a virtuous society is one in which women are not beaten. We can pass legislation and implement it to achieve this effect. We can imprison those who flout such a rule. We can use education to improve the attitudes of men toward women when they are still boys and girls. The language of rights—the language that says something is wrong because each individual has a personal moral claim against the rest of society—adds nothing. If Amnesty was to call itself the champion of human dignity, not human rights, would anything have to change? *Human dignity* is one of the phrases used by Pierre Sané in his paper for the 1993 Boston ICM. The same report also talks about obligations, human solidarity, injustice, and "existential needs."[17] These various ethical concepts are neither identical nor (necessarily) complementary in more philosophical terms, hence the need for faith in the absence of interests or identity.

The meeting with the consultant sought to remove conceptual and linguistic blockages to allow moral energy to flow. An initial discussion on terminology—not saying *nonstate actors* but naming the agent (men or a company) and dropping the feminist language of *girl-child* for *girl* had one experienced staffer actually bouncing up and down in her seat saying "yes, this is so good" as obstacles to the straightforward expression of moral sentiments were removed.

Some issues were tougher. In terms of sexuality, for example, existing policy was that Amnesty could not work on people imprisoned for consensual extra-marital heterosexual sex where that was illegal, but it could work on behalf of gays and lesbians imprisoned for having sex outside marriage.[18] And, finally, there were reproductive rights. For the women's movement, this is a key marker of belonging. At a gathering of experts on SVAW called by Amnesty in Oxford, one distinguished participant described sexual rights as the final frontier.[19] When she was told AI did not have a position on the right to abortion, she replied in disbelief, "don't be silly, you're joking" (at which point, one senior Amnesty staffer pointed out that HRW did not have a position either). Not upholding the right to abortion after rape, said another, was "colluding in silence" (yet some were wary of making exceptions because it risked legitimizing nonabortion as a position). Just sticking to what international law said was like saying nothing, said a third; at this, another senior Amnesty staffer added wryly, "that's why we're comfortable with it." Amnesty reformers wanted to move the agenda on, but were constrained by the need for the ICM to rule on the issue and by the lack of consensus within the movement.[20]

For activists with a shared identity or interest, questions such as "is domestic violence torture?" are effectively irrelevant. The issues are tactical: Is it an effective way to advance the cause of women's protection? Policy problems are to be solved pragmatically so things can change in the world. Moral authority is the opposite of tactical; it aspires to truth. There must be an answer to the question "is domestic violence torture?" that is in some deeper sense the right answer. Moral authority looks constantly for an anchorage that is not political. It craves foundations. For campaigners, the language of universal human rights is instrumental. It is a tool to further a practical aim—in this case, better lives for women.

The regional programs continued throughout 2003 to explain why their priorities were important. The Middle East Program wanted a September 11 report first, to "prepare the ground." The Asia Program talked about material "in the pipeline," and Europe's work on women was mainly about Turkey (it was chided: these were "all things you were going to do anyway"). The Americas Program wanted work on community and custodial violence and on the United States; the Asia Program suggested it had little research on domestic violence and that for credibility's sake something would have to be said on "comfort women" (Korean women used as prostitutes by Japanese soldiers during World War II). The head of the Africa Program said that researchers were "doing work on VAW irrespective of the campaign" and that there was "no lack of willingness" but it was "unclear to us what the expectations of the campaign are," leading to a "great deal of confusion on what is expected from regional programs."

A further high-level meeting in the secretary general's office heard campaigners say that they were still "looking for the big idea." There was even some skepticism in the building about whether violence in the family was a human rights issue, they said. Issues of impunity, domestic violence, and armed conflict were "conceptually difficult," policy staff told the meeting, worried that using Amnesty's traditional language of impunity made it an issue of the criminal law (not, in Amnesty terms, a human rights issue). A further question was over "traditional authorities," that is, "parallel structures to the state" (e.g., tribes). Some of the meeting participants wanted them delegitimized entirely; others wanted to pressure the state to make them "exercise their power responsibly."

As time ticked by, frustrated campaigners could not assume the necessary work on cases was being done. One complained, "we can't instruct anyone to do anything" and another said that "it's the usual blood out of a stone thing. . . . some women won't be represented at all, obviously not by Amnesty." A fund-raiser observed wryly, "We need a chain of command and please I use the term loosely, I understand the organization well." It was a question of authority and priorities. Regional programs even wanted the campaign launch report to range more widely than the two movement-agreed major themes. They sought either to continue work that did not come under the campaign priorities or to expand the priorities. In the words of one recently hired researcher:

> We've always thought to mainstream women, cases of women, so as long as that's what mainstreaming means, that's what we'll carry on doing. If it means something else, and I don't know, we'll get told eventually, that what we're doing is wrong and it needs to be something else. But again, if they're going to tell us that we have to do more women related stuff and drop other priorities, then that's going to create problems. Maybe in other countries it doesn't matter. But in a country like [name deleted] you know, the massive problems that that country has, we have our long-term priorities and they're long-term priorities for a reason. And we can't simply just drop them. So we'll have to reach some kind of compromise and weave in the new priorities into our existing work.

No wonder campaigners felt they needed someone to "walk the corridors" asking for "deliverables," that is, physically extracting the cases.

By August, just before the ICM internal launch, a meeting of those involved in planning the campaign heard that there was some concern "whether we are going to get any domestic violence cases at all." Regional programs saw any report involving women as a project for the campaign, whether or not it fit with the major themes. There were, at that stage, no cases from Western Europe, for example. The function of the launch report was also unclear: Would it set out Amnesty's thinking on these questions, or would it be a major piece of work with cases and demands for action around which sections could campaign? We deal with the ICM launch in chapter 7. We turn now to the equally fraught issue of multiculturalism.

Multiculturalism

"The face of Amnesty for research and things has for a long time been very white. . . . And I think that many people want it to remain that way." These were the words of a regional program campaigner. As a would-be global organization, undergirded by a universal ethos and a commitment to independence and impartiality, Amnesty has always been careful about even-handedness in the world of states. But it has done less well in terms of its own balance—it retains a very narrow base in terms of membership, remaining very white in terms of both members and IS staff. As its own Cultural Diversity and Equal Opportunities Policy puts it, the IS and AI "still have a mainly white, male, able-bodied hegemony."[21] In the "Change IS Report" of April 2002, under the heading "discrimination and multiculturalism," there is the following observation: "Covert racism can be found amongst staff and management. It manifests itself in lack of awareness of the global movement and in the de facto English cultural supremacy at the IS." The problems lie in geography, money, and the working culture of Amnesty. Blindness to race was a virtue not a vice for the founders, of course, and by the 1978 Cambridge ICM the movement averred: "The organization as a whole and each section, group and individual member works towards AI's objectives. No account will be taken of political, religious or other conscientiously held beliefs of persecuted persons or of their ethnic origins, color, sex or language; nor of the political, social, cultural or economic structure of the ideology of the country in which persecution takes place." The result of this blindness was, however, the same skewed outcome of a white and heavily Western central staff that we see in many other prestigious organizations. Multiculturalism provides various antidotes for this in theory—assimilation with existing public culture, the promotion of the virtues of diversity through a hybrid public culture (both varieties of republicanism), or a public sphere of homogeneity and a private sphere of difference (the liberal solution). Practically, none has proved noticeably successful at overcoming the initial distribution of influence and authority.

TABLE 6.5
Nationality and Staff Composition, 1974[a]

	British	American	Canadian	Swedish	Other
All staff	38 (60%)	7 (11%)	3 (5%)	3 (5%)	13 (19%)[b]
Senior staff[c]	6 (66%)	1 (11%)	1 (11%)	1 (11%)	—
Researchers	5 (36%)	2 (14%)	2 (14%)	1 (7%)	4 (29%)[d]

 [a] *From Agenda Item 19, FIN 03, IEC 74, 1 November 1974. n = 64 paid staff members. There were thirteen long-term unpaid volunteers listed. Three staff members were noted as being paid a lower salary than they were entitled to at their own request. The staff are labeled by "nationality" in this list.*
 [b] *Of the other category, the numbers were Dutch (2), German (2), and 1 each for Argentina, Australia, Bolivia, Chile, Colombia, France, New Zealand, and Togo. One person, a researcher, was listed as "stateless".*
 [c] *These figures include managers, as far as can be ascertained from job descriptions. They do not include researchers.*
 [d] *One researcher each from Togo, New Zealand, and the Netherlands and one "stateless."*

Although country of origin is not a perfect proxy for nationality, ethnicity, or race (British nationality does not correlate with race or ethnicity, of course, and many respondents might self-identify differently from their objective identification), we do get a sense from the historical material of the likely composition of the IS staff when staff members' country of origin was recorded. For example, table 6.5 is drawn from an IEC report on IS salaries from 1974. We can see how heavy the British presence is, unsurprisingly at this stage, although diversity increases among the researchers as the search for expertise causes the net to be cast wider.[22] Tables 6.6 and 6.7 show data from the HRP for the years 1992–2002. They record country of origin, again only a proxy for race or ethnicity, and must therefore be treated as only generally indicative. We can infer several things from these tables. Note that the proportion of staff from the United Kingdom, and from the West as a whole, has remained remarkably constant despite an increase in the size of the IS of more than 70 percent. Many of these UK staffers are in support services and are locals. This is exacerbated by a prominent feature of the states system—work permits—which makes it hard to hire staff from outside Europe for jobs where local skills are available.[23] In the search for a truly transnational organization that better mirrors global divisions of ethnicity, race, and nationality, work permit restrictions are a powerful constraint.

What happens when we look at these figures in relation to those designated Researchers? As shown in tables 6.7 and 6.8, the percentage of the total staff (with a designated country of origin) from the West in 1992 was

TABLE 6.6
Human Resources Program Data on Staff Country of Origin, 1992–2002[a]

Year (SCO)	West				Non-West				
	UK	USA	RoW	Total	Af/ME	Asia	Latin America	Eastern Europe	Total
1992 (226)	121	12	40	173	27	7	15	4	53
1993 (238)	133	9	42	184	28	6	16	4	54
1994 (254)	143	10	43	196	32	6	16	4	58
1995 (287)	157	14	52	223	36	6	16	6	64
1996 (286)	154	15	51	220	38	7	15	6	66
1997 (281)	149	13	53	215	39	8	13	6	66
1998 (297)	156	13	59	228	42	8	12	7	69
1999 (335)	167	14	78	259	48	9	11	8	76
2000 (362)	172[b]	13	88	273	57	8	16	8	89
2001 (388)	183	14	99	296	54	11	17	10	92
2002 (405)	184[c]	16	103	303	59	12	18	13	102

[a] *Af/ME, Africa and Middle East (including Iran and Iraq); Latin America includes the Caribbean; RoW, Rest of the West (western/northern/southern Europe, Canada, Australia, and New Zealand); SCO, number of staff members for whom a country of origin is recorded. One staff member, with country of origin listed as "Wed Kingdom," is not included in the total.*
[b] *The UK figure now includes one person whose country of origin is given as "Wales" and another from "Scotland." By 2001, a further person is now listed as being from "England."*
[c] *This figure includes the three staff designated "England," "Scotland," and "Wales."*

TABLE 6.7
Percentage of Staff from the UK and Western Countries, 1992–2002[a]

Year	Total IS staff	SCO	SCO from UK (%)[b]	From West (%)
1992	237	226	54	77
1993	258	238	56	78
1994	303	254	56	77
1995	364	287	55	77
1996	351	286	54	77
1997	352	281	53	77
1998	366	297	53	77
1999	376	335	50	77
2000	377	362	48	75
2001	414	388	47	76
2002	430	405	46	75

[a] *SCO, number of staff members for whom a country of origin is recorded.*
[b] *The total staff figure is always more than that for designated country of origin, and so the percentage of the total staff who come from the United Kingdom and the West falls when taken as a percentage of this overall figure.*

77 percent and of staff members labeled researcher, 67 percent. In 2002, these numbers were 76 and 71 percent.

These figures are only a rough guide. Nevertheless, the impression they give is of a heavy weighting, even among researchers—the experts

TABLE 6.8
Researchers and Country of Origin, 1992 and 2002[e]

	1992[a]	2002[b]
UK	18 (40%)	20 (31%)
USA	2 (4%)	4 (6%)
Rest of the West[c]	9 (20%)	20 (31%)
Africa/Middle East	9 (20%)	9 (14%)
Latin America[d]	5 (11%)	5 (8%)
Asia	0 (0%)	1 (2%)
Eastern Europe	1 (2%)	2 (3%)
Total	(44)	(61)

[a] N = 45, but only 44 have country of origin recorded.
[b] N = 65, but only 62 have country of origin recorded, and a further one, with "Wed Kingdom" as country of origin, is excluded.
[c] Western/northern/southern Europe, Canada, Australia, and New Zealand.
[d] Includes the Caribbean.
[e] Only staff members labeled "Researchers" in regional programs according to HRP data. These do not include campaigners or RCAs from regional programs or researchers on themes (located in the Campaigns Program). They do include two "field researchers" on Africa, and a Russia campaign researcher. Because of the small numbers, the percentages are approximate.

on countries throughout the world—toward the West. Expertise is knowledge-based not identity-based. The expert on Burundi cannot, under IS rules (WOOC), come from Burundi. Spread across all the regions and a majority of countries of the world, the places where the IS and Amnesty have often (although far from exclusively) found their country experts have been Western universities and Western human rights NGOs. WOOC privileges those who have knowledge but not the markers of identity. Work permits reinforce this. Detachment is built into research, into objectivity, into the ethos, and into the way capital-rich states and regions filter immigration.

Multiculturalism has been the conceptual heading under which Amnesty and the IS have dealt with issues of race and representation. A project team on multiculturalism composed of junior staff met several times as part of the Change IS process, but by November 2002 it was struggling with its rationale. Discussing a questionnaire the team wanted to distribute to the rest of the building, the team members found themselves disagreeing about the purpose of the group. For some it was principally about racism, with other issues—age discrimination, gender, sexual orientation—being important but not being multiculturalism issues. It was too sensitive, they said, for Amnesty to have a group solely called "racism" or "antiracism," so it never got to be an issue in its own right. Those who went to the multiculturalism workshop at a two-day Staff Forum at the Barbican in London (see chap. 7) were "mainly black" and "all knew why they were there" because "the only group that will do it is the one devoted to it" (the group that has an interest, or identity, in other words). Against this, the argument was made that all forms of discrimination should be included in the questionnaire, including the effects of class on volunteers. Multiculturalism was about encouraging diversity, it was argued, and all forms of discrimination had to be addressed.

In interviews, several staff members were unhappy with the way multiculturalism and race were dealt with. Given that minorities within the IS staff are disproportionately located at less senior levels where the percentage of staff members who are female and British is also higher, one major concern is that Amnesty and the IS are blind to problems in their own backyards. Again, what was once a virtue was now metamorphosing into a vice. Amnesty, and especially the IS, exists in central London, a real place that is in no way exempted from human rights abuses. Now, paradoxically, globalization has intensified the meaning of place. It matters more, not less, just where you are located, geographically and socially (in terms of gender, race, and class).

Blindness to local human rights concerns, which disproportionately affect the minority staff, exacerbate the whiteness of Amnesty. Early in my fieldwork, I asked a program director about multiculturalism and received a very animated reply about the IS as "abominably self-righteous, abominably pompous, abominably elitist." The outside world in London, I was told forcefully, was more multicultural than the IS (and there were plenty of people, he added, doing just as valuable work in local advice centers throughout the British capital). Later in another interview, the same manager said, "I just can't see how you are going to test that some prominent political activist who got badly treated in Chile counts for more than some women in south east London who are getting beaten up by their husbands every night of the week. But that's not called a human rights violation. It's so full and suffused with value judgements and culture and inherited from a particular period of the early sixties. It's indefensible." This brings to mind the earlier comment that in Africa human rights are domestic while in the West they are foreign policy. This is mirrored inside the IS: researchers turn outward and are concerned with other people's human rights; nonresearchers turn inward and are as concerned with their own.

For the impassioned IS manager just quoted, a working-class battered woman in London matters just as much as an imprisoned professor in Chile. The deep culture of the IS (and Amnesty) does not give them the same importance, of course, and many senior IS staff move in a transnational rather than local reality, reinforcing fears voiced by several interviewees about the "UN-ization" of Amnesty. The historical status of Amnesty with international audiences, such as those at the World Economic Forum in Davos, is related to its engagement with foreign (large-scale, symbolic, global) issues and therefore with the relations between states. The IS country-based organization consolidates this. As with gender, and class, activities and concerns that do not engage with issues of global importance lack status within the organization. Multiculturalism is one of those. Local human rights abuses do not carry the same weight, and they force the IS to engage in the political world of social justice and collective action with other, highly motivated groups that do share an identity or interest.

One junior IS staffer, talking about being black in London, said, "You know they talk about struggle being out in countries out there. For a lot of the black community, it's here." She went on, "You know I hear this word at Amnesty, recently, quite a lot. The lived experience of the individual. I don't think Amnesty has a clue, to be honest as to what that really means for people. You know, because a lot of the struggle for a lot of people within organizations is out there. And a lot of the struggle for black people is actually in their own yard. And they don't need to go anywhere else. You know we're struggling on a day to day level."

She raised a further issue having to do with the deep culture that various interviewees concerned with race raised. That is, the strong sense the IS has of its own moral superiority enshrined in the ethos. Amnesty as an institution struggles to deal with, or even talk to, other organizations (although many staff members are active in local causes outside their Amnesty work). It struggles, for example, with alternative human rights discourses that stress indivisibility and dialog.[24] For her, local community organizations mistrusted Amnesty's ability to be an equal partner in a more negotiated space (as others suggested, some human rights NGOs in Africa and Asia were skeptical, fearing Amnesty would compete with them for funding and publicity). Here are the young black staffer's words: "Human rights is always something that is a certain language. And trying to in some ways reformulate, reenergize, and actually reconceptualize some of those discussions is a struggle. And I think that, you know, perhaps organizations like Amnesty [that] are very highly structured can't necessarily enter those debates. I think that actually what we need to be doing is looking at ourselves and trying to change ourselves. And then trying to enter those debates."

This alternative human rights discourse is much closer to what we have characterized as political. It is about social change, not enduring truth. Why has making this change been so difficult in Amnesty? "Because it's traditionally had a very Western centrist approach to looking at human rights. . . . It comes back to all those things about assuming that the Western way of doing things or the Western definition and understanding . . . of human rights is actually more superior. . . . They don't really listen." Amnesty talks the talk, she suggested—"we need to listen, we need to evolve, we need to be bigger, we need to be in touch with the lived experience . . . to be wedded to people rather than texts"—but "Actually, when you see it through the practical realization in those meetings of what's going on, or even within presentations, you actually see that Amnesty . . . or the individuals who are leading those processes really aren't aware. Really aren't self-conscious of the things that they carry with them and the impressions they give to the people that they're trying to take with them. . . . You know, you can't make statements which are hollow because people see through them very very quickly." Amnesty's tendency to assume a degree of superiority was evident, she felt, in the "patronizing" attitude Amnesty took to political change in its countries. "Do they not think there's a whole world out there? You know, we are not the kings and queens of human rights. We're not the ones. . . . There are thousands of groups out there. You know. Who do this work every day."

On consultations with external experts she was equally forthright: "Who are these people? They are people who are able to [articulate] human rights language. . . . They're not people who necessarily are down there on the ground doing service provision work." She recalled an Asian speaker in the IS talking about domestic violence who offended some in her audience by using the word *black* as a political term of resistance rather than using the Amnesty language. "And I just thought to myself how dare you? How dare you say that you have the monopoly on what is right and wrong within this discourse? Because you don't. We don't have the license to say . . . you're now right, you're now wrong, and all the rest of it. These aren't definitions that, you know, we're part of that package. . . . We shouldn't be imposing. We should be evolving and [working with] others to evolve that language." Another interviewee put it succinctly: "It's not that people in Latin America, Asia, South East Asia, Africa do not know how to campaign. They obviously know how to campaign. They have driven away dictators."

The embedded culture is deep, as described by another black staff member: "It's a culturally diverse organization. I think, though, that the dominant culture is Western and is white. And middle class. And I suppose if you fall outside of those norms then, you know, you're, you're . . . I don't say that it's impossible, but it's more difficult I think. To achieve and attain. And to kind of get those informal breaks that others benefit from. I've witnessed that." How was race a problem, I asked?

It's a problem because we can't talk about it. It's a problem because of the bad practices there. Sometimes we don't know if something is race or if it's not. And because there's no mechanism for finding out what it really is. . . . It's a problem because the last secretary general was black. Which meant that it was absolutely a no-go area for discussion at the staff level. And because . . . he was in the position of secretary general, the last thing he would have wanted is to have been seen to be being partial to ethnic minorities. Either black, Indian or whatever. So everything was hush-hush. . . . And it will continue to be a problem. Especially because Irene is also Bangladeshi. She came to [a] meeting on development and, when the discussion moved to the issue of power, she was the one that chopped the discussion in half. So it will continue to be a problem.

Managerial practice was so poor, she went on, that it was difficult to distinguish whether that was the problem or race was. A former senior

IS staffer said he wrote to the IEC chair when he left complaining about the way race was dealt with inside the IS. He was adamant in saying, "I've never seen so much racism as I saw there," but then qualified this: "It was racism. Because you can't see what else it is. I'm not going to say it is purely racism. I think race plays a part." His explanation went right back to contested authority: "I think there was more a feeling. It was more that, that the staff don't want you to make decisions. And the moment that you make decisions, they'll fight you, and they'll use anything they can. To fight you on it." Within the IS, he argued, the notion of equal opportunities was "used actually as a shield. Against diversification of staff. You know . . . therefore it means if we need to have a hundred percent white people, it's fine. And I couldn't believe [it] . . . that's not fine!." In the letter to the IEC, he concentrated on his personal experiences, saying "I have never felt as uncomfortable in my life, as I have felt in, in the IS. . . . And I could only attribute some of that discomfort to the fact that I was black. And I was an African."

In my perspective, it was mostly that I call, I call it racism because I think there's a, there was a, a clear need for people to conform to their culture and the practice within Amnesty. And I cannot do it because I'm not English and I'm not part of the culture of, of the English. I've got my own culture. And I hold it very strongly. And so that . . . once you run counter to it, you are going, you are going to have a hard time to fit in. And that's what really it is. And I kept saying to the IEC, just move this office from London. You know. Even if you just go over to Manchester. That change will be good, for everybody. Because they'll, they'll start again. They've been there for so long. . . . You've just go to do something that can shake it.[25]

Overall, it seemed, the homogenous culture—monoculturalism—was the problem.[26] In both the ethos and the classical theory of universal human rights, being color blind is a principled position. Meritocracy appears to operate on a level playing field, and even if you have a staff whose members are mainly white, the ethos and culture they share takes color to be an irrelevant consideration. Over time, a strong set of culturally embedded norms about belonging evolves, reinforced by appointing and encouraging staff members in its own image. The IS is no more immune to this than any institution. Because of the effective tenure system for researchers and regional campaigners—lifelong employment in a position outside management but with significant informal authority—the turnover of staff is lower at this level. Thus, we get the culture we are reading about: masculine, white, and middle class.

This whiteness is not about open racism, and many staff members reading this will be horrified because their own beliefs and organizational self-image are the exact opposite. They will point to the difficulties of attracting good nonwhite overseas staff to a lowly paid job in an expensive city such as London. They will say that even when shortlists for jobs include nonwhite candidates, the professional skills of Westerners are often too strong when the decision is made meritocratically. But the fact remains that none of the senior directors appointed was black, very few of the researchers are black, and, apart from a few very distinguished exceptions, few of the IEC members have been black.[27] The strength is not there, in the African, Asian, and Middle Eastern sections, not to mention among the nonwhite members of Western sections.

Impartiality and WOOC have tended to legitimize such replication, but it is now a problem because Amnesty is transforming itself into a movement about being as much as doing. There is, as we have seen with gender, less and less of a private space demarcated as Amnesty International. And in this more political world, engagement is necessary. As, metaphorically speaking, the doors of the IS are flung open, the culture will be exposed to the light and, from what Amnesty and the IS is, observers will infer how "authentically" (to use a reformers' term) Amnesty fits into the struggle of the powerless and the marginalized against the strong. Being white, masculine, and middle class will distance, or even alienate, Amnesty from this struggle, a struggle that globalization is only intensifying.

For example, the number of staff members with China and India as countries of origin in 1992 was one and two, respectively, and in 2002 one and five. There was no staff member listed throughout this sample from Indonesia.[28] The IS has a profile that mirrors economic and political power (excluding Japan—there was no member of the IS staff in 2002 with Japan registered as country of origin, and the Japanese section as a whole is seen within Amnesty as moribund). Even if we take the United Kingdom

out, we see that staff from smaller countries of the West hugely out-
number those from the south.

In 2002, there was a total of twenty staff members from Belgium (two),
Denmark (six), Ireland (six), Luxembourg (one) and the Netherlands (five)
countries whose populations combined are very approximately 36 million.
There were also twenty staff members from: Argentina (one), Bangladesh
(one), Brazil (two), Congo (two), Egypt (one), Iran (one), Mexico (three),
Nigeria (six), and Poland (three). These countries have a combined popu-
lation of approximately 775 million. This excludes China, India, and
Indonesia (with six employees between them in 2002).[29]

Does this matter? Not if you are following the rules. Researchers are
sent to gather information as the embodiment of those rules. Nationality,
race, and ethnicity are irrelevant. The meritocratic criterion—the best
person for the job at that point in time—may be properly applied (indeed
the right of each applicant to be treated equally requires that it be) and
the various advantages in terms of education, money, travel, work experience, credentials, and languages that those who are Western and middle
class enjoy may well make them the best candidates. But in terms of
political authority, it matters hugely.

The situation is, if anything, worse on a movementwide scale. Here,
Amnesty is profoundly unrepresentative. Out of 2,305 groups of Amnesty
members registered in 1979, only thirty-seven could be said to be from
outside the West (including fifteen groups in Japan). As a comparison,
Belgium (Francophone and Flemish sections) had eighty-nine, Switzerland
had seventy-five, and Canada and Australia both had thirty-four. West
Germany had by far the largest number of groups, 645, followed by
Sweden (257), France (246), and the Netherlands (232) and then the United
States (177), and United Kingdom (164). This did not matter when Amnesty
was not a representative and its impartiality was embodied in the lore.
Now that it desires to be a representative, it needs markers of identity.
This is not a problem in gender terms, as long as Amnesty can learn to
speak the appropriate language and modify the masculine culture,
because women are the majority of the movement's members and staff.
But it is a serious problem for multiculturalism.

A State of the Movement exercise carried out in the middle of 2003
before the ICM looked into both membership and activism (how active
those members were). On the question of global representation, the results

TABLE 6.9
Amnesty Members in Largest Sections by Region, 2003[a]

	North America/ Western Europe	Asia Pacific	Africa
Membership	1,157,939	56,195	4,201

[a] *Six largest sections in each region.*

were salutary. As of October 18, 2002, total membership was put at 1,758,733. However, when sections were divided regionally the results shown in table 6.9 were obtained. Even in those non-Western countries where Amnesty has a presence, the story is a depressing one. Some sections have stagnated and many have either collapsed, been taken under IS management, or been closed by the IEC.[30] In Brazil, for example, where the AI section collapsed amid great acrimony, Amnesty is still involved in various messy and very costly legal battles. The section in Bangladesh, Irene Khan's home country, was derecognized in 2003 by the IEC for "non-compliance with AI's core values and principles," whereas structures in countries such as Pakistan have little depth, meeting the minimum formal requirements for section status but having no activism to back them up.[31] Soul-searching about why development has failed is continuous. As a note to the IEC in 1973 put it succinctly, "It is obvious . . . that the credibility of Amnesty as a non-European organization is wide open to challenge."[32] This comment appears after a table (table 6.10) showing sections and groups. The report goes on: "It is important to consider whether the traditional Amnesty group is not too 'unnatural' a phenomenon in countries where social concern is likely to be turned towards the indigenous problems of starvation, disease and illiteracy."[33]

A legendary IS and Amnesty figure, Richard Reoch, who worked for the organization for more than twenty years, was field secretary in South Asia in 1974, tasked with trying to encourage sections in India, Bangladesh, Nepal, Pakistan, and Sri Lanka. In an open letter to sections, Reoch was clear that "To establish its credibility in the Third World, Amnesty international must become more obviously relevant to . . . problems of social justice in underdeveloped countries."[34]

Reoch identified acutely one of the central problems that Amnesty faced and still faces outside the West:

TABLE 6.10
Sections and Groups by Region, 1973

	Sections	Groups
West Europe[a]	15	1,008
Australia/New Zealand	5	43
USA/Canada	1	26
Asia	5	9
Africa	3	3
Latin America	2	2

[a] *From AI Index: ORG 03/IEC 73, agenda item 16. Of the Western European total, 872 groups were from West Germany, Holland, Sweden, and the United Kingdom. Australian states had their own sections at this stage.*

Evidence of the particular "cultural bias" of Amnesty International . . . is also seen, significantly, in the fact that the people who are interested in joining the organization are most often members of the small educated urban elite who are very much Westernized and English-speaking. This elite, with its Western outlook, is often closer in spirit to European society that to the rural masses in their own country. On the other hand, the social activists, who provide information to Amnesty International on prisoners, do not actually see themselves as having anything in common with the Amnesty movement itself; they merely hope to use the organization's external pressure to further their own socio-political aims.[35]

This was 1975. Fast forward to an IEC meeting at a London hotel in 2003. The senior staff members of the Asia Program are presenting a development strategy to the IEC. The presenter, a researcher, says, "this is very painful, I'll warn you in advance." Although weakening WOOC will help with Asia membership, "the Western European model certainly isn't what works" (meaning formal structure, counting individuals, and setting up groups). Some Asia sections were "not a credit to the name of Amnesty International," she continued, being either facades or too middle class. The IS needed to have an office in a regional center such as Bangkok, not in Hong Kong, and more staff members devoted to developing membership, given Asia's population size.

The response from IEC members was exasperated. One said he was not prepared to see another £10 million spent to find "it's just gone. . . . It will not deliver anything more except very tired people." Others pointed out that the model of territorial control (setting up sections that then exclusively managed national territory) was flawed for an international movement, that getting human rights workers in Asia to work on other countries was not going to work, and that the diversity and geography in Asia made prospects daunting. Another added; "In my view we've got worse again at seeing everything through a European, North American lens." The IEC told the Asia Program that it was prepared to be radical and to "knock down the organizational barriers" for what successful development would require. But the movement as a whole had to agree.

In July 2003, a consultancy called Intrac produced a review of development for the IS that recommended that the term *development* be dropped in favor of a more dynamic phrase such as *mobilization*. The main operational change advocated was to try to build a human rights constituency rather than seek to replicate national sections. The report's key findings about Amnesty will come as no surprise: no clear vision of development, "grey areas" in the respective roles of the movement and the IS, an internally "political" organization "drowning in paper," poor management, "fragmentation," and little monitoring and evaluation. Of fragmentation, the consultants wrote, "IS staff do not appear to think in terms of the connectedness of what each of them are doing," which included seeing fund-raising as something separate from mobilizing other kinds of resources.

What the report could not address, of course, was the extent to which precisely what Amnesty is makes it structurally unable to build a constituency. The "one voice" principle and detachment from local concerns via WOOC were operational, yes, but they were anchored in the ethos and that goes right to the heart of what Amnesty has been. For so many reasons—a focus on civil and political rights; impartiality; WOOC; "one voice"; the white, masculine, and middle-class IS and Amnesty membership; POCs and letter writing; colonial legacies; the dominance of English operationally; and religionless Christianity—Amnesty faces a challenge in trying to develop the kind of constituency outside the West that it desires. It is just not that kind of organization. Its normative structure will not allow it to be. As one former senior IS staffer recalls an Indian human rights activist saying to him, "You, Amnesty, you are the McDonalds of human rights. You are the face of globalization in human rights terms. You come in here, you build your prefabricated restaurants, you serve your set menu, you displace local cuisine and local activism. You know, that was the sort of metaphor he used. And, I think, while that's not exactly true of India, I think it is very true of Amnesty." And if you think about it, that is just what Benenson had in mind—to resurrect some kind of global authority in the face of globalization by trying to organize on a world scale around a set of what were taken to be transcendent principles.

Conclusion

In doing good, the act itself is the only morally relevant consideration. In being good, the agent's identity and motives matter. Thus, Amnesty's whiteness, masculinity, and affluence become problematic. The IS and Amnesty are far from homogenous, and for some interviewees this diversity was one of the attractions. But in most organizations such diversity, although perhaps a desirable goal, is not an issue that goes right to the heart of their legitimacy. In the same way, a clear majority of IS staff are women, but the embedded working culture is masculine, affecting identity and internal interaction in often unproductive ways. Although we have made little of what we might call class (or status), on many occasions we have seen how such differentials work, especially when associated with the combination of higher education and research. The members of altruistic groups such as Amnesty tend to be middle class because they can afford not to spend all of their time and money protecting their own interests.

The concentration on POCs and civil and political rights means that financial redistribution has not been a core concern. The rejection of politics from the beginning marginalized the activist Left. Rules such as WOOC mean that those attracted to Amnesty tend not to be grassroots activists, who are more likely to be poor, but instead those for whom association with Amnesty, a well-known, Western, English-speaking organization, is a matter of prestige. Many IS staff members are drawn from volunteers (who by definition can afford to work some of their time unpaid in London). Once inside Amnesty, we are only too well aware of the complexity of the internal lore. Mastering this requires mastering a large and complex literature, in English. Those nonnative English speakers competent enough in English to be able to move to London and take up an IS post are rarely from the poorer classes in their own countries. The POCs were, in the beginning, often men from educated backgrounds—professors, priests, lawyers, poets—and their "crime," practicing freedom of expression, required a facility with words and ideas in the public sphere. All of these considerations predisposed Amnesty to be an intellectually demanding organization that reinforced its underlying class structure. It also has a political economy dominated by the United States and Europe. Could it change? As we see next, a determined effort is certainly being made to continue the work Pierre Sané began.

7

THE INHERITORS

what is it, I asked a long-standing IS senior manager, that the keepers of the flame are protecting? He replied:

> One is that we lose the focus on the individual. And the second is that we lose the focus on countries. And that we only identify a small group of countries to work on and we then try and do thematic work. But you can only really do thematic work through knowledge about what's happening in countries. And the problem with thematic action or campaigns is that the recommendations you make to governments are not country focused. So in a sense they're very general. And it's difficult to engage with individual governments because the recommendations are not for them. So the overall impact of a thematic campaign, I think, is potentially questionable.[1]

To this list he later added, "To maintain, at least, that we will continue to have a higher profile on physical and mental integrity."

Real responsibility for making the IS work—getting documents out, handling crises, and checking letters before they leave the building—lies "with a small handful of people," almost all in regional, policy, and legal programs. There were perhaps three people in his program who would be called in an emergency. "They're the ones that save things at the end of the day," he said. These people are keepers of the flame. They have charisma, a reputation for quality work, and long experience inside Amnesty. He saw them as indispensable: "That's what makes this organization vulnerable. We can cope with a certain rate of turnover. But if we start to hemorrhage key staff then we're in trouble." It is these staff members, the inheritors of the ethos, who needed, he said, to be persuaded by the revolution under way, and so far they were not.

That revolution, Change IS, was supposed to be different. For the first time, a more explicit deal was struck: improved management and physical space, among other things, in return for a change in working practices that would reenergize the IS for a mandateless future. The IS even shut down completely, for the first time ever, for a two-day forum of all staff at London's Barbican early in 2002. Since before the 2001 ICM in Dakar, members had been determined to remission the IS. Institutional change was the aim: from stasis to motion, from organization to movement, from impartiality to advocacy.

The forum was reported at length in a *Change IS Report* to the secretary general. Staff members identified a long list of positive values, from accuracy to accountability, from commitment to creativity, from impartiality and integrity to justice and fairness, and from respect to solidarity and team work. They were adamant that personal and professional values had to align. The report noted, "It was impossible to sever the interrelationship between our feelings and behavior as individuals in the workplace, our working relationships as colleagues and the efficacy of our work. . . . Individuals who can perform work which accords with their own personal values will be happier and therefore more productive, resulting in improved outputs and a more harmonious working environment."[2] Staff members, were frank in seeing that "the failure to identify and follow values . . . [was] a major cause of organizational dysfunction." These values were necessary to protect the standards and reputation of the IS, bind its staff together, and allow it to serve its various beneficiaries (beginning with the sufferers of human rights abuses). So what were the obstacles? Given the chance to let off steam, IS staff members were brutal with themselves.

First, bad management: too many staff members for program directors to manage, a poor structure, unclear authority, abuse and uncaringness, a lack of guidance, a lack of trust, and many more specific complaints. This was "management dithering in an organizational culture of widespread impunity."

Second, workload: too much work, too high expectations, poor prioritization. Third, staff terms and conditions: low wages, discrimination and lack of equal opportunities ("lip service paid to multiculturalism"), and insecurity (too many short- and fixed-term contracts). Fourth, fifth, and sixth were planning, accountability, and poor use of resources. The IS was seen as "claustrophobic."

A long list under the heading "Problems with Bureaucracy" had twenty-five subitems, including rigid adherence to rules at the expense of creativity and quick response (but also, "not enough guidelines"); a tedious, long-winded approval system; bureaucracy that hides behind consultation and power that hides behind bureaucracy; information control paranoia; too many meetings; and an obsession with accuracy. Staff members saw different programs as having different ideologies. An "informal culture" list was equally long. It included culture of blame, isolation, lack of respect for resource programs, and lack of positive feedback. Many themes touched on rudeness, lack of respect, inappropriate behavior, elitism, sexism, racism, and "dysfunctional hierarchy," in which "Apart from formal hierarchy in grades and job titles, there is a 'false' notion of hierarchy in terms of functions (e.g., research is seen as more important than fundraising) which in turn hampers effective integration of programs or tasks or cooperation across programs."

It was a long shadow. The list under "problems in attitude" begins with "inability to overcome low morale/negativity" and continues with, among others, "Fear of change; too much hoarding; too much nostalgia, lack of playfulness; slagging each other off; hypocrisy; unethical behavior; lack of risk-taking; failure to bury past errors; fear of "administrative punishment"; too serious/heavy-handed; lack of ownership of work; righteousness; stifled creativity; fossilized thinking; resistance to change." On this list, the one that stood out for me was "mental claustrophobia." Staff members certainly did not spare themselves. But the forum was also about removing these barriers. Many suggestions for improvement were made: more and better management, planning, fewer short-term contracts, better recruitment, accountability, and an improved physical environment. One insightful paragraph on fragmentation brought these points together:

Participants identified various reasons why this almost total fragmentation existed. There is a lack of common "mental" and "physical" space across programs. Thus participants flagged ideas such as the need to merge programs such as the "campaigning" and "research" programs or the information technology and information resources programs. The "culture" of the building was described as a culture in which neither ideas, nor experience nor problems are shared between individuals, teams or programs. The IS is a place in which the "only I know" syndrome exists and is perpetuated. This "culture" is usually linked to hierarchical positions. In fact, the lack of cohesion within the IS made it extremely territorial not only at program level but also at team level. There are, participants stated, too many "prima donnas" and little, if any, personal or institutional responsibility to pass on information and ideas and "get on" with people generally. . . sometimes it was agreed this was due to workload pressure.

These "hierarchical power structures" were also mentioned in a section on transparency, where "the failure to act transparently prevents ethical and honest working practices—resulting in a fundamental contradiction between the values the IS purports to espouse and its working practices." In advocating more attention to transparency, the report stated that "real transparency generates trust, improves morale and allows for progression." The next section noted that "the problem of respect and inappropriate behavior could in fact be the largest and most damaging problem at the IS." The language here mirrors Amnesty's external language, referring to "impunity for the perpetrators," for example, and recapitulates much we have seen about harassment, bullying, and stress. It also recorded that "Gradism again was stressed as a significant problem with some believing themselves more important than others."

The penultimate section, before a proposed new mission statement, is titled, knowingly: "Is Change Possible at the IS?" It acknowledges that "organizations don't change without individuals both changing and experiencing change." Implicit in long, long lists of comments to management, staff, and sections is the notion of a renegotiated contract. The comments are all of the kind: If you do X, I will do Y. For example, to management: "If you are more transparent and fair in . . . decision-making I will trust and respect you even when tough decisions are made." And to staff: "If 'prima donnas' reform we will like them," "I will develop a private life if you let me have one," and "I will acknowledge your work and not your grade."

Many things emerge from this. An endemic lack of trust and absence of respected authority comes through in almost every section. Amnesty staffers and members have made heroic personal efforts to try to effect moral change at a certain cost to themselves. The urge to transparency was a demand that researchers (the prima donnas), especially but not exclusively, get out of their offices—that they shed their informal authority, in other words.

Some saw the drive for change as another cycle in a continuous process and simply continued to adhere, throughout it, to the core values for which, in their view, Amnesty stands. Others saw this as the last chance for the IS. One senior movement member told me the IS might have as little as five years to reform. I put this to an IS director, who shot back, "Why, why have they given us that long? . . . If I was in a section where it mattered . . . I would be talking about competitive tendering."

The *Change IS Report* promised more and better management and a refurbished working environment in exchange for behavioral changes and a genuine engagement in transforming the IS to deliver the new mission outlined in the movement's Integrated Strategic Plan (ISP) entitled "Globalize Justice!" The IS part of this was an International Secretariat Operational Plan (ISOP) to begin in 2004. This became the central focus of numerous meetings and discussions leading up to the 2003 ICM in Mexico. At the heart of these were themes that have run throughout the preceding chapters: movement-IS relations, traditional work (individual cases, country expertise, and MAC), planning and prioritization, management authority, and the role of research and researchers. Could the ethos be redrawn, the working culture transformed, and Amnesty remain as a single, more socially active movement with the IS at its center? Or would the keepers of the flame succeed in preserving the ethos and its working culture?

The Operational Plan

At the Dakar ICM in 2001, as one ardent reformer put it, they had "danced at the fire of the death of the mandate." By January 2003, an International Management Group (IMG) composed of section directors and senior IS staff was puzzling through the postmandate future. Their deliberations are instructive. It was an innovative committee for Amnesty in that IS directors and the heads of select influential sections were meeting as a proto–executive committee for the movement as a whole (with the IEC as the board). The IS staffers, below director level, were more clearly than ever employees to be managed, a civil service for the movement and not decision makers. They were now equivalent to section staffers, and any direct input they had to the international level would be advisory. The IMG was a first attempt to give more concrete reality to international space, making Amnesty "something you join for the purpose of pushing Amnesty's goals rather than something you join to promote your country's interests." It was important to "erode national boundaries" and "globalize the movement's economy," creating, for example, a consolidated set of Amnesty accounts.

A key question for the IMG was: What work will the IS actually do? The ISP committee had consciously used metaphors such as "architecture" to jolt people out of "business as usual mindsets." This confirmed that, as only an organization without building blocks could, "We can change our organization to make it the organization we need to implement our human rights strategy." Would Amnesty cover all countries, for example? The answer IS directors gave the IMG was subtle: global coverage was a core value of Amnesty and human rights were equally important everywhere. But strategic coverage—the successor concept to MAC—was a way to "take the core values and operationalise them in a way that's contemporary and relevant." MAC entailed some ongoing capacity to speak with authority on any country and a commitment in principle to cover all countries in the Annual Report. Regional programs were deeply committed to this, but reformers saw it as a myth. For them, it simply disguised the fact that researchers made decisions on priorities of their own rather than by following the wishes of the movement.

Reformers asked researchers, "what is the declared authoritative base to justify your program of work?"[3] The mandate, they added, was "no longer a shield" that could be used to say no "even if people are dying in front of us." This senior manager went on, "For years we kept the large majority of the world's victims outside Amnesty." At this stage, the idea of no ongoing work was still being discussed. In a telling comment, a senior director said that any evaluations of work would be "more evidence-based than claim based." In short, IS directors, who wanted researchers to become more like research managers, would not take the researchers' word for it. The idea of strategic coverage was to be extended to regional strategies as a whole. Countries would be covered only for three main reasons: gravity of abuses, possibility of making a difference, or as test cases. And the decision on coverage would no longer lie with the researcher.

The WOOC guidelines had already been weakened to try to encourage section research, but small sections still found the criteria for own-research permission, carefully monitored at the IS, intimidating. The ISP envisaged a world without this oversight, in which "tough trust" prevailed—the idea that was to substitute for the lore and IS scrutiny.[4] In essence, the ISP and ISOP would lay out the work, strategically and operationally, and everyone would work within these agreed parameters. This is more or less what Pierre Sané's discussion paper from 1993 had proposed. Moreover, authority in Amnesty was to be divided as follows: those who needed to be informed (the 3s, as the IMG termed it), those who needed to be consulted (2s), and those who could exercise a sanction (1s).[5]

A final problem was that of accountability. As of 2003, in the words of an IS senior manager to the IMG, "No one could actually tell you a) what is Amnesty's core business and b) what sections and structures are actually doing. . . . no-one in the movement could actually tell you that." Monitoring that people were doing what the various protocols (i.e., contracts) specified was the issue ("but who will be the police?" whispered a long-term staff member sitting in on the meeting). Although part of this group of senior section staff at the international level, the IS directors were also responsible for delivering the ISOP. They knew what they were up against, in parts of the movement as well as the staff. Despite very strong reforming sentiment among some on the IEC, a senior IS director recalled, "Just to give you a flavor from my own experience of it. I was at an IEC meeting last year some time. . . . and in, just informal conversation, I said well, you know, part of the challenge is, you know, of course we're a social change movement. And [the question is] your assumptions about how social change takes place. And one of the IEC members, very long-standing, said to me: We're not about social change. You could have knocked me down with a feather."

The French Section introduced resolutions to the ICM on impartiality, as we see shortly, whereas the Dutch Annual General Meeting (AGM) stressed to its directors that "traditional areas of work" such as the death penalty were vital, AI Netherlands' four-year section plan including a paragraph that began "promote a strong international secretariat with a leading role in research, strategy and action coordination." Inside the IS, the keepers of the flame were just as determined, one reformer likening resistance to that of "evangelical fundamentalists . . . [who] can't hold the faith without . . . packaging it in a judgmentalism about those who don't believe the way you do."

This clash between working culture and reform was played out in numerous meetings about the ISOP. At a daylong meeting of all program heads at a university site near the IS, for example, the regional programs outlined their priorities first, thus structuring the subsequent discussion much to the anger of the other programs, which consciously referred to the ISP and Decision 10 of the 2001 Dakar ICM (the model for campaigning) as their authority to argue for things that they knew regional programs would resist.[6]

When the campaigns and communications staff addressed the meeting, the tone was transformed. If the morning had been about continuity, the afternoon was all about change. As a senior campaigns manager put it, "there is a crack in the lever" (meaning Amnesty was not having the impact it should). Media staffers described "seismic changes in the mass-media market" that meant "if it isn't now, it isn't news." This was a direct challenge to the ethos. Amnesty had to aggressively defend its "very strong brand" by building new ties, on the basis of personality and trust, with the media. Fund-raising, too, stressed "stewardship" of the brand, and both were concerned—as the regional programs had not been—with competition from other NGOs. The Campaigns Program was blunt: "Campaigning is one of the main things we are in business for . . . [we are] not set up exclusively as a think tank." Amnesty had to do more than have a "terribly clever policy and then think should we do some action about it," being more concerned with "campaigning research" rather than with "how big a square is in which a demonstration is going to take place" (or "solving interesting, arcane policy problems"). The focus had to be on impact. Membership staffers, who got almost no time at all, immediately criticized the lack of multiculturalism in the room and in Amnesty (Irene

Khan, the secretary general, was the only nonwhite member of the meeting), stressing the need for a model of Amnesty that mobilized but did not necessarily have an "Amnesty stamp" on it. Finally, the resource programs pledged that they saw their role as to "support the rest of you in your work on human rights. . . . [in fact], we'd quite like to be involved a bit more."

The meeting finished with a visibly irritated senior director warning staff that "there might be some tougher messages we want to give each other." Hard choices were not being faced. "The mandate was just a set of goals, that's all it was . . . and a bit more," they were told; the core message was that in the world of social change, AI could no longer be "who we are" but had to address the question "who [do] we want to be?" There was a mismatch, participants heard, "between core values and behavior," with the implicit class basis of the IS visible in the fact that staff members would speak to people in resources programs in a way they would never address a policy person. Finally, IS managers were told that their "antipathy to money," not babies in Kuwait, was the real threat to Amnesty's reputation.

At a subsequent meeting, even senior directors did not agree on issues such as no ongoing work ("zero-based planning"). For some, this was a way to get themes to take priority over country work; for others it was "not a realistic strategy." Amnesty's legacy was powerful. As one put it, "there is nowhere else in the world where so many people can identify what torture means" (to which the reply came, "or where so many people disagree about what torture means"). One new director even asked why 1991 had such significance. Some wanted to plan with an "unconstrained vision first"; others wanted to know the structure that would tell them "an awful lot about the vision." "We don't work in abstract," said one director, "in the end the meat is the country stuff," but he was countered by another director who was concerned about the "invisible power researchers have over Amnesty in the IS."

Who would prioritize? That was the question. Directors accepted that researchers felt "incredibly personally responsible for individual victims," a "strong, real, psychological connection" that was principled, ethical, and emotional but also "disproportionate, unrealistic and grandiose." Any move away from casework toward themes was one of the points at which the ethos and the pressure for reform met head on. The emotional cost of dropping work was heavy. In the ISOP, work on disappearances, a part of Amnesty's heritage especially in the Americas Program, was now reserved for missing activists ("human rights defenders") only. The Americas Program's response was heartfelt, one experienced researcher warning it would be "extremely painful." Some researchers had been working for thirty-five years on "exactly the same cases": "This will be the end of their fight for many people. . . . You accompany the families for so long. . . . These are people, real people, we are going to be abandoning not just cases."[7] And so it was with countries. Strategic coverage and a limited number of country action plans (CAPs) entailed that each regional program would pay dedicated attention to only a handful of places—for Asia, for example, perhaps only China, Myanmar (Burma), Indonesia, and India. A senior director stressed, "There will be some countries that will be forgotten and we have to be absolutely honest about that."

Thus, casework and MAC were under pressure. Approvals came next. By April 2003, regional managers were defending their monitoring role by pointing out that some section research had been "atrocious," relaxing WOOC would make research take ten times longer because "sections are going to feel they can do what they like and we'll have to pick up the pieces in terms of quality." They feared that if "we open up the boundaries," interest groups in the sections would pursue their special projects. The regional heads were asked "why more research being done [is] good for human rights?" and were told bluntly, "The movement will not tolerate us staying in the role of the totally unchallenged authority on this stuff."

The draft ISOP, written by reform-minded senior directors, made plenty of reference to the newly volatile international political and human rights environment—globalization, transformation of the state, identity and difference, growing political and economic divides, and the mainstreaming of human rights—as well as to the glories of AI's past (Amnesty had "earned a reputation of world standing and commands an identity that is respected across the globe"). Amnesty had to change—to mobilize, to grow, to become more gender-sensitive and more multicultural, and to be more accountable—and the IS had to change too. It was "in transition," said the report.

The key section, however, was on global impact goals (GIGs). These were the human rights themes that the IS intended to work on, drawn from the ISP. In a telling sentence, the draft says, "Setting our global impact goals in terms of themes means that in the vast majority of cases, work at country level will be defined by these themes. Comprehensive country strategies will be developed only where we judge a country to hold global significance for our work. For these we will also develop a Country Action Plan. For countries where no CAP is developed, the global impact goals will be the primary determinant of our work." Themes and CAPs would be chosen, in the final analysis, by the leadership of the movement with input from the researchers. There were eight GIGs in the first draft, policy staff pointing out that there had been a relatively low level of interest in prisoners and prisons. Apart from the death penalty, the traditional work of Amnesty—POCs, torture, extra-judicial executions (EJEs), and disappearances—was mentioned only deeper in the text accompanying the "rights of activists" and "combat human rights erosion" (even then, one director found the eight goals "conservative").[8]

The ISOP drew support from a research review conducted by the Standing Committee on Research and Action (SCRA).[9] The report said that MAC had failed "to produce real global coverage," that the probability of "full spectrum" in 2005 "would place additional demands on a research capacity already stretched beyond reason," and that "changes in *what* AI will research must be accompanied by changes in *how* AI will conduct that research."[10] As per usual, the report pays handsome tribute to the ethos: "The quality of AI's research created an unparalleled reputation of credibility and international authority during its 40 years, and it will be AI's research quality, and principles of impartiality and independence that will allow AI to continue being regarded by the world community as a key player in the international human rights movement." However, "Remaining a relevant and influential international movement within an increasingly complex and sophisticated human rights environment presents a number of significant challenges for Amnesty as it enters the twenty-first century. These challenges will require changes in the way Amnesty's research work is conceptualized and organized."

The report sought, as had CLOD, Participlan, Pierre Sané's Boston ICM paper, and the 1993 Research Review, to enhance "accessible, creative research that stimulates action," expressing a vision of integration, one "in which researchers, campaigners and development staff share a common 'skill mix' allowing them to effectively and instinctively integrate their work." It advocated a more respectful, multicultural working environment and culture that reflects the principles and values of the movement" and more monitoring and evaluation of "effectiveness." For the SCRA, "identified and agreed ISP themes [should be used] as a basis for setting research priorities." Too many decisions were made "ad-hoc, without benefit of transparent and systematic decision-making framework," and there was not enough "field-based quality research that can report back in real time and potentially prevent human rights crises from spiraling out of control." The answer to a better allocation of resources was management: *"Managers will increasingly need to be strategic decision makers rather than senior researchers with program responsibilities."*[11]

The report saw that a centralized secretariat was an institutional reality for a transnational organization, but sought to transfer authority to its managers. Change was sought by members, section staff, the IEC, IS senior managers, and other IS programs. Campaigns staffers and others proposed in June 2003 to "audit the amount of existing work we have got." Their question was blunt: "How much existing work is there?" Only the regional programs really know, and the researchers control this information.[12] The scene was set for a final showdown over the ISOP.

The Final Day Out and the Letter

Before the 2003 Mexico ICM, a further IS Day Out was held to which about 250 staff members came. It took place in a cavernous, gloomy hall in central London. It was a vast and impersonal affair, even though senior management had hoped in advance that it would be a motivational day, a dialog.[13] This meeting was the catalyst for the letter sent to the secretary general warning of the mortal danger the ethos faced. The Day Out began with the usual visionary speeches about the need for the IS to change. But there was a definite undertone. For many staff members, especially those who were new or from resource programs, the fraught business of finalizing the ISP and ISOP—along with the politics of numerous other acronyms—had passed them by.[14]

This was a conversation between the keepers of the flame and senior IS management. The question was: Will you move over? More than a year of relentless meetings had still not produced an answer to this simple question. The management itself was far from unanimous, and despite recruitment efforts a key recommendation of the SCRA report had not materialized at the level of regional program director: the heads of the five regions were all former researchers.[15] Unsurprisingly, when looking for those who might cope with the unique demands of Amnesty life, existing researchers stood out a mile.

The long energy-sapping introductory presentation outlined "AI's theory of social change," stressing that "we must make a difference in the lives of real people." In various submeetings, the different opinions showed through, from researchers, supportive of MAC, saying, "you can't just simply parachute in when it takes your fancy," to senior directors pointing out that at least seventy countries had had no meaningful Amnesty action on them whatsoever. One senior researcher was adamant that "you cannot research themes without country expertise," and that "casework will continue." Another said the ISP was not an Amnesty approach, whereas yet another long-term staffer described it as Stalinist and reiterated, "We were formed as the organization to deal with forgotten prisoners."

Reformers saw things differently. Development managers referred to what the Intrac Report "calls analysis, what we've previously called research." "Development is dead," they said; welcome to "human rights constituency building"—a new language Amnesty must learn to understand. Critics asked how phrases such as *holistic* and *systemic* translated into other languages, and what the new language would mean in Paraguay or Jordan? The conversation went back and forth. One development manager wrote on the board, "Rules, rules, rules . . . mean that big ideas don't get through." At the end, before everyone regathered, one staffer got a round of applause for asking: When, how, and from whom do we get answers to all our questions? Feedback from these meetings was reported to directors with a poignant question: "If we don't maintain systematic links with most countries, what will be the difference between Amnesty International and Human Rights Watch?" The final session to all staffers was treated to an extraordinary PowerPoint presentation that, they were later told, had been hastily prepared during the day. Few staffers seemed convinced, and senior directors rued the fact that it had been put together so efficiently, especially because it led many to fear that some kind of job changes or even redundancies were being planned.[16]

At a follow-up meeting for managers two days later, one said it had seemed like the directors were "preparing people for that moment when all will be revealed." Senior management reiterated that "the truth is there isn't a grand plan. . . . there is a grand process," pointing out that part of Amnesty's "iconography, culture" was that "contempt for management is one of the badges of honor." Another program manager stressed that staff felt there were "real risks" to "our current work . . . our current mandate" and that these were not just fears. This concern became the gist of the letter, of course. But others were openly critical of what they saw as the keepers' "intellectual bigotry" and of the research staff's desire for the kind of control that "doesn't necessarily get you access to the guts stuff where the energy is."

What followed, of course, was the letter. Recall its key sentence: "We owe it to the victims of human rights violations and to the members who believe in Amnesty International's research and action."

The keepers of the flame were the prime movers. Not necessarily the longest time servers, many had been attracted to the IS precisely because of its mix of activism, intellect, and country-based research. For one newer researcher, without concentrated country monitoring Amnesty would be unable to be impartial. She said, "If you take away the responsibility for doing that and then try to come back to countries once every six months or once every year to look for information for the new theme campaigns, for example, you're going to get it wrong and you're going to be used. . . . If I were an [country deleted] NGO I would use Amnesty if I got the chance." Those driving the change, she feared, were "people who've never been in the field and don't know what it looks like" (an added level of country expertise, of course). At the Day Out, directors had talked about Amnesty moving from outsider to insider status. She had been shocked, she said, by this sea change, of which neither she nor, she thought, the membership as a whole were supportive.[17] Amnesty was "weakening our foundations as we're taking on more weight." For these researchers, an attachment to specific countries was not simply a case of transferable skills deployed in one of many possible locations. They were experts on particular places.

When the letter to the secretary general and her deputy arrived, one senior manager said as an aside, "It's just like the good old days," adding quickly, "they do have a point although I'm not allowed to say that." The first staff meeting over the letter had been called after a key group of about twelve from the IS met to talk over their dissatisfaction with the Day Out. They discussed sending a letter to section directors and even considered trying to get it read out at the ICM. In the end, they drew up a draft copy and called the staff meeting, without approval, to discuss it. About 150 people turned up at very short notice. The principal director at this meeting was the deputy secretary general, and key architect of change, Kate Gilmore. A call was made for her to be excluded, which was hastily rejected. The packed meeting was asked who actually wanted change? There was disquiet in the movement about what was happening, staff members were told. Why the shift to themes? Why not regions and countries? The "chilling" crux, as one attendee put it, was that some didn't want the ISOP to go to the ICM as a document from the IS because it was not sufficiently agreed within the IS.

This shows beyond question that management has no natural writ over identity in an organization such as Amnesty and that authority was so dispersed that individuals felt empowered to speak even against corporate decisions of the management and movement. The letter was then opened for signing, along with space for staff to append questions. About thirty union members also met to discuss the Day Out, one researcher saying, "at stake is the future of our organization." The union passed a critical resolution using words such as *disappointed* and *demotivated*. "Trust," it said, had been "undermined," adding that "the truth is that we came along because our managers made it clear that our attendance was expected."

Compelled to respond to this level of dissatisfaction, senior directors accepted that communication may have been "a dog's breakfast," but also that "A handful of people will never be convinced that any change at Amnesty at any time will ever be a good idea." Some felt that it was the "sacred treatment of the mandate we're up against." The response to the Day Out had been anti-intellectual and visceral, and logic had to be reintroduced because "the vast majority are firmly with us." The ISOP had by now been printed in glossy format, with photographs, for the ICM. It did not differ substantially from earlier drafts, although the first of the GIGs on the reform of the justice sector had an important added sentence making it clear the IS would continue to document traditional abuses concerning unfair trials, political prisoners, torture, and POCs.

A final meeting was held in the conference room, and there Irene Khan and Kate Gilmore addressed the staff about the letter. The room was once again packed and expectant. No one was quite sure what to expect. A researcher who was one of the letter writers said, "it was a revolution so we're bound to be stamped on," whereas a senior director said, acerbically, to another key researcher looking for a chair, "come on, you belong at the front." Senior directors began with a clear admission of their communication failure and a promise to "step out of the management structure at times, and to listen to you, to understand you" (adding, "Secretaries general come and go but the IS is here to stay").

But then they stated some givens: that everyone was committed to change, that the IS was only one player in that process inside the AI movement, and that many improvements had taken place through the Change IS process (asking—to some nods from experienced staff members—when it had ever been done better). Staff members expressed their fears about the declining quality of work and its impact on "credibility and effectiveness," one researcher asking bluntly whether the secretary general cared about the dangers of failure. This drew an angry and passionate response from the secretary general that she was as committed to quality as anyone. They had never said the IS would not do country work, adding "at the end of the day people live in countries." But did work on violence against women start in Nigeria or with the global picture, that was the question? And was work on discrimination, women, or children not traditional now?

In the end, no one said, as the letter had: Why are we not doing forgotten prisoners? The movement had already decided they were not and that was, effectively, that. This clear division—between governance of the movement and its staff—had grown inexorably since the 1990s. The final disentangling would come in Mexico.

The Twenty-Sixth ICM, Morelos, Mexico (August 16–23, 2003)

There can be few more elaborate and complex gatherings of delegates from more than sixty countries than the ICM. This is transnational democracy in action. At a cost of nearly £700,000 every two years, it is expensive democracy too.[18] In Mexico, a proposal to move to a three-year cycle (until

1983 it had been annual), saving money but granting more discretion to the movement's leadership, was defeated.[19]

The ICM began in buoyant mood, a pre-Council high-level mission to Mexico by Irene Khan to launch Amnesty's campaign on disappeared young women in the Maquilladora industries on the Mexico-US border had generated substantial press coverage nationally and internationally.[20] The mothers of some of these murdered and disappeared young women made a moving appearance at the ICM and were part of the launch of the SVAW campaign.[21] Furthermore, it was clear that passing the ISP—the main business of the meeting—would be relatively uncontentious (as it was). The most extensive discussion concerned an AI Netherlands's amendment to introduce a core program for all sections to follow, precisely the sort of operational decision the IEC and IS were keen to avoid. Without a core, AI Netherlands's chair feared, common identity would be lost. She wanted "some level of activities that we would all still work on." The amendment was passed, after much redrafting, without any "specific reference to prioritization." An IEC resolution was also passed amending the Statute so that anyone paying annual dues could be a member of Amnesty (rather than just those who were active), affirming the idea of an individual member of Amnesty rather than of an Amnesty section. As an IEC member put it later, "We want to end the idea that because you were born in Holland the only thing you can ever do with Amnesty is through this rigid structure." This gave more reality to international space, requiring only that members "act in accordance with the core values and policies of Amnesty International."

Soon, however, the mood was subdued by the death of the UN human rights commissioner, Sergio Vierra de Mello, after a bombing at his office in Baghdad.[22] In the sections that follow, I draw out four issues from the meeting, held in the luxurious Hotel Hacienda Cocoyoc, an hour's drive from Mexico City: the role of the IS; members and money; Amnesty, war, and impartiality; and the internal SVAW launch.

The Role of the International Secretariat

Great sensitivity surrounds the role of the IS at ICMs. From the vantage point of a year's fieldwork in London, we are apt to forget—as many IS staff clearly do—that there are 1.7 million members out there that the IS notionally serves. We know this is not an accurate picture of the situation, but at the ICM the sense that the IS should be seen and not heard is strong. IS staff members undertake the organization of the ICM, including all the resource support and much more. At senior levels, they may make presentations but have to be asked to speak. One senior director recalled being reported to the chair because he applauded a resolution, which implied that he approved of it. In other words, a ritualistic pretence is maintained that the IS is not involved at every stage in giving serious and detailed strategic and policy advice to the IEC. The IS is part of a management and leadership structure that works to promote various options and defeat others. Particular senior directors can be heavily involved, for example, in behind-the-scenes lobbying, resolution drafting, and coalition building for IEC positions. This was a marked feature of the week in Mexico.

Yet this ICM took a further step. An AI Israel resolution passed eliminating the position of IS representative (staff rep) on the IEC. This was not a matter of great tension. There was little outspoken support and, most crucially, no push from the IEC, senior IS management, or the IS staff to keep it. Meetings at the IS with the popular campaigner who was the current IS member of the IEC attracted no more than a handful of people.[23] Senior IS managers declared themselves neutral, but they certainly had no love for a position that looked anomalous when the IS as a whole was being delinked from the movement's leadership. This was a change from 1991, when the staff rep was described as having "obviously an important [function] in giving a voice to the IS on the IEC and to the wider movement." Established in 1972 to improve the poor staff-movement relations, the staff rep—elected by permanent and volunteer staff at the IS with at least two years experience—had at various stages been both a voting and nonvoting member of the IEC. Staff reps were by convention neither managers nor IEC chairs.[24] They also did not have to be members of Amnesty. At Mexico, an extra member of the IEC was voted on to keep the total number at nine.

Members and Money

What Amnesty wanted to be, ICM delegates were told, was "a multicultural membership-based organization of human rights defenders" (the

ISP envisages 600,000 new members by 2010). But the "McAmnesty model," as the head of the movement's committee on organizational development called it, had failed. It did not help this development presentation that "four middle-aged white men" (in the words of an annoyed senior IS manager) talked at length to the delegates assembled before them behind rows of tables. This meeting was seen as something of a debacle by the IEC members, who noted that there was also "pretty widespread distrust of the IS in handling this area."

The gist of the presentations was a shift, under the ISP, to the idea of mobilization, under which section monopolies in their own countries— "exclusive rights to the AI brand, the AI name"—were to be challenged if sections did not deliver money, people, activism, and diversity. Instead of the blueprint approach, from now on form would follow function. The sections, however, were not happy. Some saw multilingualism as the key and believed the movement was not really serious about it. Others complained that the structures, protosections with as yet no voting rights, could not attend the annual Directors' Forum because they could not pay and the IEC would not pay for them.

AI India continued the theme. Structures were being told they needed a formal board, but this contradicted the notion of a looser, activism-based network. The financial relationship between Amnesty and its structures was likened to the granting of International Monetary Fund (IMF) loans, AI India's delegate telling the audience that he was "yet to see an analysis of how this difference of power is manifested in how Amnesty works." A proposal for project-based funding, rather than ongoing finance, was called a recipe for disaster, and some were concerned that other sections might be able to move into their territory, making Amnesty's local accountability problematic. This is where international space really bites, a single movement that would overcome the traditional sovereign power of each section raising fears of a kind of imperialism. Amnesty politics mimic those of globalization and sovereignty at the national level.

The skewed political economy of the movement is visible in terms of money and the brand. *The brand* is a controversial way to speak about such valued symbols as the candle in barbed wire and the Amnesty name.[25] An entire document for the ICM, written by a movement committee and titled "Managing to Protect AI's image" does not use the word *brand* once.[26] It updates Hammarberg's fears about corruption, covering

Amnesty's involvement with corporate sponsorship and the selling of products and services. (One AI Netherlands director talked at the IS about global merchandizing.) It firmly drew the sacred/profane line from the start: "The [basic] principles have their foundation in protecting the image and reputation of Amnesty International. It is AI's image and reputation that have made it a potent force in support of human rights. The focus of this statement is on protecting that image." The values underlying the image began with impartiality, independence, credibility, and consistency. The document is clear that AI "makes judgements according to its own values and principles" and that "AI's decisions and actions cannot be bought." "Everything AI does can be explained by reference to its own values and processes." Under credibility, it says, "What AI says can be believed because AI has said it. AI says only what it knows to be true, and therefore supports its decisions and actions by proper and adequate research."

This strong residual statement of the ethos (and the use of a classic Amnesty word *image* rather than *brand*) contrasts with other parts of the movement. AI Norway, for example, made a presentation on its human rights education work with the Norwegian oil company Statoil that drew criticism from other members.[27] One delegate from AI Ireland said she was disturbed to see the AI logo near the Statoil logo on the screen and worried about the "contamination of that image." But we know that the brand, protecting it (commercially) and exploiting it, are part of the financial philosophy of the movement's reformers. Furthermore, IS fund-raisers see the biggest potential for membership and money growth within the already-dominant Western sections. The payback for investment here is much greater than "tilting at windmills," as one delegate called it, by chasing more money in the south. Amnesty should get the money where it is and then spend it where the greatest impact can be achieved, he said.

The movement's economy is hugely skewed toward a handful of sections. The assessments for 2004 (the amount each section is expected to contribute to the international movement based on what it declares as its national income) are listed in table 7.1 for the eleven biggest sections. These figures are startling. The twelfth section is Denmark with £352,871, but by the twenty-second, AI Portugal, the annual contribution is down to barely £12,000, as much as we might expect from one wealthy American.

TABLE 7.1
Projected Income from Largest Sections for 2004

Country	Total (£)	Section percentage for IS	Cumulative total (%)
USA	6,221,333	24.54	24.54
UK	4,039,801	15.94	40.48
Netherlands	3,039,895	11.99	52.47
France	2,173,891	8.58	61.05
Germany	1,815,469	7.16	68.21
Switzerland	1,382,469	5.45	73.66
Sweden	955,674	3.77	77.43
Canada (English-speaking)	941,899	3.72	81.15
Italy	939,708	3.71	84.86
Australia	787,953	3.11	87.97
Norway	776,651	3.06	91.03

Most of the eleven largest sections were formed almost immediately after 1961 and still dominate the movement. Just three sections contribute one-half of the international movement's income. The first section that might be considered to be developing is Peru (twenty-seventh largest), contributing £2,428, but then Peru has had two IEC members (who are husband and wife).

That far more money can be found in the West is shown in table 7.2, which ranks the assessments for selected countries as a ratio to population for those countries.[28] Although more income can be generated from the West, without real international space most of it will stay within national domains. Indeed, unhappiness with the IS may well lead—as has happened before—to the sections withholding their "taxes." There is some doubt about whether the bigger sections want to grow at all. Having more members, seen as essential by the international leadership to enhance political authority, means more income, but it also increases administrative tasks (and all for income, a greater proportion of which may be distributed to the rest of the movement). The most obvious manifestation of sections retaining their exclusive control comes from the lack of consolidated global accounts. Even the IEC and the IS do not know how much income the sections receive because the sections are required to submit only a brief summary of their income for assessment purposes. In addition, despite constant entreaties from the IEC and IS, almost no sections have transferred ownership of the Amnesty International name and trademark candle to the international movement. (Put bluntly, if AIUSA

TABLE 7.2
Projected Assessed Income per 1,000 of Population, 2004[a]

Rank Number	Country	Total (£)	Population (thousands)	Assess (£/1,000)
1	Switzerland	1,382,469	7,261	190
2	Netherlands	3,039,895	16,105	189
3	Norway	776,651	4,524	172
4	Sweden	955,674	8,940	107
5	Belgium (Francophone)	341,863	3,718	92
6	Ireland	286,789	3,838	75
7	UK	4,039,801	58,836	69
9	Belgium (Flemish)	286,107	6,591	43
10	Australia	787,953	19,386	41
12	France	2,173,891	59,481	37
14	Iceland	7,064	286	25
16	Germany	1,815,469	82,259	22
17	USA	6,221,333	288,368	22

[a] *From AI Index: FIN 60/002/2003.*

decided to go it alone tomorrow, it could continue to use the candle and the name without any legal obstacles.)

Because the first meeting on growth had gone badly, a second was convened to try to repair some of the damage. This session was designed to be more inspirational, with senior IS managers taking a role and asking the movement to "come with us." They used the term *money without borders* and stressed that giving financially was only one way to contribute to Amnesty. The big sections were more or less silent throughout this discussion.

Amnesty, War, and Impartiality

The invasion of Iraq and the UN's use of armed force in the Ituri region of the Democratic Republic of the Congo (DRC) presented Amnesty with a dilemma. Although union members at the IS are heavily involved in the Stop the War Coalition (holding meetings, publicizing demonstrations, putting up posters, and collecting signatures), when they march the banner they use is "Human rights workers against the war" to avoid any association with Amnesty (one told me, however, she was certain that "in its heart" Amnesty was against the war). Amnesty is not a pacifist organization, but its no-position position on war is deep-seated among parts of the membership. One IS staff member, strongly against the war, recalled going with AIUK members on a demonstration outside Parliament in London on the day war broke out:

> We got this little lecture about how we had to behave ourselves properly according to the guidelines. But I've never seen any guidelines. I don't know what they thought we were going to do. This was already beginning to grate somewhat. And then they wanted us all to wear a T-shirt but wouldn't give us one . . . and then we're told it's a silent vigil and we're not allowed to carry the placards on the coach to Parliament Square in such a way as to indicate we were protesting. . . . And then as we were walking to the vigil, these two people behind me from the coach were complaining about how the school students were giving the anti-war movement a really bad name because they were being terribly anti and breaking the law and wasn't it dreadful and they clearly didn't understand the intricacies . . . and at that point I just walked off, coach or no. So I do think I'm at variance with the membership here as well.

Contrast this with a senior IS staffer, standing in the kitchen holding his tea mug, passionately contesting the IEC's decision to allow Amnesty members to march because (the IEC said) the antiwar coalition was broad enough that you could be marching against the consequences of war not against war itself. These people should not wear an Amnesty T-shirt or badge, he argued, because they would be using Amnesty for their own personal positions.

Amnesty's public position on Iraq was that war should only be used as a last resort. This was seen as a shift, a more radical interpretation of Decision 7 of the 1997 ICM, which stated, "Amnesty International currently takes no position on the desirability or otherwise of armed intervention or the use of force in any circumstances including, in particular, in crises or situations of mass human rights violations." When it came, later in 2003, to the question of sending UN troops to Ituri in the DRC, with the DRC's consent, the IEC opted to join with Human Rights Watch in supporting a rapid deployment force. It was this decision that drew fire in Mexico. Several emergency resolutions were tabled; some sections worried about the IEC making such a quick decision, and some worried about the decision itself. Some were strongly critical of what they saw as the IEC, after a short email consultation, contradicting ICM policy. Constant behind-the-scenes negotiating by the IEC—with substantial IS input— amended resolutions so the IEC could accept them. The strongest critic of the IEC's policy was the French Section, which felt that a "fundamental rule on a very important subject was not being followed." "Amnesty has never called for armed forces," the section said, whereas the "IEC acts as guardian for the rules we set ourselves." The IEC disagreed vehemently that the decision was outside policy. The armed Ituri force was to place itself between the warring factions, not on one side or the other. This left a related issue, a pre-ICM amendment on impartiality from the French Section. IS senior managers saw this as an attempt to reintroduce mandate-style language by the back door, and they urged the IEC to oppose it.

The French Section chair told delegates that Amnesty had signed the European Social Forum Charter even though it was explicitly "opposed to neo-liberalism and the domination of the world by capital." The Dutch Section agreed, unconvinced when it was told that the IEC was "building a bridge between the old Amnesty and the new Amnesty." It wanted guidelines on independence and impartiality. AI India, in contrast, asked members to have "the courage to step forward and to tell the world we are with the victims"—*that*, delegates were told, was impartiality. This view prevailed, and the resolution was lost. Although there were glimpses of the old Amnesty, many issues that had once been (pre-Dakar) deeply problematic for Amnesty—work on nuclear weapons testing, children's rights, and AIDS—were agreed on with minimal contention. Exemplifying this new world was the SVAW campaign.

The Internal Stop Violence Against Women Launch

In the end, the launching of the SVAW campaign was the highlight of the ICM. In a strongly symbolic manner, delegates (me included) painted one hand with orange, blue, purple, or green paint and placed it on one of three banners demanding an end to violence against women. They then queued to wash their painted hands in a bucket of water at the end of the table. Some kept the paint on their hand, and you could see various delegates with its remnants throughout the week.[29] One of these banners was given to the Mothers of the Disappeared from Ciudad Juarez at a ceremony where they were told "those handprints are a sign of hope and solidarity to the Mothers of Juarez" (followed by all the delegates, wearing Stop VAW T-shirts, gathering on the steps of the main meeting hall to chant, "No more violence against women," in Spanish while press photographers took pictures).

This fine visual symbolism was accompanied by tougher internal meetings. IS staff members described violence against women as "tantamount to a pandemic," stressing that although a latecomer Amnesty was in a good position to engage men in a way the women's movement was not. Rape would also be classified as torture, delegates heard. But the difficult question was abortion. The proposed policy, arising out of the Oxford meeting (see chap. 6), was the decriminalization of abortion as a first step, grounding that work in sexual and reproductive rights and in the right to health. Would Amnesty, an IEC member asked, support the right to abortion? Although it passed without too much comment at the first meeting, during which a continuous stream of IS, IEC, and section staff members spoke, concern rose that abortion rights had just been dropped on the table and that this was consultation. Sections wanted another meeting, but the IEC was worried it might "spin out of control" and Amnesty would be "hopelessly mired." Sections feared the IEC had made a decision and that the IS was just "waiting for the movement to go away again."

In the end, an open discussion was held to keep things informal and avoid a policy clash. The IEC challenged delegates to ensure that there would never again be an ICM delegation without a woman, and IS senior management told delegates the "symbol of the paint" was a stain to remind the movement that its credibility and authenticity was at stake. Most floor contributions were supportive, as it transpired, and oddly so, because listening to the questions you would have presumed there were no policy issues. It was left for a future ICM to try to move Amnesty to support the right to abortion.

Conclusion

The visionary rhetoric at Mexico drew heavily on the imagery of the past. Secretary General Irene Khan talked about "when I first took the candle from Pierre" while speeches paid tribute to Amnesty "holding the candle high in forgotten conflicts." Amnesty was about change in the lives of ordinary people, about lived experience: "Amnesty International was born a campaign and to this heritage we must remain true." But old rules and old tools had to go, she added. In a borderless world, Amnesty needed to move away from WOOC toward global themes, strategic coverage, and research management. The shift was from adopting victims to empowering individuals. For SVAW, Amnesty had to "unfurl a compelling banner of insistence." "Our promises, our dreams can become a reality," said a senior IEC member. But behind the scenes concern about realities would not abate. Sections were worried about many of the things the keepers of the flame were—loss of consistency and identity, strategic coverage, research quality, and the importance of country work. Many established Amnesty members clearly knew, of old, that the key question was: What will the researchers actually do? Intensive management by the IEC and IS was designed to avoid these operational questions from being aired, the ISP being a "leap beyond anything we have ever done before," in the words of a senior movement member.

Reservations about the speed of reform came, on the whole, from the more established European sections. AI Netherlands (on identity and priorities), AI France (on impartiality), AI Germany (on country work), and AI Sweden (on relief) all voiced concern about the pace, if not the overall direction, of change. AIUK was more progressive, having undergone a radical internal transformation (as evidenced in its work on branding), although it was strangely muted in Mexico. AIUSA, despite its large delegation and strategic weight, was no more in evidence than any other section, although several influential AIUSA senior members were present on various movement committees. There can, however, be few transnational organizations in which the U.S. voice is so relatively subdued.

The IEC immediately placated AI France and AI Germany by telling them that "country work will have to continue to be the central core to how we organize our research" but "we can no longer have a researcher who's named on each country." IS management began to use the words *global monitoring*, something short of MAC but a concession to the idea of maintaining a residual ability to monitor human rights in all countries.

The IS and the IEC worked tirelessly to manage the safe passage of the ISP. It was not always clear that even all IEC members were entirely sympathetic to what they had to say, especially in areas such as MAC and research. There was clearly movement support for more work on children, for example, and the IS once or twice tried to stiffen IEC resolve. As the ICM chair told them, if resolutions are passed outside the scope of the ISP, "you have to implement them" and this will take precedence over the ISP.

Through the many hours of discussions on resolutions, amendments, points of order, and voting, I was struck by how much it all owed to British parliamentary procedure and how advantaged were those familiar with the complex activity of drafting, especially when the nuance of words was the issue. I could also see the virtues of this process for enabling a diverse multinational movement to survive for forty years. It has been a cumbersome but pragmatic mechanism for dispute resolution.[30] Most of all, it was odd that the IS was so present and yet so invisible when so much of what the movement was proposing was for the IS to deliver.

8

AMNESTY IN PRACTICE

the perils and promises of turning moral capital into political authority could hardly have been better demonstrated than in Amnesty's 2005
broadside against the U.S. government. When it called Guantanamo a
gulag, Secretary of Defense Donald Rumsfeld replied that "those who
make such outlandish charges lose any claim to objectivity or serious-
ness."[1] For most of my year's fieldwork, the secretary general had "advocacy, not impartiality" written in red on the whiteboard in her office. The
gulag taunt, and the decision to make it, was a calculated example of that
advocacy. It clearly stung U.S. officials, forcing the Bush White House into
the open to defend itself. It is a sign of Amnesty's moral authority that it
can name and shame in this way. But as Secretary Rumsfeld's response
implies, once one is off the fence it is hard to get back on. Indeed, for the
holders of political authority there is no longer any pretense that a fence
exists. In other words, the dilemmas of previous chapters are real, not
esoteric, and a great deal is at stake. This is not, however, the place to
revisit the many claims made in preceding chapters. Instead, I take a look
at four questions that run through the entire book in more or less explicit
ways. We deal first with subjectivity and objectivity. To put it crudely, I
pit objectivity against subjectivity and then pit subjectivity against objectivity. We need to see morality as social but real. I then look at the resulting picture of Amnesty, relate it to the advantages and limitations of
Durkheim's account, and propose a way forward that leaves behind the
dualism of agency (subjectivity) versus structure (objectivity). The key
role of IS practice as an interpreter of these binary oppositions is highlighted, drawing on the work of Pierre Bourdieu, and some reservations
made about the way in which constructivists deal with identity-action

issues in international politics. The final section is about ethics. It includes some reflection on my fieldwork in Amnesty, and asks how we might think about our personal morality under modernity.

Keeping It Real

For Amnesty, two claims to objectivity have been important: factual and moral. Is unflinching realism evidence of constructed or discovered truth? An objective reality is one that can be seen and described by you, me, or anyone, in more or less identical terms. The meaning of what we see is inherent in the thing that is seen, not in our interpretation of it. If it is an example of X, we all see an X and describe it thus. Richard Wilson's view, in contrast, is that the truth of X is constructed out of a few bare facts (e.g., that someone was killed) and a great deal of interpretation: "The indeterminacy of the event and the heterogeneous nature of bystanders' narratives hamper the coherence of a single inte-grated plot, which is highly disconcerting for those seeking actionable certainties. Human rights reports must therefore impose meaning on the chaos and incoherence of events. Further, occurrences are universalized, that is, they are re-presented in human rights reports in such a way that the event can be comprehended by readers on the other side of the globe."[2]

I have no real quarrel with this account. But I do want to suggest that we can conceive of "truth"—of meaning—as existing in precisely the few bare facts, preelaboration. Central to this is the awareness of individual human frailty, of the physical vulnerability of a person alone. The elabora-tion of this "truth" in the classic Amnesty style is designed not to tell a story but to try to do the opposite (as far as the inherent limitations of language allow). It would be most affecting if we could all just see it, without words and in the first person, but in the absence of proximity words and pictures become our telescope. This is why pictures are often more powerful than words but also why the most effective words paint a picture that connects the reader as fully as possible to the sensations that she or he might have experienced being there. Any word from the writer—an adjective or adverb or sentiment that reminds us the writer is there—jars with this unadulterated access. It confounds, rather than con-structs, the truth. We cease, all of a sudden, to be fully a subject, focused wholly on this external event, and become existentially aware that we are an object too. There is someone else, in our relationship with the victim, watching us respond.

Take an iconic late-twentieth-century image: the young Chinese man standing in front of a column of advancing tanks near Tiananmen Square in June 1989. What was the meaning of this act? According to Richard Gordon, when Chinese television broadcast the film widely it was as evidence for the restraint of the soldiers in the face of a "lone scoundrel." In the West, of course, it symbolized one man's courage in the face of brutal state power and became the defining image of Tiananmen for millions.[3]

The fact was: man stands in front of tanks. We need some background knowledge (to know what a tank is, for example). What if the man was blocking a tank in Berlin in 1945 to protest against the downfall of the Nazis? Would we view his act the same way then? Perhaps not. But it would still be courageous, on its own terms, and besides we are doing something else now: explaining, categorizing, politicizing. Isn't there a moment before that, perhaps fleeting, but real nonetheless, of recognition? One when we recognize courage and sacrifice, and sense violence fear, and death? The most potent bare facts concern death—its occurrence, imminence, possibility—all without context, and all saturated with the presumption of innocence. Richard Wilson wants context, as do many critics of Amnesty's classic style. I suggest moral authority relies on its absence. Only then can we hope to make plausible the claim that there is a normative sphere somehow beyond politics, with all of its conflicts of interest and identity. The bare facts are like fleeting glimpses of this sphere, a place where we see our true vulnerability both as individuals and as a species. We do this absent motive. Before we ask why, we just see. The ideal-type case may be self-immolation. Is there any way to see pictures of someone self-immolating, engulfed in the flames, and escape that frozen moment in time when the fabric of our mortality is briefly revealed in full to our senses? Only then come the words, the rendering of this transcendent insight into narratives of innocence and guilt, choice and responsibility, rationality, morality, and blame. This is the process of construction: unflinching realism, however unsatisfactory, is an attempt to avoid it. The more purely descriptive the words, the nearer we approximate pure recognition.

Let me be clear. Recognizing courage and human mortality in this way is, I think, learned, not innate. It is neither natural (inherent in the human condition, universal, or eternal) nor God-given (there are, after all, many kinds of god). It may be, and perhaps is, to anticipate Marx, bourgeois ideology. And it clearly resonates fully only with a particular audience, one largely, although far from exclusively, rooted in the idealism of the West and its often sentimental, uncritical, unreflective, and contradictory attachment to notions of innocence, enlightenment, and moral progress. And it is not a product of thinking either—reason cannot tell us how to feel.

In chapter 1, I said it was like an archetype. It is embedded so deeply in our cultural heritage that it seems like a natural fact. Its specific manifestation in Amnesty's case was the POC. Unflinching realism aimed at stirring the recognition of something that was already there, deep within. Words are a medium, and something cultural but real lies beyond them. For some, these words spark a sense of where meaning can be seen and touched when we cannot see it or touch it ourselves.

Amnesty is mobilized around this truth. From POCs to torture to women's rights, its core concern has been with the worst abuses, with those that deal with the darkest human shadow—death, violence, and emotional and physical pain. Amnesty has taken us as close as it can to the threshold between life and death, where sacrifice and extreme suffering are the norm.

Objectivity, Identity, and Need

"How can an *I* that has taken on the perspective of impartiality be left with enough identity to live a life that respects its own interests?"[4] This question, asked by moral philosopher Bernard Williams, can just as reasonably be addressed to Amnesty. It was described in chapter 1 as a first-person point of view. We may think about ethical questions by taking a step back, but when we come to act we must act in the first person. And for that we need an identity, to know who we are and where we are in the world. We need to be someone or something with discernible qualities and characteristics.

It is in situations in which we are called on to act, rather than reflecting on action in the abstract, that our moral options become clearest. For Bonhoeffer:

There can be ethics only in the framework of history, in the concrete situation, at the moment of the divine call, the moment of being addressed, of the claim made by the concrete need and the situation for decision, of the claim which I have to answer and for which I have to make myself responsible. There cannot be ethics in a vacuum, as a principle; there cannot be good and evil as general ideas, but only as qualities of will making a decision. . . . In ethical decisions we are brought into the deepest solitude, the solitude in which man stands before the living God.[5]

Amnesty was founded as the embodiment of universality—open to all, concerned with all. Its space is third-person space. It was precisely not representative of a particular identity or interest. This meant it had no thick social and cultural identity to reason from in making choices. If there was any danger of this, and we can see that it is to some extent unavoidable given its class, gender, and ethnic origins, a whole series of mechanisms were created to try to prevent it. It tried actively to discourage the first-person voice.

How, then, did Amnesty make choices? Initially it did not have to. The POCs made up the whole work, and the perpetuation of this basic technique obviated the need for any explicit evaluation of what Amnesty was and what it stood for. Universal human rights were a rhetorical device for spreading the word; they were not the reason why Amnesty existed. It was never going to release more than a tiny proportion of POCs, but then again it did not need to. It just needed to keep the flame burning in the darkness and gather people around it.

In a 1998 speech, Pierre Sané observed, "Amnesty was not established to free prisoners of conscience. Amnesty was established to contribute to the full realization of Human rights for all." He went on, "And we chose at the beginning to work for the release of prisoners of conscience because, at the time, the prisoners of conscience were maybe the best symbol of Human rights and maybe was the best way to introduce Human rights to the great public."[6] The mandate, he added, was not a core value but a strategy. This is, I think, both right and wrong. Yes, a certain spirit lies behind Amnesty—and behind human rights for that matter (they are not bedrock)—which Benenson expressed as the "benevolent influence of a universal, uniting, indomitable power usually referred to as compassion" and which I have described as a kind of faith in the spirit of natural rights. POCs were a perfect symbolization of this spirit. But practice is real; it is how ethics get meaning, as Bonhoeffer suggests. Thus, the mandate was a self-validating core practice, and Amnesty was what it did. After AI's success, and as its focus expanded, the prisoner orientation remained. In campaigns and reports on torture, the death penalty, and disappearances, attention remained on those who could not speak for themselves (hence, the still-crucial notion of victims).

Once it began to move away from this solitary figure without social content toward issues in which there was more politics—gay rights, women's rights, economic rights—it was choosing sides. But the advocates of *a* moral law cannot be the judges (who must arbitrate in terms of *the* law). By what principles was AI now choosing, when any choice diminished the purity of the ideal. Here's a senior manager talking about choosing:

> We need to prioritize. And someone actually said to me she thought it was dirty to prioritize. To try and make comparisons between human rights abuses. Because that was, you know . . . somehow it was unacceptable. That, you know, it was dirty. Those were the words she used. So. You know. And so there's a huge amount of emotion there around having to try and let go of some areas or even a recognition that you can't do everything. A difficulty is actually subjecting that thinking of bearing witness to a more pragmatic approach. . . . How do you bear witness to everything simultaneously?

Choices have been made by researchers for more than thirty years in the context of the lore and in their position as the experts. Here's one of Amnesty's most experienced researchers talking about the movement setting priorities: "Somebody in my perspective would think they were interfering too much or they were interfering on the basis [of] ignorance and actually distorting the program in order to conform to the needs of the membership. That became a tension. *We who were working on the countries themselves knew what the countries needed in Amnesty terms.* You know, and our first sort of clientele, if you will, was the contacts or the victims in the countries."[7]

Moral authority is not political authority. Politics is based on difference, on competing interests, on the distribution of scarce resources. You cannot stand for the whole *and* for restitution between one part of the whole and another. After the 1980s, and especially after the end of the Cold War, the search began for new, inevitably more political moorings. Subuniversal identities and interests were drawn to Amnesty's moral authority, its disinterested detachment having created moral power that advocates of various partial rights saw they could use. The metric was: "Help people like us." And social progress mattered. As one reformer put it, "What you get from being right is just self-satisfied." Taking sides and prioritizing the greatest need—this is the reformers' strategy for the future. It is no longer "what's right is right" but "what can we achieve and for whom?" A strategy paper on economic, social, and cultural (ESC) rights, the main umbrella for introducing many new, more political rights, issued on Human Rights Day in 2002, was actually called "Making Choices on Economic, Social and Cultural Rights." In it, Amnesty acknowledges the difficulties involved in choosing among rights on principle. But, if all rights are equally important, how do you choose one? The old answer was to symbolize how important they all were. "Making Choices" continues:

In the strategic decisions human rights organizations take, they should be guided as much as possible by the gravity of the abuses, and more specifically, by the gaps that exist in the protection offered against those abuses. A focus on gravity of abuses also leads to a focus on individuals and communities that have suffered the most abuse, and to the relevance of the prohibition of discrimination as a tool for offering protection. In addition, it suggests prioritizing issues that can be demonstrated by stories of individuals and communities that have been affected.

The gravity of the abuse, discrimination, impact—all these reasons have an underlying metric that takes us to consequences, to the questions: Whose suffering is worst, and who needs us most? "Making Choices" is frank:

All human rights organizations face resource constraints, and need to select areas of work in order to guarantee the accuracy of research, but also to ensure that the workload is manageable. Selection is inevitable. It is important to communicate explicitly on the arguments that support the choices made, in order to avoid raising expectations the organization will not be able to fulfil. A prerequisite for good external communication is that the organization is explicit and clear internally on the limitations of its work.

This pragmatism—anchored in increasing utility, not in incontrovertible rights and wrongs—has been most marked in the United States.[8] Within Amnesty over the last twenty years, the most powerful single section, AIUSA, has pushed for the kind of democratic authority that owes a great deal to pragmatist philosophy. It was referred to earlier as being politically smart, understanding that you need members, money, and influence to change policy, that outcomes are what matter, and that U.S. power is a reality to be harnessed, tamed, and redirected rather than resisted. One senior AIUSA official in a meeting at the IS, for example, bemoaned the fact that Amnesty could not speak out in favor of democracy, rendering it "obsolete to the point of making us irrelevant" in the United States after September 11 and the Iraq war. AIUSA was even censured by the movement for speaking out on its own against the demotion of the United States from the Human Rights Commission.

Several prominent and influential academics in the United States advance the pragmatist argument philosophically and politically. For Michael Ignatieff, for example, "Elevating the moral and metaphysical claims made on behalf of human rights may be intended to increase its universal appeal. In fact, it has the opposite effect, raising doubts among religious groups and non-Western groups who do not happen to be in need of Western secular creeds." He goes on, "It may be tempting to relate the idea of human rights to propositions like the following: that human beings have an innate or natural dignity, that they have a natural and intrinsic self-worth, that they are sacred. The problem with these propositions is that they are not clear and they are controversial. They are not clear because they confuse what we wish men and women to be with what we empirically know them to be." He fears metaphysical claims "fragment commitment to the practical responsibilities entailed by human rights," the intrinsic contestability of such claims inescapable in terms of whether and how human beings might be thought of as sacred. He concludes, "Foundational claims of this sort divide, and those divisions cannot be resolved in the way humans usually resolve their arguments, by means of discussion and compromise. Far better, I would argue, to forgo these kinds of foundational arguments altogether and seek to build support for human rights on the basis of what such rights actually *do* for human beings."[9]

David Kennedy shares this emphasis on what human rights actually do, as does Richard Rorty, who sees hope in the replacement of the question: "what is our nature?" by the more pragmatic "what can we make of ourselves?"[10] For Kennedy, human rights advocates "have too often treated our norms as true—rather than as reminders of what might be made true."[11] He, like Ignatieff, is wary of idolatry. His is an argument for a kind of disenchanted pragmatic renewal, one that is world-weary, focused on consequences, vigilant about the betrayal of humanitarian ideas, and yet all too aware of the shadow side of humanitarianism and its inherent limitations. It is always a work in progress. Human rights activists are rulers, for Kennedy, and they should rule responsibly, both "speaking to power and as power."[12] He is strongly critical of the imperviousness to criticism of human rights advocates and humanitarians who, despite the "global flood of law," see their projects as "weak and marginal": "Thinking we light only a single candle, we fail to look beyond its dim light to see the consequences—also the darker consequences—of our humanitarian work."[13] He says, "We should foster our will to power and embrace the full range of our effects on the world. Thinking of our humanitarianism as force, we will no longer be tempted to nurture it protectively, preserving its knowledge and clarity, that it might one day express itself as counterforce to the power and politics of others. We can turn our attention to building a terrain for politics and political choice, letting go the will to know, but not to do."[14]

This kind of pragmatism has been marked in AIUSA. It is illustrated in an exchange between IS researchers in the Americas Program and AIUSA staff concerning how to release three Mexican POCs in the year 2000 (one of them was General Gallardo). AIUSA asked the IS whether the new president-elect Fox had the power to free them. The IS replied that he did but that AI policy was not to advise the government how to do it but just to do it. AIUSA came back that this was not helpful, that the first days of a new presidency were a good time politically to apply pressure and that pointing out the ways in which it could be done prevented the government from making excuses. The IS replied again that "immediate and unconditional release" was the only demand—no political considerations, questions of fair trial, torture or mistreatment, or procedural irregularities were relevant in POC cases. This went back and forth again with AIUSA eventually saying to the IS, "L'etat ce n'est pas vous," after Americas Program staff told them the IS was only faithfully following AI's approach. One side was prepared to try all available means; the other wanted to stick close to the principle of unconditional release (the view of the staffer who showed me the emails had shifted in the intervening years closer to the AIUSA position).

But, in the end, doesn't pragmatism depend on agreed social and cultural values? Doesn't it make so much sense in the United States because it is ultimately grounded in political liberalism? And doesn't political liberalism make so much sense in the West because it is consistent with core aspects of the legacy of Christianity and capitalism? Isn't there a political ideology behind universal human rights, making the "new Amnesty" a more self-aware advocate for values that *are* ultimately best observed in Western societies? Is this why membership is skewed as it is? At the ICM in Mexico, Eastern European and Asia-Pacific members invited delegates to a party with a flyer headed, "AI 2020 Party, The Colonies Strike Back!" It had a graphic that imagined AI membership in 2020, showing only 5 percent in the United States and 5 percent in Western Europe. Eastern and central Europe had 15 percent, Africa, Central America, and Latin America had 20 percent each, and Asia-Pacific had 35 percent. That this is simply inconceivable should make us pause for thought. One Asian IS staffer said that when she goes home she does not even tell her family she works for Amnesty (they think it is just part of the UN anyway, she said).

As pragmatists recognize, choices must be made and choices can only be made from a point of view. This means that to choose and act ethically we must move into the first person (be ourselves, be Amnesty) and weigh the consequences of our actions accordingly. An interest in this sense means not "what is good for us" but "on what reason will I turn reflection into a decision to do A or B." This is taking an interest, taking action. Thus, I argue, impartial morality must become consequential to be practical. Someone or something with concrete properties must choose under conditions of scarcity (when everything we all want cannot be met). Amnesty is as near to pure impartial morality as we are ever likely to get. But moral problems are irredeemably practical.

Identity, Reflection, and Action

Even if our interests are linked to who we are, to our identity (our first persons), it is nonsensical to argue that our identities determine our interests because this leaves out deliberation entirely.[15] Unless behavior is compulsive, wholly explained by physical urges, or we become automatons mindlessly implementing rules, there is a gap, in John Searle's terms, that needs to be filled. In fact there are three gaps: between beliefs and decision, between decision and action, and between an initial action and its continuation.[16] The IS researchers, the architects of human rights practice, exist in these gaps within a material and moral structure, possessing beliefs that make what may once have been contingent possibilities seem like certainties but also with the awareness and practical skill to engage in self-conscious social action that conforms neither to the dictates of structure nor the open vista of unbridled agency.

Within the academic theory of international relations, it is only more recent critical approaches that have opened up the study of this gap (ironically, given that politics *is* the gap). More orthodox theories have taken the positivist view that one fully constituted subject, say Amnesty, impacts on an object, say Burma, trying to get the latter not to change its interest—for that is always the same (i.e., pursuing its own power)—but how it conceives of what will best achieve that interest. This particular example is of no relevance to mainstream international relations—there, Amnesty's moral power is considered no kind of power at all. Even liberal critics of this account, who see some hope for cooperation and progress, stress the given nature of identities, interests, and strategic interaction.

From the 1980s onward, poststructuralists, critical theorists, and feminists have succeeded in widening the cracks in this hegemonic account. In the 1990s, a group of constructivist scholars much closer to the mainstream—close enough to be called a "domesticated critique"[17]—have made inroads into the orthodoxy by asking how identities and interests get formed, by asking where ideas come from, and by studying the emergence and dissemination of international moral norms.[18] Martha

Finnemore argues, for example, that NGOs can teach states what to want, international norms changing state-preferences (a thin term for identity) and so their interests.[19] Margaret Keck and Kathryn Sikkink have charted this process historically, whereas Thomas Risse, Stephen Ropp and Sikkink again have looked at the mechanisms by which these norms are exported and embedded.[20] There are then empirically richer accounts that look in more detail at workings within the gap.[21]

Keepers of the Flame belongs, broadly, in this tradition. Critiques of more conventional, domesticated constructivism have alleged it pays too little attention to language and that it "obscures the politics already involved in representing reality."[22] This account of Amnesty's internal processes avoids some of these pitfalls.[23] Its intention has been to focus our attention on practice, understood neither as derived solely from structures (of language, morality, and materiality) nor as the product of heroic agency. In chapters 3 and 6, for example, we locate Amnesty and especially the IS very firmly within its historical-cultural background, whereas in chapters 4 and 5 we see how practice has evolved over time. The IS and Amnesty leaders still innovate, problem solve, and develop strategies for action. The choice of the word "gulag," for example, sent Amnesty down one path rather than another. Amnesty has not been the inevitable unfurling of some logic inherent in universal human rights.

In fact, one of this book's stronger claims is that there is nothing self-evident about the meaning of human rights at all. They are made, not discovered. They get their meaning through practice. They are what they have become. I argue in the first section of this chapter that underlying this was an historical-cultural sentiment about death and moral courage so deep as to be, in effect, an objective moral fact. But the moment this recognition is cast into words, interpretation and mobilization, the triggering of the will begins, and then we are fully in the world of social construction.

Amnesty had no preordained historical role to play. Practice came before identity. It was made, not from nothing, but from bits of other things. There is a plasticity about words, concepts, beliefs, and social action for which positivist, rationalistic, and structural theories cannot account.

This jars with Durkheim's structuralism, in which rules can exist even if no one applies them.[24] His argument has served us well this far, as summarized in the following claim: "No society can exist that does not feel the need at regular intervals to sustain and reaffirm the collective feelings and ideas that constitute its unity and its personality."[25] This reminds us of two important things. First, religion is about social integration and self-recognition, not divine presence. Religious behavior can be present in the most secular of settings. Second, human beings create meaning for themselves through their collective endeavors, especially when these concern emotionally potent life experiences such as death and suffering. A spirit is generated that makes the whole seem more than the sum of the parts. We are at our best, and our worst, when we are organized together for action because we are at the closest point to the threshold between the sacred and the profane, between meaning and day-to-day existence. It is only here that we feel strongly enough to contemplate transcending our bonds.

Amnesty is potent evidence for a kind of secular religiosity born of collective action, sacrifice, and suffering. But the IS and its toiling staff have not been unwitting ciphers or transmitters of iron laws. They have helped make and shape morality—in the language of universal human rights—to be what it is. Thus, we have focused a great deal of attention on practice. This necessitates, as the method and approach of this book have shown, taking an anthropological and sociological look at key features of the international system.[26]

One example of taking these shapers seriously as structured structurers is through the work of Pierre Bourdieu. The virtue of Bourdieu's theoretical scheme, and one that conventional constructivists ought to heed, is that of giving a qualified independence to agents while accepting that much of what they think, believe, and value is the product of historical structures. In seeing this, we cannot separate an international NGO—funded, staffed, and run from the West—from those historical structures (of capital, culture, ideology, law, and morality) of which it is a product. To look at the formal distinction between an international NGO and a state is to miss all that is shared, taken-for-granted, and too obvious to mention. This is why constructivists persist in arguing that norms can be bad but focus only on the good. In theory yes, in (current) practice no. The only practices that can plausibly be called international norms in the modern era are, for deep historical-structural reasons of state and capital power, those that accord with liberalism and the hegemony of the West.

The key concept for Bourdieu is *habitus,* defined as "principles which generate and organize practices and representations that can be objectively adapted to their outcomes without presupposing a conscious aiming at ends or an express mastery of the operations necessary in order to attain them."[27] This habitus is a product of history and, in turn, produces history; it can be "creative, inventive" but only "within the limits of its structures, which are the embodied sedimentation of the social structures which produced it."[28] There is a script, in other words, but actors may improvise and ad-lib within its structure and text. In this way we can both explain the practical mastery that keepers of the flame have shown in elaborating the practice of human rights activism and not neglect the ways in which they have nevertheless reproduced various structures of meaning, of which they themselves have not necessarily been consciously aware.

If I have not used Bourdieu more explicitly in this book, it is because that would decenter the practitioners and this book is about them and their practice. Bourdieu's scheme can help us in a way that no orthodox international relations theory, and precious little constructivism, can. What we learn is that identity emerges partly out of ongoing practice. It cannot be read off from theory, as if in a manual, and when phrases such as *the logic of appropriateness* and *moral entrepreneurs* are used, we need to know a great deal more about what is appropriate, why it is considered so, and what is meant by moral. Thus, we have the irony that although Amnesty is the core case for the advocates of the spread of global human rights norms and those who believe that we live in an age of emerging global civil society, it is not first and foremost a human rights organization at all. It is much more like a Free Church whose main product, thus far, has been moral authority, not social change. If it has championed the cause of human rights, it has been as a means to broadcast that moral authority, to carry its core message that its main work is to symbolize transcendent principles. It remains part of a nascent global civil society, but it must be theorized in a very different way as a result.

How Should We Be Now?

For MSF president Jean-Hervé Bradol, humanitarian action is "an art of living founded on the pleasure of unconditionally offering people at risk of death the assistance that will allow them to survive."[29] This is seeing the glass half full. Altruism produces just as much misery. That morality hurts is a sign that it is indeed morality (see later discussion of Kant). Why not earn 50 percent more doing a commercial job and give half of that surplus to a worthy cause? Must it really be *you* who does the work? And yet, don't we desire employment that does not alienate us from our real selves? Work that is a calling? Recall an earlier quotation (chap. 5) from 1991: "Several IS staff expressed the fear that there seemed to be a conflict between the values of staff and volunteers which at times of tension can appear to be exploited. In this context the work of volunteers is regarded as being of greater moral worth. . . . At times there appears to be a strange perception that real activism is only undertaken by the volunteer segment of the movement. Given the composition of IS staff the RC finds it difficult to understand how such a perception can rationally be sustained."[30] At first I could not see how such a perception could not be rationally sustained—working all day and only then devoting yourself to writing letters, raising money, or going on marches. Then, I understood better. To do Amnesty work for a living, with its endemic stress, sense of guilt, and poor material rewards, was seen by those who did it as at least an equal sacrifice. Must a veteran IS researcher really see a member giving money as a *more* moral contribution? One long-serving researcher said it was her "duty to protect Amnesty's reputation." It is not a job. For keepers of the flame, it is not like being part of the human rights movement, with its higher salaries, career structure, and mainstream profile. This is why the revelation at the Day Out that senior managers envisaged a shift from outsider to insider status came as such a shock.

This sense of duty, central to the ethos, is highly redolent of Kantianism—the "what's right is right" side of the equation from chapter 1. For Kant, in order for an act to be morally good, it had to not only conform to the moral law (i.e., be good in actuality), but it also had to "be done for the sake of the law." This gives true moral worth only to acts undertaken from duty (because you should) rather than from inclination (because you want to).[31] Richard Rorty considers it astonishing that Kant claims "sentimentality has nothing to do with morality, that there is something distinctively and transculturally human called the sense of moral obligation which has nothing to do with love, friendship, trust, or social solidarity."[32] The problem, as Kant would be the first to point out, is that this has no moral purchase on those who are not inclined to help. What can we say to them? Rorty says we should tell them sad stories, Martha Nussbaum advocates "education for world citizenship," and David Kennedy retains faith in the "humanitarian impulse."[33] These answers seem to me no more promising than Kant's arid transcendentalism. Indeed, the overzealous inculcation of virtue is one of the things rights are supposed to protect us from.

The question of why we should be moral remains famously difficult to answer. To convince the indifferent, the agnostic, and the reluctant, morality relies in the end, I suggest not just on the exercise of our own reason, nor on inclination, but also on the recognition of an authority whose judgment we take in place of our own. One that we respect and trust and follow, even if we don't agree with it. This might be characterized as moral leadership, as leading by example. It certainly takes us closer to the level of the archetype, and to the charismatic authority that Benenson, for instance, had in such abundance. It may be harder to lose such authority than people think, but real risks are run in the dual maneuver of deconstructing existing authority and trying to rebuild or transform it in new ways. This makes authority inherently conservative. It must be founded on what has gone before, emerging from within it. It is also implicitly inegalitarian in terms of influence. It may require us to listen more attentively to our "olders and betters." But our age seems particularly brutal in dispensing with all that we might term traditional authority and although this may be no more than a presentist misconception on my part, the catalog of public and personal authorities whose reputation stands tarnished seems to grow inexorably. Yet, if we can't trust our parents, and especially our fathers, or our priests and professors, our prime ministers, presidents, teachers, and state officials, who will be able to unite us, without coercion, into acting for the betterment of our societies as a whole? Who will we regard as wise? Who will disseminate social solidarity between generations and embody the public interest? Even the idea of such a singular "public" is fading. Perhaps a moral as much as a political neo-medievalism beckons? In furthering this deconstruction, human rights have played a prominent role with their rationalism (giving tradition short shrift) and individualism (with its ambivalence towards society). Amnesty was a subtle and complex response to this dilemma. It contained the seeds of a transformed authority to which it clung for four decades and more, creating and retaining a remarkable degree of trust. Are the seeds of a new authority found within the human rights ideology as a whole?

One senior researcher feared the new rhetoric of Amnesty was increasingly about "problems for human rights" rather than for a specific suffering human being. Human rights have taken on a life of their own. Martin Ennals, Amnesty's first proper secretary general, observed, as an underlying belief for Amnesty members, that they shared "a certain skepticism about ideologies and 'isms.' "[34] Amnesty is faith in action. And reformers run very real risks in meddling with it.

First, by removing the tangibility, the concrete practice, the face of precisely this person, you diffuse responsibility, making it harder to identify with the victim and increasing the apparent impossibility of effective intervention. Denial is made easier, like not catching the eye of a beggar on the street.[35] Second, by removing what for reformers is the myth of foundational truth and entering the more political world of interests and identities, a united front becomes impossible to sustain. Third, the sense of suffering and sacrifice that suffuses Amnesty is a signal of purity and integrity. The search for a more concrete identity—being not just doing—gives staff and members a reason for being there that is not "because it is right." This drains away moral authority precisely as it increases political authority.

Fourth, globalization cares nothing for what is intrinsically ethical about Amnesty's work. It is only attracted by the value, in capital terms, of the symbol. Amnesty is not a service provider—it does not create utility by meeting needs in any real sense—thus, its attractions for the market are contingent and fleeting. Furthermore, money risks tainting the symbol the moment it touches it, polluting the very thing it desires. Money has an obvious and inherent interest, something morality (to be convincing as such) cannot have. And when the money moves on, as it will, Amnesty will be left restructured in the language of efficiency and growth. More than any other organization of its type that I can think of, Amnesty's name is its whole being. It has turned itself into moral authority. And the world of morality and the world of utility, efficiency, alienation, and money are at some point irreconcilable.

Reformers reject this kind of sacred-profane bipolarity. A way can be found that avoids the entrenched view that one senior director attributed to the keepers of the flame: "They serve as black and white, good and evil. . . . I am the one with the faith. I am the one who knows. I can't just mildly disagree with you. You are threatening the whole movement by disagreeing with me. . . . We've built a culture based on fear. And it's the fear of being wrong. And . . . we have imagined an apocalypse. That will come as a result of giving in to the devil of doubt."

What reformers argue is that Amnesty must adapt or die. This is simply a stark reality. If it cannot keep pace with its rivals, as more and more better-resourced humanitarian organizations move into the human rights field, then it will shrivel in the shade of these larger canopies. The Integrated Strategic Plan had a one-word financial strategy, grow! This could equally well have been survive. And Amnesty's more partial and political style is having an impact. We have seen its brave intervention against the Bush White House. The external SVAW campaign has also had its successes, especially highlighting domestic violence against women in Sweden, considered by many the world's foremost gender-equal state, and drawing praise from the UN special rapporteur on VAW, Yakin Erturk, for its work on the implementation of legislation (so-called "due diligence").[36]

And what of my position? In comments on this book's first draft, the secretary general asked for some reflection on the "nature of the access you were given to the IS and to the broader AI community and on the trust and openness with which people received you." The IS staff, and almost all AI members I met, did honor me with a remarkable degree of trust. In many ways, the individuals themselves were more open than the institution as a whole has been historically—for reasons of detachment and authority we now understand all too well. Transparency about itself is a brave new world for a moral authority like Amnesty and my unprecedented level of access was a courageous first step.

I had imagined that the IS would be a very singular entity inside, deeply suspicious en masse of interlopers like me and of one mind, as it were, on the mission it pursued in the world. Yet, as we can see, once one is beyond the hard shell there is significant internal diversity and division, a strong commitment to the ideals of Amnesty overlaid by an equally strong and permanent conversation about how best to go forward. To be true to this ongoing contestation, and to the account contained in both the written historical record and staff interviews, these disagreements, about principles as well as strategy, needed to be drawn. To sanitize the story, to let observations and comments about gender or race, or stress, slip from the record of my fieldwork, or to let the principled disagreements about how best, if at all, to reform Amnesty for the twenty-first century, would have been indefensible. It would have rendered IS life anodyne, emotionless, and bland, rather than as what I hope readers have in places felt it to be, a fascinating story of practical morality and its possibilities and problems. All the voices I heard during a year in the IS deserve to be heard as part of that story.

On the first draft I received extensive feedback from many sources that has had an appreciable impact on the text. The secretary general made only very minor suggestions about the removal of material that was potentially offensive, or damaging but unsubstantiated. If my interpretation, for that's all it can be, helps Amnesty in any way in understanding its own identity in the era of the War on Terror and late globalization, and to survive and thrive in that difficult environment, then I hope that is some reward for being so open.

So what did I do? One evening in Mexico I talked with an Amnesty stalwart about his motivation. He had been a socialist and an anarchist, he said. No mention of human rights. He had chosen Amnesty because as an anarchist it seemed a natural fit, despite all the rules. He just felt at home. It was, paradoxically, somewhere you could be an individual in solidarity with other individuals.

And it was practical. It meant doing something, saying (unfortunately, alongside the troubling figure of Martin Luther); "Here I stand, I can do no other." This is the beginning of practice and end of theory. On this basis, I joined Amnesty as I finished the book—as an act of solidarity against unaccountable power, and as a positive identification with those Amnesty members and especially IS staff for whom sympathy with the underdog is a kind of instinctive reaction. It is power, in all its guises, that lies behind depredation, misery, pain, and suffering. Watching it, mitigating it, and controlling it, even when it is our own, is, in the end, all we can do. I can see the virtues in both the reformers' and keepers' positions. How do we know how it will play out? Will the use of a word like "gulag" to describe Guantanamo Bay be a sunset or a dawn? There is a place for a trusted authority, but is that authority of any use if it can't be turned into social change? Without changing as society has changed,

Amnesty risks charges of arrogance and a future as a kind of museum piece of the Cold War. And yet, with rapid expansion a more transient membership might ossify it from within rather than without, creating hollowness where once there was such active commitment that any external blow could be absorbed by those who were "Amnesty" to their core. If new members do not feel such deep obligation, they may not share in the sense of corporate responsibility if things go wrong and may just leave with little soul searching. Being "Amnesty" is not in their soul, and does not derive from their shared sense of the faith.

Then again, does Amnesty have to be "useful"? One word that irritated some keepers of the flame was "relevance." For them, Amnesty's role as a sentinel was timeless, immune to passing fashion and vigilant about things that matter, they say, in any era. Entering the turbulent sea of political authority may engulf this beacon. And then, will the same degree of effort be forthcoming—forty-five years worth—to construct an equally tall lighthouse with parallel authority? There is something powerfully attractive in being an organization of record, in witnessing. In saying: This person lived. It is a kind of humanistic solidarity, well expressed by Pierre Sané in a statement surprisingly close to the core of the ethos for someone identified as an arch-reformer:

> Many organizations work for Human rights but they do not necessarily have a focus on the individual victim. Amnesty started with the individual victims, with the POCs. Forty years later, even when we are dealing with genocide in Rwanda, we try in our report to name individuals, to give the stories of their lives because we want to bring out the humanity of each individual in spite of the big numbers. It's only by bringing back the individuality of each victim that we can make sense of the atrocities we are dealing with. These victims are not just numbers or are not just Hutus or are not just street-children. They have a name, they have a date of birth, they have a history and the history of their life is what we need to talk about.[37]

abbreviations

AI	Amnesty International
AIUK	Amnesty International United Kingdom
AIUSA	Amnesty International USA
CAP	Country Action Plan
CAT	Campaign Against Torture
CCC	Cambridge Crash Committee
CLOD	Committee on Long-Range Organizational Development
ESC	Economic, social, and cultural
FMP	Facilities Management Program
GIG	Global Impact Goal
HORO	Head of Research Office
HRP	Human Resources Program
HRW	Human Rights Watch
ICJ	International Commission of Jurists
ICM	International Council Meeting
ICRC	International Committee of the Red Cross
IEC	International Executive Committee
IMG	International Management Group
IS	International Secretariat
ISOP	International Secretariat Operational Plan
ISP	Integrated Strategic Plan
LRPC	Long Range Planning Committee
MAC	Minimum Adequate Coverage
MAV	Media and Audio-Visual Program
MRC	Mandate Review Committee
MSF	Médecins sans Frontières
NGO	nongovernmental organization
POC	prisoner of conscience
RCA	research and campaign assistant
RMP	Research and Mandate Program

SCRA   Standing Committee on Research and Action

SGO   Secretary General's Office

SMF   Senior Management Forum (senior management)

SVAW   Stop Violence Against Women

UDHR   Universal Declaration of Human Rights

VAW   Violence Against Women

WOOC   Work On Own Country rule

notes

Preface

[i] Luis Muñoz has now told his own remarkable story in *Being Luis: A Chilean Life* (Exeter: Impress Books, 2005).
[ii] George Orwell, *Nineteen Eighty-Four* (London: Penguin Books, 1983): 230.
[iii] Orwell, *Nineteen Eighty-Four*: 231.
[iv] "American Gulag," *Washington Post*, May 26th, 2005, at www.washingtonpost.com/wp-dyn/content/article/2005/05/25/AR2005052501838.html.

1. Between Two Worlds

[1] The letter was signed by more than 100 staff members out of about 450. Some may have been volunteers who are not part of the total of 450. This quotation is from the draft for staff approval emailed on 30 July 2003.
[2] Boldface in original.
[3] On principled NGOs, see Ann Marie Clark, *Diplomacy of Conscience: Amnesty International and Changing Human Rights Norms* (Princeton: Princeton University Press, 2001); on transnational advocacy networks, see Margaret E. Keck and Kathryn Sikkink, *Activists Beyond Borders: Advocacy Networks in International Politics* (Ithaca: Cornell University Press, 1988); on transnational social actors, see James Ron, Howard Ramos, and Kathleen Rodgers, "Transnational information politics: Amnesty International's country reporting, 1986–2000," *International Studies Quarterly* 49, no. 3 (2005), 557–88.
[4] See Joseph Raz, *The Morality of Freedom* (Oxford: Clarendon Press, 1986), chap. 3.
[5] R. B. Friedman, "On the concept of authority in political philosophy," in *Authority*, edited by Joseph Raz (Oxford: Basil Blackwell, 1990), 67.
[6] Ibid., 76.
[7] Stephen Toulmin, *Cosmopolis: The Hidden Agenda of Modernity* (Chicago: University of Chicago Press, 1990), 197.
[8] Richard A. Wilson, "Representing human rights violations: Social contexts and subjectivities," in *Human Rights, Culture & Context: Anthropological Perspectives*, edited by Richard A. Wilson (London: Pluto Press, 1997), 149.
[9] Ibid., 155.
[10] Bernard Williams, *Ethics and the Limits of Philosophy* (London: Fontana Press, 1993), 69. Williams is talking about individual reasoning, but this seems to me to hold for organizations.
[11] I make no claims, one way or the other, for its resonance beyond the core realm of Christianity.
[12] Quoted in Tom Buchanan, " 'The truth will set you free': The making of Amnesty International," *Journal of Contemporary History* 37, no. 4 (2002): 593–94.
[13] Ibid., 593. The young and "women past their prime of life who have been, unfortunately, unable to expend in full their maternal impulses" were among his key target groups.
[14] Peter Jones, *Rights* (London: Macmillan, 1994), 79.
[15] In introducing an edition of *The Rights of Man*, Tony Benn, Benenson's contemporary on the British Left, writes, "It is evident to anyone who reads Paine's writings or studies

his life that the concept of inherent rights is fundamental and that everybody possesses them whether they are rich or poor, men or women, black or white"; see Thomas Paine, *Common Sense, and The Rights of Man* (London: Phoenix Press, 1993), xviii.

[16] E. P. Thompson describes *The Rights of Man* as one of the two "foundation texts of the English working-class movement" (along with John Bunyan's *Pilgrim's Progress*); see *The Making of the English Working Class* (London: Penguin Books, 1980), 34.

[17] Peter Benenson, *Amnesty International Bulletin*, no. 2, May 1963, 1.

[18] See Peter Beyer, *Religion and Globalization* (London: Sage Publications, 1994), 89.

[19] *Lore* is defined here as collective knowledge or wisdom.

[20] Some IS staff who responded to the first draft of this book were unhappy with what they saw as an oversimplification that left out those whose views were somewhere between the keepers of the flame and the reformers. And of course this *is* a simplification. But that there are two broadly coherent alternative conceptions of Amnesty visible within its institutional history is entirely manifest. As one long-serving IS staffer commented on the draft, "In the end the two camps you presented exist all too obviously, although again perhaps in less black and white terms than they often come across."

[21] Even though all IS and Amnesty staff and members could be characterized as keepers of the flame, this book is named for the guardians of Amnesty's traditional symbolic moral authority in recognition of their historical contribution to Amnesty's reputation.

[22] See Orlando Patterson, *Slavery and Social Death* (Cambridge: Harvard University Press, 1985), for historical examples of the links between not belonging and authority.

[23] Friedman, "On the concept of authority," 76.

[24] Benenson, *Amnesty International Bulletin*, May 1963, 1. This was Amnesty's second birthday.

[25] Once you are locked within a bureaucratic career structure, there may be limits later on in terms of changing your mind, and participatory benefits—of being personally associated with a prestigious and esteemed organization such as Amnesty—may become correspondingly more important as compensations.

[26] Émile Durkheim, *The Elementary Forms of Religious Life*, trans. by Carol Cosman (Oxford: Oxford University Press, 2001 [1912]), 46 (emphasis in original).

[27] Ibid., 317.

[28] Benedict Anderson, *Imagined Communities* (London: Verso, 1991), 55–56.

[29] Durkheim, *Elementary Forms of Religious Life*, 326.

[30] Ibid., 317.

[31] Ibid., 230–31.

[32] Ibid., 267, 266.

[33] Ibid., 317–18.

2. Shadows and Doors

[1] The IS has regional offices in several places, the most sizable of which is in Kampala. It also maintains small staffs in New York, Hong Kong, Geneva, and Paris.

[2] The other side of the street, No. 28, was bought in 1987 at a cost of about £2 million.

[3] However, other staff members had stories of the impressive lengths to which the IS had gone in helping them with personal traumas. Although the working culture as a whole was seen as chaotic and unsympathetic, it was still capable of individual acts of great sensitivity.

[4] *Amnesty Bulletin*, no. 11, April 1965, 2. Amnesty renamed its publications regularly at this early stage, looking for the most effective format.

[5] Norman Marsh, AI Oral History interview, June 1984. The Amnesty International Oral History is housed at the International Institute for Social History, Amsterdam. This history—interviews with sixteen of the prime movers in Amnesty's foundation and development, including Peter Benenson—was compiled as a pilot study by two AIUSA members, Andrew Blane and Priscilla Ellsworth; the former was an ex-member of the

IEC and the latter was the wife of Whitney Ellsworth, influential AIUSA and IEC member.

[6] An exception was Benenson himself, who in 1964 entered Haiti by posing as a tourist on a painting excursion. See Egon Larsen, *A Flame in Barbed Wire* (New York: W.W. Norton & Co, 1979), 26–27.

[7] Peter Calvocoressi, a British international relations professor, helped Amnesty draw up its five-region department plan in the early 1970s.

[8] Maureen Teitelbaum, "Memorandum on the Present Position of the Library Department of Amnesty International, for the International Executive Meeting in Dublin, March 1966."

[9] In Europe Program meetings, I was told, discussions about operational change were met by some with the response: "How long is Irene's contract?"

[10] Special Report for Information, no. 28, re: Architect, from Secretary General to All IEC Members, 28 May 1982, IEC 1982.

[11] This has a gender dimension (see chap. 6).

[12] One senior director was skeptical it could be easily found.

[13] Old newspapers were stacked up, blocking a fire door, for example. Another senior manager joked that they should call the fire department themselves because it would at least mean an enforced holiday.

[14] AI Index: ACT 77/009/2002. All AI documents are now identified by means of a unique index number.

[15] In the 1980s, two staff members guesstimated informally that perhaps one-third of the staff was ex-Catholics (without the belief, but missing the comfort of the church structure).

[16] Carl G. Jung, *Memories, Dreams, Reflections* (London: Fontana, 1995 [1963]), 106–7.

[17] Carl G. Jung, "On the psychology of the unconscious," in *The Essential Jung*, edited by Anthony Storr (London: Fontana, 1983), 87.

[18] Ibid., 90.

[19] All emphasis in the original. This survey was shared with the IS senior managers in June 2003 at an all-day bilateral meeting with AIUK's reformist directors.

[20] For one senior researcher, being out of the building was the interesting and gratifying part of the job; being inside was "an absolute nightmare for researchers."

[21] Amnesty's core work lends itself to such humor; one staffer said that there were "some people within Amnesty I'd take out and shoot without a trial."

[22] It is hard enough to read these accounts; see, for example, those in Amnesty International, *Broken Bodies, Shattered Minds: Torture and Ill-Treatment of Women* (AI Index: ACT 40/001/2001).

[23] In a perfect echo of Durkheim, this researcher talked about the IS in the 1980s when "the energy was derived from this sense of collective belonging."

[24] This is Report 2 of the Administration Committee, 15 September 1967. It has no AI Index number. Its authors were Goran C.-O. Claesson (of the Swedish section's executive) and Cornelis van der Vlies (of the IEC and the Dutch Section). The Dutch Section, today one of Amnesty's most influential, all but collapsed at this stage due to disillusionment with the secretariat.

[25] One former program head considered these stories to be myths, however, and was skeptical that by the late 1970s Secretary General Martin Ennals was spending any of his time on reception, for example.

3. Lighting the Candle

[1] Beyer, *Religion and Globalization*, 106. My analysis here draws heavily on Beyer, who in turn draws on the work of Niklas Luhmann, for example, *The Differentiation of Society*, trans. by Stephen Holmes and Charles Larmore, (New York: Columbia University Press, 1982).

[2] Beyer, *Religion and Globalization*, 98.

[3] Ibid., 90.

[4] Ibid., 88. For an illuminating example of competition between liberal and conservative variants, see David Stoll, *Is Latin America Turning Protestant?* (Berkeley: University of California Press, 1990).

[5] Buchanan, "'The truth will set you free,'" 594. See also Tom Buchanan, "Amnesty International in crisis, 1966–1967," *Twentieth Century British History* 15, no. 3 (2004), 267–89. Buchanan's work is the best on the foundations of Amnesty.

[6] Max Weber, "The social psychology of the world's religions," in *From Max Weber*, trans. by Hans H. Gerth and C. Wright Mills (London: Kegan Paul, Trench & Trubner, 1947), 295.

[7] Peggy Crane, interview, 17 June 1985, Amnesty International Oral History.

[8] See, for example, the obituary written by Peter Archer, in *The Guardian*, 28 February 2005, p. 21.

[9] Flora Solomon and Barnet Litvinoff, *Baku to Baker Street: The Memoirs of Flora Solomon* (London: Collins, 1984), 149.

[10] Flora Solomon was a well-known Zionist who pioneered staff development at the British department store Marks and Spencer. Peter changed his surname to Solomon-Benenson at the request of his dying grandfather (and later changed it to just Benenson).

[11] Justice became the British section of the International Commission of Jurists (ICJ).

[12] Buchanan, "'The truth will set you free'," 576 n. 6.

[13] In addition to Buchanan, for general reviews of Amnesty's origins see Larsen, *Flame in Barbed Wire*; Jonathan Power, *Like Water on Stone* (London: Penguin Press, 2001), 119–64.

[14] Peter Benenson, essay and interview, 12 November 1983, AI Oral History.

[15] At Eton they raised enough money to bring three boys from Germany; the sister of one, Marlys Deeds, later became a founding staff member of Amnesty.

[16] The Church of England is often described as "the Tory Party at prayer." If we define the British establishment in narrower terms, emphasizing its Englishness, its political Conservatism, and its Anglicanism, very few of those associated with Amnesty fit into this influential class, a class that dominated the state (if not the government).

[17] Benenson, interview, 12 November 1983.

[18] Peter Benenson, dedication, 28 February 1989 (emphasis in original).

[19] Benenson, essay, AI Oral History.

[20] Benenson, interview, 12 November 1983.

[21] Reinforcing this was Benenson's interest in Frank Buchman's Moral Re-Armament Movement and in the work of Danilo Dolci, the Sicilian social reformer; see Buchanan, "'The truth will set you free'," 581–83.

[22] Peter Archer, interview, 4 June 1984, AI Oral History. Archer wrote the Benenson's *Guardian* obituary.

[23] Dorothy Warner, interview, 18 June 1985, AI Oral History; Diana Redhouse interview, 4 June 1984, AI Oral History.

[24] Tom Sargant, interview, 22 June 1985, AI Oral History.

[25] Christel Marsh, interview, 7 November 1983, AI Oral History.

[26] Louis Blom-Cooper, interview, 6 June 1984, AI Oral History.

[27] Peggy Crane, interview, 17 June 1985, AI Oral History.

[28] Marlys Deeds, interview, 19 June 1985, AI Oral History; Keith Siviter, interview, 5 June 1984, AI Oral History.

[29] Joyce Baker, interview, June 1983, AI Oral History.

[30] Margaret Benenson was "from three generations of [Anglican] missionaries"; interview, 14 June 1985, AI Oral History.

[31] Archer, interview, 4 June 1984.

[32] Sharon Erickson Nepstad, "Popular religion, protest, and revolt," in *Disruptive Religion: The Force of Faith in Social Movement Activism*, edited by Christian Smith (New York: Routledge, 1996), 110–11.

[33] On liberation theology's decline in the face of evangelical Protestantism, see Stoll, *Is Latin America Turning Protestant?* chap. 10.

[34] By July 1961, Baker was joint director of the Appeal with Benenson. In his 1983 essay, Benenson said the bar on adopting violent POCs was a pragmatic decision to aid in "uniting public support."

[35] Joyce Baker, interview, June 1983.

[36] Eric Baker, memo for IEC, 6–9 October 1967, on IS reorganization (italics added).

[37] In *Amnesty* no. 6, 9 August 1961, 5. *Amnesty* was published biweekly out of Benenson's legal chambers from 27 June 1961.

[38] Benenson later claimed he included so many churchmen to "give the whole initiative more respectability": interview, 6 June 1984.

[39] *Amnesty*, no. 6, 6 September 1961, 1.

[40] *Amnesty*, no. 11, 15 November 1961, 4.

[41] *Amnesty*, no. 12, 29 November 1961, had an article by a Catholic lawyer, R.A.G. O'Brien, on the Christian attitude to unjust laws, titled "The justice of the law." O'Brien argued that the authority of all law came ultimately from God.

[42] John A.T. Robinson, *Honest to God* (London: SCM Press, 1963), 7–8, chap. 5. This book was in its sixth printing within two months.

[43] Ibid., 25.

[44] Benenson, interview, 12 November 1983.

[45] Amnesty is not, however, a pacifist organization. Bonhoeffer had prayed that "God will give me the strength not to take up arms" when Hitler came to power; Renate Wind, *Dietrich Bonhoeffer: A Spoke in the Wheel*, trans. by John Bowden (Grand Rapids, Mich.: Wm. B. Eerdmans, 1991), 93.

[46] In his AI Oral History interview, 5 June 1984, Siviter said of the Congregationalists, "We are under the surface here in Amnesty, but we've been there all along." Warner, interview, 18 June 1985. Benenson also mentions Irmgard Payne, who may have been Bonhoeffer's niece. He met Bonhoeffer's sister when she visited Payne in England; interview, 12 November 1983.

[47] Some writers have drawn explicit parallels between Bonhoeffer's death and that of Jesus; see Stephen R Haynes, *The Bonhoeffer Phenomenon: Portraits of a Protestant Saint* (London: SCM Press, 2004), 144–47. Evangelicals have also sought to claim Bonhoeffer for their own, pointing among other things to his constant use of the Bible; (89–97).

[48] Ibid., 99.

[49] Letter to Eberhard Bethge, 27 June 1944, in Dietrich Bonhoeffer, *A Testament to Freedom*, edited by Geffrey B. Kelly and F. Burton Nelson (New York: HarperCollins, 1990), 507.

[50] Stephen Plant, *Bonhoeffer* (London: Continuum, 2004), 130.

[51] See Haynes, *Bonhoeffer Phenomenon*, chap. 6. Robinson's *Honest to God* played a major part in popularizing Bonhoeffer's theology.

[52] André Dumas, *Dietrich Bonhoeffer: Theologian of Reality*, trans. by Robert McAfee Brown (London: SCM Press, 1971), 172, 185.

[53] Letter to Eberhard Bethge, 21 July 1944, in Bonhoeffer, *Testament to Freedom*, 510.

[54] Dumas, *Dietrich Bonhoeffer*, 289.

[55] Siviter, interview, 5 June 1984.

[56] "After Ten Years," a letter to family and conspirators, Christmas 1942, in Bonhoeffer, *Testament to Freedom*, 486.

[57] "Thoughts on the Day of the Baptism of Dietrich Wilhelm Rudiger Bethge," May 1944, in Bonhoeffer, *Testament to Freedom*, 505.

[58] Wind, *Dietrich Bonhoeffer*, 180.

[59] Norman Marsh, interview, June 1984, AI Oral History.

[60] In Buchanan, "Amnesty International in crisis," 289.

[61] In Buchanan, "'The truth will set you free,'" 582.

[62] The phrase *International Secretariat* was first used in *Amnesty*, no. 4, 9 August, 1961.

[63] Larsen, *Flame in Barbed Wire*, 15.

[64] Benenson had one large room and two small ones on the ground floor of his chambers and two small cellar rooms.

[65] All references in this account are to Christel Marsh, interview, 7 November 1983 (with written additions made 1 June 1984).

[66] According to Keith Siviter, case information arrived as a few lines on one-third of an A4 sheet of paper; interview, 5 June 1984.

[67] Blom-Cooper, interview, 6 June 1984.

[68] Peggy Crane, interview, 17 June 1985.

[69] Siviter, interview, 5 June 1984.

[70] Amnesty *Bulletin*, no. 2, May 1963, 2.

[71] Deeds, interview, 19 June 1985. Other examples are also given in the Oral History interviews, many showing both a gender division (men tended to make policy; women tended to enact it) and the pressure on women to run families and meet limitless working demands.

[72] Deeds, interview, 19 June 1985.

[73] *Amnesty*, no. 3, 25 July 1961, 7.

[74] Sean McBride, interview 8 June, 1984, AI Oral History.

[75] *Amnesty Quarterly*, no. 3, 1962, 7.

[76] Benenson, essay, August 1983.

[77] Ibid.; Larsen, *Flame in Barbed Wire*, 17–18.

[78] A code of this sort was first published by Amnesty on Human Rights Day, December 10, 1962, Benenson describing its contents as moral principles that would one day be part of the law of civilization; *Amnesty Quarterly*, no. 4, 1963, 7,8.

[79] Amnesty *Bulletin*, no. 5 [misprinted on orig. as 3], November 1963, 4.

[80] Blane and Ellsworth, in submitting their oral history to Amnesty (in September 1992), told the leadership in a cover letter that Amnesty had been forced to stop doing this when tax officials found out.

[81] Financial affairs were so badly managed that one treasurer resigned because he was not told by Benenson that £3,000 was being spent on refurbishing new premises.

[82] Buchanan, "Amnesty International in crisis," gives an extensive account, on which this paragraph draws. Key to the crisis was a falling out between Benenson and the British state, their previously good relations soured by Amnesty allegations about the use of torture in Aden.

[83] On the CIA-ICJ link, see Kirsten Sellars, *The Rise and Rise of Human Rights* (Stroud: Sutton Publishing, 2002), 107.

[84] Joyce Baker, interview, June 1983, AI Oral History.

4. Telling the Truth about Suffering

[1] Wilson, "Representing human rights violations," 151.

[2] Ibid., 152–53.

[3] *Bulletin*, no. 17, November 1966, 2.

[4] The report is AI Index: ASA 33/17/99; the campaign document is AI Index: ASA 33/18/1999.

[5] A senior manager from AI Netherlands told IS staffers that they found people were "no longer prepared to commit themselves to ten years of boring work," the old way having been to "give people a disappearance case and say goodbye, we'll see you in fifteen years time."

[6] On symbolic capital, see Pierre Bourdieu, *The Logic of Practice* (Cambridge: Polity Press, 1990), book 1, chap. 7.

[7] Eric Baker, memo for meeting of IEC, 6–9 October 1967, on secretariat reorganization, Secretary General's Office files.

[8] Thomas Hammarberg, "AI's Identity in the Late 'Eighties," memo, 5 October 1983 (emphasis added).

[9] Amnesty's British origins also meant the IS worked inductively and empirically, basing its claims on cases and precedents, not first principles. In this it reflected English Common Law.

[10] Goran C.-O. Claesson and Cornelis van der Vlies, "Report 1 from the Administration Committee," 1 May 1967 (emphasis in original), AI Index Number: ORG 06.

[11] "Memorandum on the Present Position of the Library Department of Amnesty International, for the International Executive meeting in Dublin, March 1966."

[12] "The Investigation Bureau–Staffing and Needs," Amnesty International Executive Meeting, October 1967, Secretary General's Office (SGO) files. There is a document from June 30, 1967, signed by Stella Joyce of the Investigation Department and indexed as ORG 06, that contains very similar language.

[13] In April 1971, the countries where most prisoner cases were either adopted or under investigation were, in the West, Rhodesia (120), Spain (250), and Greece (196); in the East, USSR (250); and in the nonaligned, Brazil (150).

[14] One researcher from this era recalled that as preparation for her first mission she was advised to read Evelyn Waugh's satirical novel about British foreign correspondents abroad, *Scoop*.

[15] Stella Joyce, "Investigation Department," June 1967, ORG 06.

[16] "Structure of Amnesty International: A Working Paper Prepared by the International Secretariat for the International Executive Committee Meeting May 1970," AI Index: ORG 01, IEC/9–10 May 1970.

[17] Memo, McKinsey & Co to Martin Ennals, 21 April 1972, SGO files.

[18] "The Present State and the Future Development of the Research Department," IEC/28–29 November 1970.

[19] "Amnesty International Five Years Hence—Report and Recommendations," 31 May 1972, ORG 03. The authors were Lothar H. Belck (Swiss Section and international treasurer), Dirk Borner (German Section), and Arnout Ruitenberg (Dutch Section). This report estimates the likely 1977–1978 IS budget to be £263,500, compared with the 1972–1973 figure of £134,850.

[20] Ibid. (emphasis in original).

[21] Memo, Martin Ennals to IEC and staff, 30 March 1973, POL 05/IEC 73.

[22] See Clark, *Diplomacy of Conscience*, chap. 3.

[23] Sherman Carroll, "Restructuring of the Secretariat," memo, 8 January 1976, submitted in revised form to the IEC, for Information 33, January 1976 (emphasis in original).

[24] Ibid.

[25] "Report of the Evaluation of the Campaign Against Torture," AI Index: ACT 40/003/2002. I mentioned this to a young researcher, who pointed out that this did not mean the campaign*er* should drive the research.

[26] "'Administrative' Responsibilities for Heads of Department/Region/Unit," memo, 11 November 1978.

[27] "Responsibilities, Consultations and Decision-Making within the International Secretariat," memo, 20 October 1978.

[28] "Background Information on Case Sheet Quota," ACT 02/IEC 04/79. In the 1974–1978 period, the number of released prisoners varied: 1974 (1,403), 1975 (1,688), 1976 (1,274), 1977 (1,536), and 1978 (2,037). Each released prisoner meant a new case had to be found for the groups concerned.

[29] "Research Department Planning," memo, AI Index: POL 04/IEC 01/79.

[30] "Report of the Crash Committee (CCC) Appointed to Advise on AI Development and Planning," July IEC 1977. It may have had the growing AIUSA membership in mind.

[31] See Laurence R. Iannaccone, "Why strict churches are strong," *American Journal of Sociology* 99, no. 5 (1994): 1180–211. I thank Karen Melham for bringing this to my attention. This bears on the question of liberal and conservative responses to globalization—strictness can, in the end, be counterproductive as well.

[32] "Re: CCC Report," Thomas Hammarberg to IEC, July IEC 1977, POL 05/IEC 77.

[33] "Report of the Committee on Administrative Structure," AI Index: ORG 61/IEC01/80, IEC July 1980.

[34] There was much unhappiness in the IS about the selection of candidates for these interviews, including the feeling that not enough researchers were consulted.

[35] "Status Report on Committee Work and Procedures," 26 November 1979, to IEC from A. Whitney Ellsworth.

[36] Documentation Center, Program Department (dealing with campaigns and membership), Legal Office, Administration Department, and Research Department.

[37] Although the Research Department thrived under Hammarberg, one current researcher who began work at the IS during his tenure felt that Hammarberg was naturally more sympathetic to campaigners, mentioning the Research Department only once during his leaving speech in 1986.

[38] "How Should the IS Be Managed?" IEC October 1981, for Information 11 (emphasis in original).

[39] "Staffing of the Research Department," memo, Clayton Yeo to Thomas Hammarberg, 9 March 1980. One current researcher recalls Yeo telling her (as she moved to cover a new, complex, and combative country), "Focus on one issue. Take two years. And write a report."

[40] "Quality of Research: Some Points for Starting a Discussion," memo, IEC July 1980, Index No: POL 04/IEC 03/80.

[41] Ibid. (emphasis added).

[42] During one 2003 meeting at which fundamental changes to the Annual Report were discussed, a senior researcher (referring to the modernization efforts of Pierre Sané between 1993 and 2001) said "not even Pierre tried to touch the Annual Report."

[43] "Interim Report on the Review of Amnesty International's Impartiality," 6 August 1984, AI Index: POL 01/06/84. The final report is indexed as POL 01/03/85. Written by the IS, it clearly states, "All AI actions start with research and the availability of information."

[44] "Quality of Research."

[45] The use of the mixed pronoun *s/he* in 1980 shows a gender awareness that would have been unusual, but the whole tone of the memo is one of paternal, even fatherly, authority, the male heads of research disciplining the unruly movement.

[46] For an informed view of the mandate by an academic and ex-IEC member, see Peter R Baehr, "Amnesty International and its self-imposed limited mandate," *Netherlands Quarterly of Human Rights* 12, no. 1 (1994), 5–21. See also Peter Pack, "Amnesty International: An evolving mandate in a changing world," in *Human Rights: An Agenda for the 21st Century*, edited by Angela Hegarty and Siobhan Leonard (London: Cavendish Publishing, 1999), 233–46. Pack (of AIUK) is the most influential movement figure on mandate matters.

[47] "AI's identity in the Late 'Eighties," memo, 5 October 1983.

[48] Hammarberg, Larry Cox (U.S. section and later deputy secretary general), Nigel (later Sir Nigel) Rodley (legal advisor, IS staff representative on the IEC, and future UN Special Rapporteur on Torture), Martin Ennals, and Clayton Yeo.

[49] "Report of the Meeting of the Mandate Committee held in London on 5th and 6th December, 1978," (emphasis in original), AI Index: POL 21/IEC 01/79.

[50] "AI's Identity in the Late 'Eighties" (emphasis in original).

[51] This memo has no index number. It is dated 5 July 1988 and is from Yeo to MRC members.

[52] "Final Report of the Review of Amnesty International's Impartiality," 26 June 1985, AI Index: POL 01/03/85.

[53] This was the view of the Research and Mandate Program, writing to senior managers in 2002.

[54] There is a common language other than English for the Americas Program (Spanish) and the Middle East Program (Arabic), and in the Europe Program the strength of the sections puts a premium on researchers having linguistic skills. In the Africa Program there is an Anglophone-Francophone tension, but given the diversity of local languages only Swahili, perhaps, is a feasible local option. In Asia, of course, the linguistic diversity is vast.

[55] In 1984, Secretary General Hammarberg listed the "controversial twenty" on which questions about balance most often arose: United States, Cuba, Nicaragua, Guatemala, El Salvador, South Africa, Namibia, Zimbabwe, Ethiopia, Israel, Lebanon, Syria, Iraq, Iran,

Afghanistan, Vietnam, China, United Kingdom, USSR, and Poland (with North Korea and Kampuchea as other possibles).

[56] The transcript of this talk is part of the AI historical archive boxes in Easton Street. I have corrected minor errors of spelling in the transcript, but have left the text unedited otherwise.

[57] One IS staffer recalled that in Thailand in the 1980s UN officials would move rather than sit next to him at the night market for fear they would be seen by the authorities associating with human rights workers. "They treated human rights work like the plague," he said.

[58] "An International Personality: Notes on the International Consultation on AI's Public Image," IEC June 1982, agenda item 2.4, Index: NS 05/IEC 02/82.

5. Politics and Democratic Authority

[1] In Thomas Nagel, "Moral conflict and political legitimacy," in *Authority*, edited by Joseph Raz (Oxford: Blackwell, 1990), 300.

[2] Ibid., 301.

[3] AIUSA has recently been embroiled in a bitter internal row, in which notions of solidarity and victimhood feature prominently, over whether to believe one of its own volunteers who alleges her life was threatened by agents of the Guatemalan state. See Ian Parker, "Victims and volunteers," *The New Yorker*, 26 January 2004.

[4] For an informed view of these changes from an academic who has been chair of the AIUSA board and a long-time member of the international movement, see Morton E. Winston, "Assessing the effectiveness of international human rights NGOs," in *NGOs and Human Rights*, edited by Claude E. Welch (Philadelphia: University of Pennsylvania Press, 2001).

[5] One of AIUSA's first chairmen was Michael Straight, former editor of *The New Republic* and a member of the notorious Cambridge spy ring (having been recruited at Cambridge by Anthony Blunt).

[6] Lyons refers several times to U.S. skepticism about the level of "amateurism" that is tolerated "in England." The memo was written to AIUSA board members on June 14, 1967.

[7] In the event it was never used.

[8] The key figure in the West Coast operation was Ginetta Sagan.

[9] "AI Membership Statistics," AI Index: ORG 40/02/93.

[10] The group, a kind of localized solidarity, is a further sign of Amnesty's ambiguous relationship to "globalizing modernity" with its integral drive toward individuation.

[11] "Notes of Group of Sixteen Meeting," 10 April, 1987, SGO files.

[12] James Henke, *Human Rights Now!* (London: Bloomsbury, 1988), 10.

[13] Healey's relationship with then IEC chair, Franca Sciuto, was by all accounts highly tempestuous; one interviewee described it as "the war of the worlds"–"the irresistible force [Healey] meeting the immovable object [Sciuto]."

[14] "Notes of Group of Sixteen Meeting," June 1987, SGO files.

[15] "Report of the Committee on Long-Range Organization and Development to the 1987 International Council." AI Index: ORG 31/01/87 (bold face in original).

[16] "IS—Project," from Sophie (Tomoko Shinozaki) and Walter (Roevekamp), to CLOD members, 23 March 1986, SGO files (emphasis in original).

[17] "Sexual Orientation and the AI Mandate," Luxembourg section, for 1982 ICM, AI Index: 21/01/82.

[18] "Research Project on AI and Homosexuality," George Siemensma, IEC agenda paper, November 1986, POL 03/IEC 12/86.

[19] "AI and Homosexuality," November 1986, from Head of Research Department, POL 03/IEC 12/86.

[20] This letter was sent on December 4, 1990 and distributed to AI sections by AI Canada's English-speaking section, of which Schelew was a member. Secretary General Ian Martin immediately sought and received assurances from the other MRC members

(including two IEC members) in a statement to the movement dated February 23, 1991, that they did not share Schelew's view.

[21] There were two members from the IEC and one each from Sweden, Kuwait, Greece, Canada (English-speaking), India, and Chile. Michael Schelew was the Canadian representative.

[22] Letter, Paul Hoffman to Franca Sciuto, October 31 1988, IEC files.

[23] "Final Report of the Mandate Review Committee," April 1991, AI Index: POL 21/15/91.

[24] "Comments from AI USA on First Three Reports of MRC," Index: MRC 9.10, 29 October 1990.

[25] For detailed material on ICM discussions, I am extremely grateful to David Matas, a member of the Standing Committee on the Mandate (1993–1999) and delegate for Canada (English-speaking) to every ICM between 1987 and 2001 (excluding 1991 when he was a rapporteur). His reports on each ICM since 1987 are collected in Matas, "The Amnesty Mandate Story," unpublished manuscript.

[26] AIUSA was soon writing again to the IS and IEC alleging that researchers were deliberately not seeking out cases of gay POCs. In the end, it published its own report, *Breaking the Silence*, in 1994.

[27] Matas, "Amnesty Mandate Story."

[28] See Sellars, *Rise and Rise of Human Rights*, 153–57.

[29] See the update to *Iraq/Occupied Kuwait: Human Rights Violations since 2 August*, AI Index: MDE 17/03/91. See also William Langewiesche, "The Accuser," *The Atlantic Monthly*, March 2005, which centers on Hania Mufti, who is now Human Rights Watch's researcher on Iraq but who was in 1990 Amnesty's and so responsible for AI's publication of the Kuwaiti babies story. "The Accuser" is a good account of the life of an Amnesty-style researcher.

[30] One senior member of the movement regularly introduced his speeches with stories about his early days, at the 1987 Brazil ICM, when it seemed to him that his task was to rewrite the rules "so people couldn't do things," with the secretary general (Martin) telling delegates, "you've passed 67 resolutions and we can't do any of them."

[31] Ian Martin, letter, 8 February 1991.

[32] Peter Duffy, letter, 11 February 1991.

[33] "Statement to IEC and Senior Management," Dick Oosting, 24 February 1991.

[34] "Report by Participlan to the 1991 ICM: A Study of Decision-Making in Amnesty International," 13 May 1991, AI Index: ORG 30/05/91.

[35] Ibid. (boldface in original).

[36] "The IS Management Response to the Participlan Report," 2 July 1991, AI Index: ORG 30/07/91.

[37] Review Committee Report, AI Index: ORG 60/04/91.

[38] Shortly before his death, in 1999, Duffy represented Amnesty before the House of Lords in the Pinochet case.

[39] Sané had for fifteen years worked in Senegal for a Canadian organization, the International Development Research Center.

[40] "Strategic Directions 1995–1998: A Discussion Paper," June 1993, AI Index: POL 50/03/93.

[41] "Review of Amnesty International's Research: Final Report," submitted to IEC March 1993, AI Index: POL 40/02/93.

[42] This was a disagreement about where violence stopped and torture started; on the core meaning and practice of torture, there was no dissent.

[43] "Recommendations from a Staff Working Group," 14 April 1993.

[44] The following material comes from the contemporaneous files of one of the researchers involved.

[45] The Lawyer's Committee has now rebranded itself as the more media-friendly "Human Rights First."

[46] One ex-senior researcher from the 1980s recalled giving a junior researcher an apple after she had written a particularly good report. He had no money to give her a bonus, he told her, so he gave her an apple instead.

[47] Eliot Freidson, *Professionalism: The Third Logic* (Cambridge, UK: Polity, 2001), 33.

[48] This letter was posted on the electronic noticeboard for IS staff, IntSec Forum. The sections signing the letter were United Kingdom, United States, France, Germany, Netherlands, and Belgium (Francophone and Flemish).

[49] The 1983 membership report has no index number. The 1993 report is AI Index: ORG 40/02/94.

[50] "Rwanda 1994 Evaluation," October 1995. It was written by IS Crisis Response Project Manager Peer Baneke and Deputy Executive Director of AIUSA Curt Goering.

[51] According to an IS researcher involved with the Rwanda crisis, one (now ex) AIUSA official told them it was essential AI got a representative to Kigali before Human Rights Watch. The main contention through weeks of IS meetings was, he said, whether to support the dispatch of an extra UN armed force. He described the Baneke-Goering evaluation as "remarkably polite about our inability to do anything useful (or to think of anything useful to do) once the genocide started."

[52] One researcher described this as thirty angry people in a room shouting at one another for a month, which has since made the Africa Program wary of ever going into crisis response mode again.

[53] However, Human Rights Watch's influential former director Aryeh Neier devotes almost no attention to Amnesty in his book *Taking Liberties: Four Decades in the Struggle for Rights* (New York: Public Affairs 2003).

[54] In this letter, dated April 15, 2002, Schulz also says how surprised he was to see Roth refer to HRW as an "international human rights organization" rather than a U.S.-based one, Roth's usual means of distinguishing HRW from AI.

[55] See Claude E. Welch, "Amnesty International and Human Rights Watch: A comparison," in *NGOs and Human Rights* edited by Claude E. Welch (Philadelphia: University of Pennsylvania Press, 2001), 95–97.

[56] Consider, also, our earlier observations about donors and members as two different categories in the United States. Seen in this light, HRW looks like the shadow Amnesty—a more typically American way to organize human rights work rather than the group-based, money-averse, European-inspired AI.

[57] The song may be moving to hear, but the lyrics call for an end to religious belief. Do the words matter or just the tug on the heart? Amnesty would not endorse the specific statements, but could it even endorse the sentiment?

[58] One area of IS life that I have been forced to underplay due to space constraints is the role of the union. It reflects many British-style trade union values that seem similar to the voluntaristic vocational side of the ethos, the competition within Amnesty for the moral high ground, and the intellectually demanding culture. It remains an important arena for staff expression and one in which skeptics about corporatism can unite.

6. Being and Doing

[1] A State of the Movement report produced for the ICM in mid-2003 found that in all but one northern section female members outnumbered male. The pattern was similar in Latin America. In Africa and the Middle East, there tended to be more male than female members (data on Asia Pacific were too incomplete to use).

[2] We were discussing the feelings of a male regional campaigner who said he often wished there were more men around. He recalled an email from the secretary general's office just after Irene Khan had started suggesting staff members should feel free to chat with her at any time, "even in the toilets." The presumption was, of course, that all staff members could meet her there.

[3] AI Index: FIN 03 IEC 73. This is deduced from the first names of the staff, one or two of which (e.g., *Jean*, which I counted as female) were ambiguous. One researcher who worked at the IS in the 1970s said, "It was mostly women," young men only joining when "it began to be sort of quasi respectable enough as a job."

[4] These figures are indicative not definitive, and they can change quickly. A look at the March 2003 staff list gives a total figure for Africa of forty-nine, for example. The regional

offices in Kampala (sixteen staff members), Hong Kong (six staff members), Costa Rica (one staff member), and Paris are included, as are development staff and campaign coordinators in the regional programs.

[5] See "Women 'choose to have lower pay than men,'" *Sunday Times*, 6 June 2004, 25.

[6] She went on to say the problem was more acute with lesbian and gay issues, which were not the priority in her region and which local gay groups didn't, she said, want raised.

[7] However, of the human rights activists that organizers chose to represent the tour to the world's press and who traveled on the planes, four were women.

[8] These comments are from a copy of her speech retained by a campaign coordinator.

[9] AI Index: ACT 10/IEC01/01.

[10] The 2003–2005 IEC had a female majority, however.

[11] These quotations are from notes circulated by a campaigner after the meeting. Bunch noted the prominent role that AIUSA had played on women's rights in the United States.

[12] Internal memo, "Report on the VAW Campaign Consultation Forum," Mark Neuman (Campaigns Program director) to program directors, 14 November 2002. Gender issues were simply not "mainstreamed" in research, the memo says.

[13] "Violence Against Women Campaign Draft Strategy," AI Index: ACT 77/009/2002 (bold face in original).

[14] Various acronyms were used for the senior management at this time, which comprised by January 2003 the secretary general and her deputy and six newly appointed senior directors (SDs). These weekly meetings were termed Senior Management Forums (SMF), and I use this term to refer to the senior management collectively.

[15] I have this poster on my wall as I write these words, and it was frequently on display in parts of the IS. It can also be seen on the wall of Sam Seaborn's office in an episode of the popular U.S. TV series, *The West Wing*.

[16] The SMF was also told that women's NGOs Amnesty had consulted had warned them off issues involving prostitution and sex workers in the SVAW campaign because they raised questions about women's right to choose. Also, the trafficking of women was considered too complex an issue to take on despite the interest of European sections in tackling it in the campaign.

[17] Pierre Sané, "Strategic Directions 1995–1998: A Discussion Paper," June 1993, AI Index: POL 50/03/93.

[18] For one senior campaigner, this contrast was explained by the lesbian and gay network being a "constituency" for change within and outside Amnesty (there being no equivalent lobby of Muslim women demanding that imprisonment for extra-marital sex be taken up).

[19] Until this meeting, the campaign had always been awkwardly titled the VAW Campaign; afterward it became the Stop VAW or SVAW Campaign.

[20] No Amnesty report would tackle abortion head on, whatever the talk, predicted a veteran staffer. The operative paragraph would be cut at some point by someone with enough authority, she said, not to have to refer it back. During these discussions on violence against women, inside the almost ironic surroundings of an Oxford college, complete with heavy wooden furniture and portraits of dead white men on the walls, a loud smash of crockery echoed through the room and one senior Amnesty member remarked, "they thought we were changing our policy."

[21] This policy document, from 1992, was from HRP. *Hegemony* is defined as "leadership."

[22] A report by Whitney Ellsworth in 1986 puts British/Irish IS staff at 66.8% and Others at 33.2% (ORG: 63/IEC 03/86). The more senior the grade, however, the lower the British/Irish (BI) domination. By grade, it was A, BI = 85%; B, BI = 60%; C, BI = 54%; D, BI = 62.5%; E, BI = 25%; and SG/DSG (secretary general and deputy secretary general), BI = 0%. There were, however only eight Ds, four Es, and two SG/DSGs.

[23] UK legislation constrains the employment of nationals from outside the European Economic Area.

[24] Indivisibility—that social, economic, and cultural rights are inseparable from civil and political rights—is a core message of the SVAW campaign. It brings rights back home by pointing to the poverty, marginalization, and injustice that are marked within all Western societies, disproportionately so for women, minorities, and the poor.

[25] The still-active Cultural Diversity and Equal Opportunity (CDEOP) policy from 1992 recognized three core principles: valuing diversity, ending discrimination, and ending *unnecessary conformity*.

[26] Under IS works, the IS will have a multifaith prayer space. It also had a Christmas Party in the middle of my fieldwork, although Christmas decorations were evident only in parts of the building that dealt with resource provision—not with research or campaigns. In previous years, a specifically Christmas party, named as such, had not been held for fear of causing offence.

[27] The recently appointed head of the Africa Program (in 2004), previously a legal advisor at the IS, is African. There isn't space to deal with the sixteen-strong Kampala office, the most ambitious effort by Amnesty to decentralize research, campaigning, and development to Africa itself. It is also too early to say whether this policy of deconcentration, as it is called, is wise or effective. IS senior managers certainly wanted to take a searching look at whether it had yielded positive results, one observing that it was often easier to travel to somewhere in Africa starting in London than in Uganda.

[28] I realize this is a crude measure. There are plenty of members of the transnational class from these countries, the old north-south certainties looking less and less appropriate under globalization when rich-poor draws a very different and much more complex map of wealth and power.

[29] At this more senior level, where local conditions ought to be proportionately less relevant, twenty researchers still have the United Kingdom as their country of origin.

[30] AI sections and structures (aspiring sections) with problems include Argentina, Bangladesh, Brazil, Colombia, Ecuador, Ghana, Nigeria, Pakistan, Palestine (groups), Paraguay, and Senegal.

[31] One senior member thought that no Amnesty section that is a net contributor to the movement (pays for itself *and* contributes to the international movement rather than taking money out or breaking even) has been formed since 1973.

[32] AI Index: ORG 03/IEC 73, agenda item 16.

[33] This insightful observation is followed by the comment: "Surely, in this context, the group must be seen as a sophisticated product and not regarded automatically as a unit of growth."

[34] "Amnesty International in the Third World," 18 July 1975, Richard Reoch and Jane Ward, AI Index: NS 134. The co-author Jane Ward, another IS and Amnesty stalwart, was Reoch's wife. The letter notes in passing that sending Christmas cards to all adopted prisoners, as Amnesty did, took little account of those prisoners who were Muslim, Hindu, or Buddhist.

[35] Being so diligent about not accepting government money was a boon for Amnesty's reputation in South Asia, said the letter, whereas being in a colonial-era capital such as London was a drawback. The Indian Section of Amnesty was very prominent during the emergency under Indira Gandhi and several key figures (such as George Fernandez) later made names for themselves in Indian politics. After this period, the section declined. India is now a test case for "constituency-building." Rather than forming a section, AI is trying to link into existing local human rights networks as a partner.

7. The Inheritors

[1] "Recommendations" are the crux of the classic Amnesty report—the specific demands AI makes on a government to take remedial action ("we all sweat over recommendations," said one ex-researcher).

[2] As we have seen in chapter 2, this assertion is questionable for an organization with no building blocks.

3 These comments were by senior IS managers at an All Programs Forum in February 2003, following the IMG.

4 One section director said quietly during a break at the IMG, "I think we need more rules, not less."

5 The IEC and ICM were the only 1s. Managers joked that, although IS staffers thought they were 2s, in reality they were 3s.

6 The banter at this meeting was often brutal, various jokes about the Axis of Evil centering on the Middle East Program, whose delegate responded, "we felt our program was multicultural, dynamic, friendly and fun, and I don't want any comments about that," to much laughter.

7 Having the mothers of the disappeared (from Ciudad Juarez) actually opening the ICM in Mexico was scotched by senior directors as being too much "old Amnesty."

8 Commenting on the draft of this book, one policy person said, "Whoever said the stuff about the dangers of failure was right. And the GIGs! All the old work is in there—there won't be any diminution of work if we take those as the priorities."

9 The report's authors talked to numerous local and international NGOs, including HRW, ICRC, and Médecins sans Frontières (MSF) in order to get an external perspective on Amnesty.

10 Emphasis in original. SCRA is a movement committee. The discussion about full spectrum (working on all human rights) is intricate; suffice it to say that the Dakar ICM in 2001 saw a shift from the status quo to core concept with the intention that by 2005 there would be full spectrum. From the mandate prescribing limits on work, the idea was to expand the boundaries of work as widely as possible and then, through the ISP and ISOP, set shorter-term plans that prioritized for a finite period. The Mandate Review Report 1997–2001 (POL: 21/01/2001) opened up the field for *any* right to be a potential Amnesty concern. This open-ended commitment effectively creates a huge internal political space for battles over prioritization. Compare this with the more conservative core concept, the basis of the AI post-Dakar mission statement in the Statute: "AI opposes grave abuses of the rights to physical and mental integrity, freedom of conscience and expression, and freedom from discrimination."

11 Emphasis in original.

12 There is no central database of POC cases that staff and members can access and use. Some material is kept by researchers on their own standalone PCs, and is not even held in files that can be networked. Some is even unknown, as are the contact lists, by campaigners and RCAs working day-to-day with certain researchers. If the researcher left, no institutional memory would remain at all in those cases. Some researchers even take their voluminous files with them (and some bitterly resisted IS Works efforts to make them deposit in the library and archive things that are a collective resource for Amnesty as a whole).

13 The continual use of PowerPoint presentations was indicative for many staff of a marketing approach to consultations that they found unpersuasive.

14 In HRP, for example, there was unhappiness. It was "supposed to make people feel less alienated," said one staff member, the acronyms (MAC was something that few people were aware of, and yet it was such a central issue on the day) were off-putting and never explained ("that's very Amnesty," said another). One staff member said she left early "to do some work," and another added, "I had to come back for a meeting and I was actually quite relieved."

15 During my time, the key post of senior director for the Regional Programs was a source of constant trouble, with interim appointments, failed recruitment, and early resignations. It was eventually filled by an existing senior director who was a long-serving IS staffer and former researcher. By 2004, out of the original six senior directors who met in January 2003 (interim or permanent), only one remained in his original post.

16 I wrote in my contemporaneous notes, "This must have been prepared in advance—just wheeled out." In a strongly worded, post–Day Out memo, senior directors were adamant there would be no job losses.

17 Despite intense criticism of the way things were unfolding, she said the IS was a far happier place than during the late 1990s. She also said, "[It] still is a great job and it's

amazing to be able to come in every day and be paid to follow what's going on in these countries that I care about."

[18] This works out at £200 per delegate per day for eight days full board.

[19] As the lore is weakened, collective rituals that reaffirm the faith may be more, not less, necessary. The deep collective memory about past ICMs, and their consecutive numbering, is a sign of their function as a continual and predictable replenishing of the spirit, as is the quarterly cycle of IEC meetings, with their highly structured agenda headings and reports, which has remained more or less the same since Sean MacBride was chairman in the 1960s.

[20] See Amnesty International, *Intolerable Killings: Mexico: 10 years of Abductions and Murder of Women in Ciudad Juarez and Chihuahua,* August 2003, AI Index: AMR 41/027/2003.

[21] One comment I received pointed out that this high-profile report on violence against women did not come under the two campaign priorities for SVAW yet reformers were happy enough to share in its success.

[22] Also killed was Arthur C. Helton, the refugee lawyer, well known to senior Amnesty personnel.

[23] Whether one of the powerful researchers who had occupied the post in the past would have been better able to mount a defense is an interesting question (of authority, of course).

[24] "Role of the IS Staff Representative on the IEC," January 1993, AI Index: ORG 70/02/93.

[25] Naomi Klein, who wrote the influential book *No Logo* (London: Flamingo, 2000), actually visited the IS and told management, "you've got a good brand, you've got to hold it up."

[26] AI Index: FIN 21/005/2003.

[27] AIUSA holds a few Exxon Mobil shares, much to the dismay of some other Amnesty members, so that it can table shareholder resolutions. It also holds shares for the same reason in various other multinational companies.

[28] We can also rank countries in terms of their contributions as a proportion of their national disposable income. The top five are the Netherlands (0.00134%), Switzerland, Norway, Sweden, and the United Kingdom (at 0.00046%). France is ninth, Germany thirteenth, and the United States fifteenth (at 0.00013%).

[29] This hand image was unpopular with some sections; delegates from Greece and Zimbabwe, for example, argued that an outstretched palm had negative social and political connotations for them.

[30] At the Mexico ICM, I was asked by the ICM chair to address all four hundred delegates for five minutes to describe my research. I was told that if I could tell them what really went on in the IS I would sell four hundred copies before I left the room. One IEC member did ask me later, surprisingly, if I was going to name Amnesty. My ambiguous existence came to an abrupt halt at the end-of-ICM party when one IS manager asked me, "is this the participant bit or the observation bit?"

8. Amnesty in Practice

[1] "Rumsfeld decries Amnesty rights report," *Washington Post*, 1 June 2005, at www.washingtonpost.com/wp-dyn/content/article/2005/06/01/AR2005060101224.html.

[2] Wilson, "Representing human rights violations," 139.

[3] See Richard Gordon, "Covering China," *Media Studies Journal*, (1999), available at www.tsquare.tv/film/tank.

[4] Williams, *Ethics and the Limits of Philosophy*, 69.

[5] Dumas, *Dietrich Bonhoeffer*, 287. The last sentence expresses the idea better than I can about the moment of transcendence in witnessing acts of courage and suffering.

[6] Pierre Sané, address to Amnesty intersection meeting "Local Groups of Year 2000," Paris, August 1998.

[7] Emphasis added.

[8] On pragmatism within international relations thinking, see Molly Cochran, *Normative Theory in International Relations: A Pragmatic Approach* (Cambridge, UK: Cambridge University Press, 1999). See also "Pragmatism in international relations theory," *Millennium: Journal of International Studies*, special issue, 31, no. 3, 2002.

[9] See Michael Ignatieff, "Human rights as idolatry," in *Michael Ignatieff: Human Rights as Politics and Idolatry* edited by Amy Gutmann (Princeton: Princeton University Press, 2001), 53–54.

[10] Richard Rorty, "Human rights, rationality, and sentimentality," in *On Human Rights: The Oxford Amnesty Lectures* 1993 edited by Stephen Shute and Susan Hurley (New York: Basic Books, 1993), 115.

[11] David Kennedy, *The Dark Sides of Virtue: Reassessing International Humanitarianism* (Princeton, NJ: Princeton University Press, 2004), 352.

[12] Ibid., 342.

[13] Ibid., 348.

[14] Ibid., 349.

[15] See Searle, *Rationality in Action* (Cambridge, Mass: MIT Press, 2001), 73.

[16] Ibid., 62.

[17] Karin M. Fierke, "Links across the abyss: Language and logic in international relations," *International Studies Quarterly* 46 (2002), 332.

[18] The most comprehensive statement of constructivism is in Alexander Wendt, *Social Theory of International Politics* (Cambridge, UK: Cambridge University Press, 1999).

[19] Martha Finnemore, *National Interests in International Society* (Ithaca: Cornell University Press, 1996), 12–13, 27. See also Michael Barnett and Martha Finnemore, *Rules for the World* (Ithaca: Cornell University Press, 2004).

[20] Keck and Sikkink, *Activists Beyond Borders*; Thomas Risse, Stephen C. Ropp, and Kathryn Sikkink (eds.), *The Power of Human Rights: International Norms and Domestic Change* (Cambridge, UK: Cambridge University Press, 1999).

[21] For more ethnographic research, see Michael Barnett, *Eyewitness to a Genocide: The United Nations and Rwanda* (Ithaca: Cornell University Press, 2002); Hugh Gusterson, *Nuclear Rites: A Weapons Laboratory at the End of the Cold War* (Berkeley: University of California Press, 1998); and for a more historical approach, Jutta Weldes, *Constructing National Interests: The United States and the Cuban Missile Crisis* (Minneapolis: University of Minnesota Press, 1999).

[22] Maja Zehfuss, *Constructivism in International Relations: The Politics of Reality* (Cambridge, UK: Cambridge University Press, 2002), 250; also Fierke, "Links across the abyss"; Jeffrey T Checkel, "Social contructivisms in global and European politics: A review essay," *Review of International Studies* 30 (2004), 229–244.

[23] Doubtless it falls into others.

[24] Pierre Bourdieu, *Outline of a Theory of Practice* (Cambridge, UK: Cambridge University Press, 1977), 27.

[25] Durkheim, *Elementary Forms of Religious Life*, 322.

[26] For one unsatisfying but influential attempt at a sociology of the world system, see John Boli and George M. Thomas, "INGOs and the organization of world culture," in *Constructing World Culture: International Nongovernmental Organizations since 1875*, edited by John Boli and George M. Thomas (Stanford: Stanford University Press, 1999). See also Arjun Appadurai, "Global ethnoscapes: Notes and queries for a transnational anthropology," in *Modernity at Large: Cultural Dimensions of Globalization* (Minneapolis: University of Minnesota Press, 1996); Jonathan Xavier Inda and Renato Rosaldo (eds.), *The Anthropology of Globalization* (Oxford: Blackwell, 2002).

[27] Bourdieu, *Logic of Practice*, 53.

[28] Loic J. D. Wacquant, "The structure and logic of Bourdieu's sociology," in Pierre Bourdieu and Loic J. D. Wacquant, *An Invitation to Reflexive Sociology* (Cambridge, UK: Polity, 1992), 19.

[29] Jean-Hervé Bradol, "The sacrificial international order and humanitarian action," in *In the Shadow of 'Just Wars': Violence, Politics and Humanitarian Action*, edited by Fabrice Weissman (London: Hurst & Co/MSF, 2004), 22.

[30] AI Index: ORG 60/04/91.

[31] Immanuel Kant, "Foundations of the metaphysics of morals," 1785, in *Kant: Selections*, edited by Lewis White Beck (New York: Scribner/Macmillan, 1988), 246, 249.

[32] Rorty, "Human rights, rationality, and sentimentality," 122.

[33] Rorty, "Human rights, rationality, sentimentality"; Kennedy, *Dark Sides of Virtue*; Martha Nussbaum, *Cultivating Humanity* (Cambridge: Harvard University Press, 1997), chap. 2.

[34] Martin Ennals, "Amnesty International and Human Rights," in *Pressure Groups in the Global System*, edited by Peter Willetts (London: Francis Pinter, 1982), 67.

[35] Stanley Cohen, *States of Denial* (Cambridge, UK: Polity, 2001), 16.

[36] The *International Herald Tribune* featured a story on the impact in Sweden of Amnesty's report; see "Sweden faces facts on violence against women," *International Herald Tribune*, March 30th 2005, at www.iht.com/articles/2005/03/29/news/letter-4909045.html.

[37] AI intersection meeting address, Paris, August 1998.

bibliography

Amnesty International. *Broken Bodies, Shattered Minds: Torture and Ill-Treatment of Women.* AI Index: ACT 40/001/2001.
———. *Intolerable Killings: Mexico: 10 years of Abductions and Murder of Women in Ciudad Juarez and Chihuahua,* August 2003. AI Index: AMR 41/027/2003.
Anderson, Benedict. *Imagined Communities.* London: Verso, 1991.
Appadurai, Arjun. "Global ethnoscapes: Notes and queries for a transnational anthropology." In *Modernity at Large: Cultural Dimensions of Globalization.* Minneapolis: University of Minnesota Press, 1996.
Baehr, Peter R. "Amnesty International and its self-imposed limited mandate." *Netherlands Quarterly of Human Rights* 12, no. 1 (1994), 5–21
Barnett, Michael. *Eyewitness to a Genocide: The United Nations and Rwanda.* Ithaca: Cornell University Press, 2002.
Barnett, Michael, and Martha Finnemore. *Rules for the World.* Ithaca: Cornell University Press, 2004.
Beck, Lewis White, ed. *Kant: Selections.* New York: Scribner/Macmillan, 1988.
Beyer, Peter. *Religion and Globalization.* London: Sage Publications, 1994.
Boli, John, and George M. Thomas. "INGOs and the organization of world culture." In John Boli and George M. Thomas (eds.), *Constructing World Culture: International Nongovernmental Organizations since 1875.* Stanford: Stanford University Press, 1999.
Bonhoeffer, Dietrich. *A Testament to Freedom,* edited by Geffrey B. Kelly & F. Burton Nelson. New York: HarperCollins, 1990.
Bourdieu, Pierre. *Outline of a Theory of Practice.* Cambridge, UK: Cambridge University Press, 1977.
———. *The Logic of Practice.* Cambridge, UK: Polity, 1990.
Bradol, Jean-Hervé. "The sacrificial international order and humanitarian action." In Fabrice Weissman (ed.), *In the Shadow of "Just Wars": Violence, Politics and Humanitarian Action.* London: Hurst & Co/MSF, 2004.
Buchanan, Tom. " 'The truth will set you free': The making of Amnesty International." *Journal of Contemporary History* 37, no. 4 (2002), 575–597.
———. "Amnesty International in crisis, 1966–1967." *Twentieth Century British History* 15, no. 3 (2004), 267–289.
Checkel, Jeffrey T. "Social contructivisms in global and European politics: A review essay." *Review of International Studies* 30 (2004): 229–244.
Clark, Ann Marie. *Diplomacy of Conscience: Amnesty International and Changing Human Rights Norms.* Princeton: Princeton University Press, 2001.
Cochran, Molly. *Normative Theory in International Relations: A Pragmatic Approach.* Cambridge, UK: Cambridge University Press, 1999.
Cohen, Stanley. *States of Denial.* Cambridge, UK: Polity, 2001.
Dumas, André. *Dietrich Bonhoeffer: Theologian of Reality,* trans. by Robert McAfee Brown. London: SCM Press, 1971.
Durkheim, Émile. *The Elementary Forms of Religious Life,* trans. by Carol Cosman. Oxford: Oxford University Press, 2001 (1912).
Ennals, Martin. "Amnesty International and Human Rights." In Peter Willetts (ed.), *Pressure Groups in the Global System.* London: Francis Pinter, 1982.
Fierke, Karin M. "Links across the abyss: Language and logic in international relations." *International Studies Quarterly* 46 (2002), 331–354.

Finnemore, Martha. *National Interests in International Society*. Ithaca: Cornell University Press, 1996.

Freidson, Eliot. *Professionalism: The Third Logic*. Cambridge, UK: Polity, 2001.

Friedman, R. B. "On the concept of authority in political philosophy." In Joseph Raz (ed.), *Authority*. Oxford: Basil Blackwell, 1990.

Gordon, Richard. "Covering China." *Media Studies Journal* (1999). Available at www.tsquare.tv/film/tank (accessed 04.03.2005).

Gusterson, Hugh. *Nuclear Rites: A Weapons Laboratory at the End of the Cold War*. Berkeley: University of California Press, 1998.

Haynes, Stephen R. *The Bonhoeffer Phenomenon: Portraits of a Protestant Saint*. London: SCM Press, 2004.

Henke, James. *Human Rights Now!* London: Bloomsbury, 1988.

Iannaccone, Laurence R. "Why strict churches are strong." *American Journal of Sociology* 99, no. 5 (1994): 1180–211.

Ignatieff, Michael. "Human rights as idolatry." In Amy Gutmann (ed.), *Michael Ignatieff: Human Rights as Politics and Idolatry*. Princeton: Princeton University Press, 2001.

Inda, Jonathan Xavier, and Renato Rosaldo, eds. *The Anthropology of Globalization*. Oxford: Blackwell, 2002.

Jones, Peter. *Rights*. London: Macmillan, 1994.

Jung, Carl G. "On the psychology of the unconscious." In Anthony Storr (ed.), *The Essential Jung*. London: Fontana, 1983.

———. *Memories, Dreams, Reflections*. London: Fontana, 1995 (1963).

Keck, Margaret E., and Kathryn Sikkink. *Activists Beyond Borders: Advocacy Networks in International Politics*. Ithaca: Cornell University Press, 1998.

Kennedy, David. *The Dark Sides of Virtue: Reassessing International Humanitarianism*. Princeton: Princeton University Press, 2004.

Klein, Naomi. *No Logo*. London: Flamingo, 2000.

Langewiesche, William. "The Accuser." *The Atlantic Monthly*, March 2005, at www.theatlantic.com/doc/200503/langewiesche.

Larsen, Egon. *A Flame in Barbed Wire*. New York: W.W. Norton & Co, 1979.

Luhmann, Niklas. *The Differentiation of Society*, trans. by Stephen Holmes and Charles Larmore. New York: Columbia University Press, 1982.

Matas, David. "The Amnesty Mandate Story." Unpublished MS, 2003.

Muñoz, Luis. *Being Luis: A Chilean Life*. Exeter: Impress Books, 2005.

Nagel, Thomas. "Moral conflict and political legitimacy." In Joseph Raz (ed.) *Authority*. Oxford: Blackwell, 1990.

Neier, Aryeh. *Taking Liberties: Four Decades in the Struggle for Rights*. New York: PublicAffairs, 2003.

Nepstad, Sharon Erickson. "Popular religion, protest, and revolt." In Christian Smith (ed.), *Disruptive Religion: The Force of Faith in Social Movement Activism*. New York: Routledge, 1996.

Nussbaum, Martha, *Cultivating Humanity*. Cambridge, Mass.: Harvard University Press, 1997.

Orwell, George. *Nineteen Eighty-Four*. London: Penguin Books, 1983.

Pack, Peter. "Amnesty International: An evolving mandate in a changing world." In Angela Hegarty and Siobhan Leonard (eds.), *Human Rights: An Agenda for the 21st Century*. London: Cavendish Publishing, 1999.

Paine, Thomas. *Common Sense, and The Rights of Man*. London: Phoenix Press, 1993.

Parker, Ian. "Victims and volunteers." *The New Yorker*, 26 January 2004, 50–61.

Patterson, Orlando. *Slavery and Social Death*. Cambridge, Mass.: Harvard University Press, 1985.

Plant, Stephen. *Bonhoeffer*. London: Continuum, 2004.

Power, Jonathan. *Like Water on Stone*. London: Penguin Press, 2001.

"Pragmatism in International Relations Theory." *Millennium: Journal of International Studies* 31, no. 3 (2002).

Raz, Joseph. *The Morality of Freedom*. Oxford: Clarendon Press, 1986.

Risse, Thomas, Stephen C. Ropp, and Kathryn Sikkink, eds. *The Power of Human Rights: International Norms and Domestic Change.* Cambridge, UK: Cambridge University Press, 1999.

Robinson, John A. T. *Honest to God.* London: SCM Press, 1963.

Ron, James, Howard Ramos, and Kathleen Rodgers. "Transnational information politics: Amnesty International's country reporting, 1986–2000." *International Studies Quarterly,* 49, no. 3 (2005), 557–588.

Rorty, Richard. "Human rights, rationality, and sentimentality." In Stephen Shute and Susan Hurley (eds.), *On Human Rights: The Oxford Amnesty Lectures 1993.* New York: Basic Books, 1993.

Searle, John R. *Rationality in Action.* Cambridge, Mass.: MIT Press, 2001.

Sellars, Kirsten. *The Rise and Rise of Human Rights.* Stroud, UK: Sutton Publishing, 2002.

Solomon, Flora, and Barnet Litvinoff. *Baku to Baker Street: The Memoirs of Flora Solomon.* London: Collins, 1984.

Stoll, David. *Is Latin America Turning Protestant?* Berkeley: University of California Press, 1990.

Thompson, E. P. *The Making of the English Working Class.* London: Penguin Books, 1980.

Toulmin, Stephen. *Cosmopolis: The Hidden Agenda of Modernity.* Chicago: University of Chicago Press, 1990.

Wacquant, Loic J. D. "The structure and logic of Bourdieu's sociology." In Pierre Bourdieu and Loic J. D. Wacquant, *An Invitation to Reflexive Sociology.* Cambridge, UK: Polity, 1992.

Weber, Max. "The social psychology of the world's religions." In *From Max Weber,* trans. by Hans H. Gerth and C. Wright Mills. London: Kegan Paul, Trench & Trubner, 1947.

Welch, Claude E. "Amnesty International and Human Rights Watch: A comparison." In Claude E. Welch (ed.), *NGOs and Human Rights.* Philadelphia: University of Pennsylvania Press, 2001.

Weldes, Jutta. *Constructing National Interests: The United States and the Cuban Missile Crisis.* Minneapolis: University of Minnesota Press, 1999.

Wendt, Alexander. *Social Theory of International Politics.* Cambridge, UK: Cambridge University Press, 1999.

Williams, Bernard. *Ethics and the Limits of Philosophy.* London: Fontana Press, 1993.

Wilson, Richard A. "Representing human rights violations: Social contexts and subjectivities." In Richard A. Wilson (ed.), *Human Rights, Culture & Context: Anthropological Perspectives.* London: Pluto Press, 1997.

Wind, Renate. *Dietrich Bonhoeffer: A Spoke in the Wheel,* trans. by John Bowden. Grand Rapids, Mich.: Wm. B. Eerdmans, 1991.

Winston, Morton E. "Assessing the effectiveness of international human rights NGOs." In Claude E. Welch (ed.), *NGOs and Human Rights.* Philadelphia: University of Pennsylvania Press, 2001.

"Women 'choose to have lower pay than men'." *Sunday Times,* June 2004.

Zehfuss, Maja. *Constructivism in International Relations: The Politics of Reality.* Cambridge, UK: Cambridge University Press, 2002.

index